Dogs in Mind

JACKIE DRAKEFORD

SKYCAT PUBLICATIONS

Published in 2014 by Skycat Publications
Vaiseys Farm, Brent Eleigh, Suffolk CO10 9 PA
Email info@skycatpublications.com
www.skycatpublications.com

ISBN 978 0 9927451 0 3

Printed in England by Lavenham Press Ltd
Arbons House, 47 Water Street, Lavenham, Suffolk CO10 9RN
Telephone: +44 (0)1787 247436
Email: enquiries@lavenhamgroup.co.uk

Cover photo courtesy of Pete Trott.

About the Author

JACKIE DRAKEFORD is a Kennel Club Accredited Instructor with many years of experience in studying dog behaviour. Based in southern England and working with a holistic veterinary practice, she is involved in a broad spectrum of training issues and dog breeds. Her specialist areas are sighthounds, scenthounds, terriers and lurchers. Jackie also lectures widely on dog aggression.

Acknowledgements

Warmest thanks are due the following, without whose help this book would have been far more difficult to write:

Emma Judson, an innovative and inspirational dog behaviour consultant, who has been so generous in discussion and explanation (www.canineconsultant.co.uk).

Jules Morgan, who has taught me so much about gundogs (www.thedogbusiness.com).

Michele Richardson of *Horses In Mind* who has kindly allowed me to parallel this title from her own horse and rider psychology work.

All who came to the rescue when injury prevented me from taking sufficient photographs: Jules Brittan (www.pawsandprintsuk.co.uk), Chris Chappel, Di Morgan, Fay Sechiari and Pete Trott.

Skycat Publications for their patience and support during the unavoidable delay to the manuscript's completion from the same cause.

Contents

Introduction

THE MODERN dog owner faces a barrage of conflicting advice from a wide range of sources, while the modern pet dog leads a more restricted and artificial life than any of its predecessors. What we want from our dogs and what our dogs need from us is not always straightforward to achieve, and solutions are often hidden behind a bewildering array of differing "expert" opinions masquerading as fact. When we want the dog to do something, or more often to stop doing something, we need to be able to engage its co-operation and provide a good answer to its implied question of "What exactly is in it for me?". To achieve the standards we want from the dog, to understand what is reasonable and what is not, we need guidance to show us what the dog is thinking. Once we know why it behaves in a particular manner, we are halfway to solving what we might previously have thought were insurmountable problems. Unravelling the way the dog's mind really works, while casting unreal expectations aside, gives us a far better starting point for any behaviour modification.

No matter how many dogs we have kept, each has the potential to offer different challenges, and no matter how much we know, we can sometimes end up at loggerheads with the dog. This is not anything other than miscommunication. Every dog and owner experiences these hiccups from time to time, and this book shows how to smooth out those misunderstandings, making it straightforward to restore the happy relationship that both dog and owner seek. In doing so, I have challenged a number of accepted ideas and favoured interpretations. Some of my conclusions are a long way from received wisdom, and may make uncomfortable reading in places, but everything is based soundly on what I have seen and learned from real dogs in the real world over a lifetime of study.

The purpose of this work is to remove the mystique attached to dog behaviour analysis, showing the everyday dog owner that they have a perfectly normal dog. By explaining how the dog thinks, behaviour modification becomes straightforward and simple to understand. We can work with the dog not against it, improving our relationship rather than upsetting it, and so obtain results that are satisfactory to each of us. Although reading the work must be done by owners, it is written very much with *Dogs In Mind*.

Chapter One

Myths and Legends

Popular Fallacies Explained

EVERYBODY KNOWS about dogs; many of us grew up with them, most of us know someone who has a dog, there are magazines and papers devoted to dogs, television shows about them featuring genius trainers who fix other people's problem dogs in a single one-hour programme, and occasionally we come across a book or film about a family's struggle to live with a "naughty" dog, or else the story of a wonder dog that saves people's lives, because after all what could a dog do better than that?

And an awful lot of it is nonsense.

Dogs have thrown their lot in with people for tens of thousands of years, and yet we know so little about them, and they must despair of us from time to time. Dogs are skilled communicators, people too, but despite this we often find we are at odds with each other. Then there is all the conflicting information – there is a saying that if three dog professionals are in one room, the only thing two will agree on is that the third one is wrong. What do we believe is right, and is it really right? Do any of the theories stand contact with reality?

So this book is for us. We want to live in harmony with our dogs, we want to know what they are trying to tell us, and we want to be able to take our dogs out and about without fear or embarrassment. We need to go with "the art of the possible" to be reasonable with what we expect from our dogs and avoid that feeling of crashing failure when what we want does not accord with what the dog does. To find out the best ways to get what we want, we have to keep in mind that management training technique of working towards the "win-win" situation, that is "I win and the dog wins" because too much dog-training is still locked into "I win – you lose". The double "win" means kidding the dog into thinking that what we want is what it wants also. This is not being weak, and forcing a dog to comply with our wishes by frightening or hurting it is not strong. We are a clever species intellectually, yet so often we revert to force or punishment as default mode when we actually want co-operation. Willing co-operation is far more effective than unwilling, and it lasts longer too. So let us discard our impression of human superiority, leave our egos at the gate, and look into the dog's mind together. There isn't a dog in the world that won't appreciate us for it.

Behaviour, Training and Management

What is the difference between these terms? What is the best way to have a dog that is easy and pleasant to live with? How does a behaviourist differ from a trainer?

Behaviour is the way a dog wants to act. Some behaviour is instinctive, some genetic, and some is learned. For instance, it is instinctive to be afraid of strange things, but dogs can learn that something they were afraid of is not dangerous, and so stop fearing it. Genetic bias makes some dogs more inclined to act a certain way in response to a given situation than others, because they have been bred to do so. Training is what we do in an active sense in order to modify behaviour. For instance, as far as a dog is concerned, behaviourally it does not want to soil its sleeping area, but it has no concept of "indoors" and "outdoors" in terms of house-training, until we teach it to empty itself outside. We can equally well passively teach it to soil its sleeping area by not giving it the chance to void itself elsewhere, and countless numbers of dogs are kept confined beyond what is a reasonable time and so learn to soil where they sleep because they have no alternative. Management is a way of getting the behaviour we want by making it impossible for the dog to display the behaviour we don't want. For instance if a dog steals food off the worktop, we either put the food away or close the kitchen door. Management is a perfectly sound way of achieving wanted behaviour, and there are many occasions when management is quicker and more reasonable than training. Some dogs can be trained not to touch food on the worktop, but it is extremely stressful for them, and not all will be willing to comply. More sensible in this instance is to use management, which is stress-free for both owner and dog.

Management also guarantees 100% success, where training never will, because we are dealing with sentient beings. Behaviour is what the dog will produce if untrained: that behaviour is always perfectly reasonable to the dog, and what it chooses to do unless we train. Training modifies behaviour but management manipulates it. All of these are perfectly reasonable ways of helping dogs to live in harmony with us; depending on the situation, we can use one or the other to better effect.

Behaviourists study dog behaviour so that when behaviour problems occur, they are able to get to the root of the dog's desire to perform that behaviour and then divert it into something more acceptable. Trainers show people how to get their dogs to respond to commands as well as how to act in the way the owner wants: for instance police dogs need to know a different array of responses from household pets. It is not necessary to have in-depth knowledge of behaviour in order to train, but it is never wasted if we do. All behaviourists can train but not all trainers know about behaviour, which is why behaviour consultants are more expensive than trainers. Equally, although behaviourists can train, many of them choose to refer simple grassroots training with normal dogs to trainers, and instead use their expertise on more difficult or complex problems. There are also specialist training disciplines within the working dog world, such as gundogs, military dogs, assistance dogs, show dogs and so on, where dogs are taken to trainers who are very experienced in such spheres. None of these sets of skills is superior to the others; behaviour, training and management knowledge is all helpful if we want a harmonious relationship with our dogs. We can also achieve that without recourse to any of those skills if we are content with the dog behaving exactly as it wishes; many people do this and are perfectly happy with the result. Everyone has different standards and nothing is right or wrong as long as owner and dog remain within the law, don't cause misery to others, and are happy together. Training, behaviour consultation and management skills are only ever needed where there is disharmony in the human/dog relationship.

Science and Dogs

Science is the benchmark against which we measure our observations, but we need to understand that science continually evolves. Yesterday's "scientific truth" is today's "we used to think"; today's "anecdotal" is tomorrow's "exciting discovery". Science does not create truth: it catches up with it from time to time, but the truth was always there to be observed. Some truths cannot be worked out until other truths have been found. For instance we have learned a lot more about wild animals once we had designed superior telemetry and remote filming equipment, and so could study them over a period of years in their own environment. Science is a good servant but a bad master.

When applied to dogs, old science can linger for far longer than it ought, because its theories pass into the public domain as "fact" rather than deduction. When this happens, only people who are deeply involved with dogs continue to challenge what they don't find acceptable or believable, and keep up with

Indian wild dog. Photo: C. Chappel.

the endless stream of new discoveries and interpretations. Science's weakness is in its interpretation, often by people who have little general understanding of animals. What do we know of dogs if we only know dogs, or don't know much about dogs at all to begin with? If we have a good general knowledge of animal behaviour from first-hand experience, we are less likely to be overawed by experiments that show that dogs can recognise their owners' voices or can remember people they have met before (each recent "scientific discoveries" at time of writing). Academia is of necessity out of date by the time it reaches the student, and it is all too easy to read a dedicated publication without realising that its information has been updated several times since. Therefore, while respecting all the good that science has given us on the road to understanding our dogs, we should never automatically believe it, nor anything we read, including this book, nor anything anyone else has told us, without question. An ounce of experience is worth a ton of theory (metric calculations are your responsibility if you prefer those) and whenever the dog tells us something that the scientist said didn't happen, listen to the dog. It has no hidden agenda: it simply wants to be a dog.

Some of the old scientific theories, such as pack rules and dominance, are really seductive to the human mind. This is only to be expected because we humans think like humans: it is an effort for us to change our attitude and think like a different animal, but at least we have the ability to do it. Dogs can only think like dogs, and how we must bewilder them with some of the things we do. Let's look at some of these theories that are so hard to let go.

The Wolf Business
Dogs are sufficiently closely related to wolves in physical terms that they can crossbreed, albeit with human intervention, as if left to their own inclinations,

4

the wolves would prefer to eat the dogs, and the dogs know it and would prefer to avoid the wolves. So, while crossbreeding can happen physically, behaviourally it isn't likely to happen without artificial assistance. This is an important distinction. Early studies on captive wolves led scientists to apply the results to dogs, but these studies were flawed in that wolves do not choose to live either in confinement or as a group of unrelated individuals. Wild wolf packs are extended family groups, not a random mix of strangers that met in the woods one day. Modern behaviourists liken those studies to observing humans in prisons and then taking the results to be normal behaviour, but they were all we had at the time, and their legacy lingers on. Experiments and studies are only as good as our interpretation of their results, and it is inevitable that some mistakes are made along the way.

While wolves and dogs have great physical similarities and some behavioural ones (there is a fair bit of wolf behaviour observable in the dog, but a lot of dog behaviour which is not found in the wolf) they split from their common ancestor millennia ago and grew into the divergent species we see today. Wolves are not dogs, dogs are not wolves, and neither is going to evolve into the other. It has taken wolves almost as long to evolve into wolves from this common ancestor as it has taken dogs to become domestic dogs, but dogs continue to change because we humans manipulate their genes by selective breeding. So while we learn about wolves by studying wolves, we learn a lot more about dogs by studying dogs. Given that domestic dogs are so easy to find in conditions that make study easy, one wonders why they have not been studied more, but maybe wolves were more glamorous.

African hunting dogs.
Photo: Chris Chappel.

Pack and Dominance Theory

Dogs are social rather than pack animals. They can choose to live in extended family groups, they can work as a team for specific reasons, notably the hunting of prey, they can seek out the company of other dogs and actually enjoy specific "friendships" with individuals, but what they have actually evolved to do is live with people. Such is the bond between domestic dogs and people that a litter of four-week-old puppies will make great efforts to approach and interact with humans, wagging their tails and giving every impression of pleasure at the touch of a human hand. Dogs of any age that have not been abused by people, and infinitely sadly, many dogs that have, will choose to approach people in a friendly manner. You don't get that with wolves, even hand-reared ones, including those beasts that have been raised with and learned to tolerate an individual human. Knowing how dogs like to be with us, some ethologists made a false link between wolf packs and our relationships with our dogs, and concluded that dogs lived with us in a hierarchal situation. Therefore, they thought, if we allowed the dog certain "privileges" our relationship with them would suffer because they would take over the family, and probably, given time, the rest of the world. Sorry, I made that last bit up just to show you how ludicrous the concept is, yet it was until recently widely accepted that a dog would "dominate" the family it lived with if given the slightest chance.

Therefore to avoid being eaten in our beds, we had to work hard to keep the dog under our authority. We were supposed to feed the dog after we had eaten, never let it on the furniture because it would see itself as above us in status as well as in height, never let it go through a doorway in front of us or run ahead on walks, not let it sleep on the bed with us, or even go upstairs, never to give it affection when it asked for it but only when we wanted, never let it "win" a game of tug, and ignore its greetings when we came home. A dog was deemed "dominant" for a whole range of harmless or normal behaviours: if it didn't like its food and so left it, if it stole or chewed up our possessions, if it didn't come when called, if it growled or snapped when it was scared, if it chased rabbits and squirrels, this was all due to "dominance". I'm ashamed of my species even writing that lot, but more extreme examples include our being told that we should wipe a child's used nappy on the wall above the dog so the dog knows it is below the child in status, and that when a dog is resting in its bed, we should step into the bed and force the dog to move so that it knows we are in control. We should also pretend to eat out of the dog's bowl before we give it its food, to prove we are above it in status, but we should not watch our dog eat because then it would think it was above us. Amazingly, there are trainers and behaviourists who still use dominance and pack theory, including some who are part of the examining team for certain respected behaviour qualifications. How on earth did we get into this appalling mindset?

Dominance and pack theory is very seductive to humans. We are a hierarchical species who like to think of a leader who is brave, strong, wise, historically male though there have been exceptions (whose sexual completeness is usually criticised) first in the fight, who dares and wins, gets all the best food, the most valuable treasures and the prettiest women. Studies of "pecking order" in chickens showed an apparant strict hierarchy in domestic poultry (from observation, this is also debatable), and somehow this idea was extended to all domestic animals despite the readily-available experiences to the contrary of those who looked after them. Poultry, herbivorous herd animals, and humans, are not dogs; anyone can see that and dogs certainly can, but actual observation didn't stand in the way of this wonderful theory that underlined our human superiority. In fact, subsequent studies on herd animals indicated what stock keepers have always known: the single male's job is not to rule the females but to impregnate them in due season. Anything the dog did that we didn't like was allegedly because it wanted to be above us in an inter-species hierarchy that just doesn't exist. Dogs know that they aren't people, and they know that people aren't dogs. How they would despise us if they thought in human fashion! They can hear far better, have an infinitely superior sense of smell, are weight for weight far more powerful, can run faster and further for longer, are more agile, have better teeth and stronger jaws, better vision in terms of detecting movement and making the best use of available light in night-time – they would think us pretty poor dogs if that was the way their minds worked. The dog is a co-operative species: given the chance and shown what we want, it is programmed to work with us, not to rule over us. We humans do so love our ranks and titles, but dogs couldn't care less. They don't want to rule anything. So what do they want? They want what works for them. They want what rewards them. And crucially, they want to feel safe. If our dogs feel safe with us, our relationship will be sound.

This is a good time to look at some of the behaviours that were blamed on dominance for so long.

Eating First
This was based on the idea that when a dog pack killed large prey, the "pack leader" i.e. the strongest male, ate first, and his underlings slunk to the feast after he had finished, in turn and in strict hierarchical order, with the pups last. This happy concept was not based on any proper pack study, but on those captive groups of unrelated wolves, who did pretty much eat in order of the strongest. When we started studying wild wolves in their natural environment, we discovered that wolf pups were allowed to feed right alongside the adults, and there was no waiting list – everyone got hold of some food and then took it away to eat it, rather than eating at the long table with the chief and only the finest warriors being allowed at the

top end above the salt. And these studies were made, let us remember, on wolves, not dogs, so were about as relevant as studying apes in order to find out about people. So the whole idea was incorrect and in any case about a different animal and in a highly artificial and rather unpleasant situation, for the wolf is a roamer and in its chosen habitat covers very long distances. Confinement does not suit wolves.

Domestic adult dogs in a biological family group will let pups feed alongside them, and even take food out of their own bowls, up until around six months of age, when "puppy amnesty" finishes and the young adolescent starts to be taught to mind its manners. However it is fairly uncommon to have domestic dogs in a family group as pets, and more likely there will be a new puppy introduced to a household of older dogs, often different in breed/type and therefore mindset. Whether it is allowed to eat from other dogs' bowls is better never discovered, as the unrelated group will vary in its level of acceptance, and many adult dogs are uncomfortable around puppies; after all, they mostly never meet one until one of the horrid things appears in their house taking up their owner's attention and competing for resources. Rather than stress out every dog and human involved, it is better to feed adults and puppies where they cannot get at each other and so can eat in peace. This is absolutely nothing to do with dominance and pecking order, and everything to do with common sense, especially as puppies need to be fed more often than adults. So, it really doesn't matter if you eat before, after or at the same time as your dog: what does matter is that everyone including us gets to eat without challenge, irritation or fear. Good

Pecking order.

stockmen used to see to all the animals in their care before their own needs, and that includes feeding; who can honestly enjoy their own meal while their animals are hungry? In terms of doing things the easy way, it is a lot easier to teach dogs to stay away from the table when people are eating if the dogs are not hungry, or expecting the end of our meal to signal the start of theirs.

Dogs on Furniture

Dominance theory argues that dogs get up on furniture because they want to be higher and therefore "superior" (note the human concept – high equals superior) than their owners, and we should not let them do so because of course we are higher and better – after all, we do pay the mortgage. What a way to mystify a perfectly simple situation! Dogs like furniture because it is raised, and therefore out of draughts and giving a great viewing area. Furniture is also softer than the floor. Therefore the dog feels both safer and more comfortable up on furniture than it does on the floor. If we do not want our dog on the furniture, then we need to commit the whole family to this concept, make sure that the dog has a raised comfortable bed, and never allow the dog up onto furniture, not even when it is a cute puppy we are desperate to cuddle. Instead, we get on the floor to interact with our dog right from the beginning. The furniture never becomes an option. We cannot expect a dog to comply when we are not there, though, so part of this system involves either closing the doors to rooms with furnishings on which we don't want the dog, or else barricading access, such as by upending chairs on the sofa, when we go out. This is training and management working in tandem to create desired behaviour.

If we have taken on a dog that has previously been allowed on furniture, and we wish to change this, then we retrain by attaching a short house lead to the collar – a short length of ribbon will do – and quietly returning the dog to its (lovely comfortable) bed with a combination of edible treats on the bed and leading with the house-lead. This will take quiet persistence and the patience of several saints, but the dog will get there in the end as long as it is never ever rewarded by anyone allowing it on the furniture at all, even "just for five minutes". The dog either has access to the furniture or it does not – anything else is unreasonable. However, dogs are smarter than we think, and people are often less smart, so we do get situations where people expect to allow the dog up beside them when they want it, and prefer it to stay off at other times. Many dogs will learn to comply with the specific invitation up, especially if that is preceded by putting a particular towel or other cover on the furniture before inviting it, and so will make the connection of "towel goes on sofa – I can get up on it". However, do not expect the dog to stay off the furniture at other times, as it then has an ambivalent situation of changing circumstances, and adapting to changing circumstances is one of the things at which dogs are very good indeed.

On and Off

Assuming the dog is to be allowed on furniture, it is useful to teach it to get off on command, for those occasions when we have visitors who would like to sit on the furniture also. We do this by making a training game of "On" and "Off" and luring with treats. Our body-language is important while we do this. Many people get into a hot-and-bothered confrontational position where they want the dog off the furniture, and the dog sinks down and growls. It is not being dominant – it is being misunderstood. First of all, a lot of us say "down" when we want a dog off the furniture, but if we have previously taught the dog to lie down upon being given the "down" command, then it is obeying us by sinking down on the sofa – it is doing exactly as it has been taught, and we are the numpties by thinking it can transpose one word to two different actions. Dogs do not speak our language: they simply link a word or phrase with an action. So we need to teach a different word – I use "Off" but you can say whatever you like, as long as you never use that word in a different context. But before we use the word, we "set ourselves up for success" by giving the dog a space to get off into. This is where we unconsciously make obedience more difficult, because we humans are great space-blockers, and space is incredibly important to animals because being hemmed in without a clear escape route frightens them. So – first think where the easiest space is for the dog to get off into, stand so that the dog can get into that space and if there is a direction you do not want the dog to go in, use your body to block it. Avoid anything threatening such as bending over the dog, and instead stay upright, relaxed and pleasant. Keep light thoughts in your mind because these will be echoed in your body-language, so rather than frowning out thoughts such as "damn you, dog, get off the sofa right this minute" think "come on then, off you get and go to your bed, and here is something nice for you when you get there". Dogs will welcome the softer body-language where they might feel uncomfortable with the annoyed stance. Remember, being nice doesn't mean you are weak, and being hard doesn't mean you are strong. Your objective is the dog off the sofa, but not to leave the matter there because that is only half the job – you need to inform the dog where you DO want it, not just where you don't. Dogs are more secure when we make their choices for them, and our wishes abundantly clear. It is unfortunate that we humans can be mighty negative and so easily focus on what we don't want rather than what we do, but animals need to know what we do want rather than what we do not.

What if the dog still won't get off? Cunning, trickery and opposing thumbs have got us where we are today, and there are better ways – oh such better ways – than losing our tempers and dragging the dog off the sofa. The thing is, we want the dog to get off willingly every time, but being confrontational will probably only succeed the once. Experience will result in the dog pre-empting, and where some will hurry off next time because they didn't like the way you acted last time, others will have figured out that they should raise the bar and snarl you a warning. This is not "dominance" but the dog only having limited communication skills. What it is trying to convey is that it is comfortable and happy where it is and does not want you to attack it like you did last time. But it manifests as a snarl or growl. If you have trained a solid On and Off, the dog has a comfortable bed to go to and you are offering sufficient reward, you should never get into this situation, but sometimes we take on a second-hand dog that has learned to fight its corner regarding staying on the sofa. It takes two to fight, and again you are not being weak by refusing to make a fight of it. There are better rewards for a dog than being on the sofa. We can put our shoes on and waggle the lead – and if we do, we must take the dog out, even if only for ten minutes round the block. We can hasten into the kitchen and open the fridge door and say "ooh look, what have I got here?" and if we do, we must provide a tiny food reward and then another on the dog's bed so it knows where we want it. Never lie to a dog, because it confirms their belief that you are unreliable and therefore not a safe place to be. They always remember lies, and they always remember people who are straight with them. It may be a smaller intellect, but it accompanies one helluva good memory.

"Changing the subject" to lure the dog into behaviour we want instead of bullying the dog out of behaviour we don't want, is not showing weakness or allowing the dog to "win". This is not a competition or a battle: it is all about communication. Laying foundations for willing co-operation in the future is far more dastardly than direct confrontation. Moreover, we always get what we want, and crucially, the dog gets what it wants as well.

Hierarchy

Though dogs do not get hierarchical with humans, there is an ebb and flow about how they see each other, and it is more intriguing than the clumsy old-style concept that this one rules over that one all the time. Resources are what matter to dogs: food, water, territory, attention, toys – because resources are all about survival. Though the modern pet dog may never have its survival threatened, it still retains the instinct to survive by whatever means, and this gives us our trump card because we are the ones who hold the resources, and we are (or should be) the ones who protect the dog. Therefore we too are a valuable resource if we have the right relationship with our dogs. Different resources matter most to different dogs. For instance, a very food-oriented dog might become challenging towards another dog over its meal, or a scrap of leftovers, while a less stomach-oriented dog does not see the food as sufficiently valuable to cause conflict. One dog might be consumed with pleasure at the thought of playing with tennis balls and footballs, while another couldn't care less. Another might be an attention-hog, and try to claim all the human attention, while a few might be indifferent to or even dislike it. So the dog that growls over its food, collects all the toys or always has its head ready for your hand, isn't being dominant over the others, but instead is demonstrating that these are the resources that matter so much to that dog at that time that it is worth competing for them.

Alpha

"Alpha" in the sense of the all-powerful chief ruler does not happen with dogs, but there are degrees of confidence and social adroitness. Because the word "Alpha" has been so misunderstood with old-fashioned interpretation of dog social structure, I prefer to avoid using the term. Yet we easily see the confident, urbane type of dog that other dogs respect, not in a kowtowing forelock-tugging deference, nor in cringing fear, but in a glad recognition that this is a very "together" canine, and so less confident dogs will feel safe around this one. Crucially, peer respect is not demanded by such dogs, nor is it necessary for them to reinforce their status by posturing or fighting. It is instead something offered by the others, and they offer it because that dog's presence gives them security. In a domestic situation involving several dogs, such dogs are worth their weight in gold for the stability they give their own group, and when that dog dies, the effect on the others can be seismic. Sometimes another dog assumes the mantle, sometimes not, for it is not in the personality of every dog to radiate calmness and confidence.

Combative Dogs

The truly respected dog does not normally need to fight for its position: it can quell most upstarts with the smallest changes of body-language. Most of us will remember a teacher like that from our schooldays, who only had to walk into a classroom for everyone to fall silent. Human nature is inclined to think that combative dogs are rulers-in-waiting, ready to challenge the calm dog for "leadership". But dogs that fight are the underconfident ones, seeking to bully other dogs in order to raise their own courage. Other dogs recognise their lack of true confidence, and so challenge them in turn, which is why we get dogs that always seem to be in a skirmish, and others that never get involved.

Peacemakers

Some dogs become agitated when other dogs posture, and will get between them and drive them apart. Peacemakers are not interested in "leadership" but they retain the instinct that says fighting weakens individuals and brings unwanted attention. This type of dog may never stand out in an established group, but its absence can have a significant effect on stability.

Play and Predatory Drift

This phrase refers to those occasions when two or more dogs are apparently playing nicely, and then one or more turns on one of them. The interpretation of this according to the "predatory drift" theory is that the attacking dog suddenly "forgot" that the other was a dog and in a primitive reversion to predatory behaviour, saw it as prey. It's an interesting theory but like so many others, needs a far fuller investigation.

Play in animals is not the sweet, benign, mutually enriching friendship display that we humans like to imagine it is. In fact, play in the human sense isn't either. Puppies play as a rehearsal for adult behaviour. They stalk, pounce, chase, hump, tussle, bite, run away and hide and come back for more, or else refuse to re-engage until the other puppy is more polite. All this is a good and necessary part of puppy development. Adult dogs, however, see other dogs as rivals rather than friends. Individual dogs can indeed have a few other dogs as "friends", and some become very happy in each others' company, but for the most part, other dogs are identified as potential competitors for resources. The "play" we see is actually dogs testing each other for strength, speed, courage and social adroitness. "Friendly" play occurs a lot less frequently than we think. You can see when a game of chase is friendly as the dogs will take it in turns to be chaser and chased, and if one dog is faster, it will slow down to let the other catch up with it. There will be play-bowing, relaxed body language and softly wagging tails. But far more often one dog chases and the other is chased, one dog will be giving appeasing signals and the other dog, instead of responding

Play bow.

Puppy play – a rehearsal for adult behaviour.

to them by backing off, will be getting more fired up. Having assessed the other dog as weaker, the stronger dog will attack. It knows full well that the other is a dog, not a prey animal, and it does intend to frighten it or do harm. Aggression is not part of predator behaviour when hunting: we don't feel aggressive towards our lunch. If that sounds a difficult concept, stop and think of humans "playing" at sport. Some of us don't even have to be playing the sport, merely watching or talking about it, to become aggressively aroused. Some people get so worked up over sport that they would risk losing a friendship rather than losing a game. Some are so tanked up after watching sport that they are spoiling for a fight afterwards. This is because the underlying theme of even human sport is not happy entertainment but the far more sinister and primitive aspect of assessing which of us is weaker.

So, getting back to "predatory drift", we can now see that it is nothing of the kind. The "playing" has simply done what was intended all along, and exposed the weaker dog. When we see this one-on-one it is bad enough, but with a group of dogs a nasty attack may follow with all or most of them pitching into the weakest one, as the primitive reaction to weakness in any social animal is to either kill or drive it away. This is hard to forgive if we see it, but it does not mean the dogs are "bad". They are simply being dogs.

Conclusions

In summary, we then see the dog not as a rival or competitor, but a species that has evolved to be with us, work with us, and accept direction from us in return for protection. They are not failed or substitute humans but successful domestic animals. It is their otherness that should make them so special to us. They are not better or worse, but different, and the sooner we can realise that, the sooner we can achieve the co-operation that they are capable of giving, if we only ask them in the right way.

Chapter Two

Jobs for the Boys

*Breed-Specific Behaviour – why you
can't train a collie the same way as a mastiff*

ALTHOUGH we don't yet know how the dog was domesticated, we do know why. The initial skills that we needed from the dog were hunting and guarding, and as our own species developed, we are likely to have used dogs for hunting first, during those times when mankind was still largely nomadic. Guarding meant property and therefore settlement, from which evolved the flock guards, and keeping livestock extended both the hunting and guarding dogs' remit to vermin control, personal protection, and warfare. Many dogs suited to these activities still exist, sometimes in somewhat diluted form, and occasionally wrongly categorised by task in the show world, which for instance gives us terriers that aren't terriers e.g. the Russian Black, spaniels that aren't spaniels e.g. the Tibetan, and sighthounds that aren't sighthounds e.g. the small Podengo. And of course, a great many dogs were dual or even multi-purpose, because then only one dog had to be fed, and it could perform a variety of tasks, so of necessity the categories overlap here and there.

Breed Traits

First we have a mammal, then we have a predator, then we have a dog, then we have a type, then we have a breed and finally we have an individual. So as a mammal, there are certain specifics with regard to physical matters e.g. warm-blooded and producing live young that are suckled, as a predator we have to understand the physical ability and mental desire to hunt and kill prey, and as a dog we see a particular mindset as well as a basic physique. By the time we get to type, our picture becomes really interesting – what are the genetic traits of this dog that affect the way it behaves? Breed refines type, such as with scent-hunting hounds that can be short or long-legged, rough or smooth coated, small, medium or large, specifically for this quarry or that and suitable to work over any particular type of terrain. Individuals have specific traits they share with all others of their type and breed, going right back in sequence to the basic mammal, but also special traits that come from their own ancestral lines. Hunt staff will often point out a hound that has a particular ability remembered in its forebears, and these talents come through generation after generation. Before addressing any behavioural issue, or ideally before even choosing the dog, we need to know what its original breed tasks were. We also need to understand the earlier links in the sequence. Although we can change the shape of a dog's body, its colour or coat in a very few generations, it takes a lot longer to alter its mindset. Although all dogs embrace broadly the same traits, selective breeding makes some better at or more willing to do some jobs than others. For our purposes, we need to know what the dog wants to do most of all, how it wants to do it, whether it is an independent worker or a team player, if it is programmed to work away from or towards us, whether the bark is important or only used as a last resort, whether it is people-friendly, dog-friendly, both or neither. We need to know what it finds most rewarding if we are going to train it with reward-based methods, and what is likely to go wrong first or most if we press the wrong buttons.

Bred-in traits can be controlled both by environmental management and training, but it is important to realise that we can never change what the dog wants to do. Where the dog's needs are at variance with our particular lifestyle – for instance we may not want a dog that can catch its own dinner

Foxhounds live and work in packs.

16

– we have to acknowledge the existence of the inbuilt need and then satisfy it in a way that does fit in, rather than just suppress it. Where instinctive behaviour can endanger the dog or ourselves, for instance by extreme guarding, we need to take care that the dog is never put in a position where the full behaviour has a chance to flower, because once expressed, it is so rewarding to that dog that it will seek to repeat that behaviour and develop it further, and practice makes perfect. This does not make the dog bad, vicious or any other such word: it is simply the product of its genes, which are the result of selective breeding for particular traits. Because a dog can do something does not mean it will. We need to be aware of breed characteristics in order to manage our dogs more skilfully, and avoid developing those behaviours that we would rather were left dormant. The following descriptions therefore express potential, and we should be aware that this potential, properly managed, never needs to become reality unless we wish it so.

Mastiff Types

Also known collectively as "molossors", mastiffs had several tasks, all of which involved working on their own initiative and if necessary, killing either man or beast. These dogs were characterised physically by large broad strong heads, punishing jaws, sizable bodies and loud voices, and were capable of fast short sprints as well as maintaining a steady trotting gait for hours in the course of duty. Some were confined on the premises they had to guard by means of fence or chain, while others patrolled flocks or property freely. Their job was not to

Molossor type.

search for trouble, but deal with it when it occurred, so if they chased a wolf or a robber, they were not required to pursue their victim indefinitely, but return to the confines of their flock or property once they had chased it to a suitable distance, or caught it and dealt with it. The mastiff was as much a deterrent as a protector, its very presence suggesting that wild animals or human intruders would be better to walk wide of that particular area. Mastiffs needed great strength and courage and an independent nature to perform their tasks. They had to be able to tell friend from foe, to be indifferent to human contact outside their immediate circle, and to stay in their own domain. Such dogs could have several owners in the course of their lives; human lives tended to be short in any case, and good dogs were commonly sold, bartered or gifted for diplomatic reasons, so mastiff types needed to be wedded to their tasks rather than their owners.

From some of these, great dogs were bred on for war. The Celts were famous for their war dogs, some reputed to be "the equivalent of four men in battle" according for instance to the Irish legend of Cuchulain. A war dog needed to be faster and more aggressive than a guard, and so it may be surmised that the larger, lighter types of wolf-killers were bred from for this purpose in preference to the more solid types. Many of our modern flock-guards could easily provide the baseline for a war-dog if crossed with something faster; the late Brian Plummer was experimenting with this just before his death, trying to recreate the Alaunt, a "running mastiff" noted for its aggression as well as its agility. The original "running mastiff" was more of a hound type, being used for hunting large game that was inclined to fight back. Its evolution paralleled that of European social development and its very efficiency, coupled with the development of firearms and a changing landscape, brought about its end as a functional animal once hunting methods changed. Though the type is extinct, fast strong dogs of mixed breeding are still used to hunt feral boar in Australia and New Zealand, and it would not take long to recreate useful running mastiffs under a dedicated breeding programme, for the basic ingredients still exist. So does the mindset, for although most pedigree mastiff types have been changed into far less agile beasts due to the fashions of the show ring, if the right situation presents, most mastiffs will still want to guard. A few years ago a very elderly mastiff surprised an intruder in its garden, charged at him baying loudly, and while the would-be burglar was trying to climb the fence, ripped the shirt off his back, then seized his ankle, pulled him off the fence and held him until his owner arrived. In all their years together, the owner had never seen this side of his dog.

Behaviour

In summary, the modern mastiff retains most of its early characteristics. It is independent, indifferent to humans outside its own immediate circle, has a desire to patrol, is defensive of the property it lives on and areas which it regularly visits, protective of its own people, suspicious of strangers, vocal in warning before it responds physically, and capable of both man and animal aggression if the wrong buttons are pressed. It doesn't much care for canine society and can be threatening towards unknown dogs. Owners of these therefore need to socialise their puppies very thoroughly towards all kinds of people, as many dogs of different sizes and types as they can, and put a lot of effort into training them to be safe with livestock too. Such dogs should be taught from puppyhood to behave impeccably on and off the lead, for they are far too big and strong to be allowed to pull and lunge. Owners should not expect them to be friendly with strangers, dogs or other animals, but instead aim for their dog ignoring these. Mastiff types have a good line in ignoring, appearing to think that the rest of the world is beneath consideration rather than needing intense investigation. They are not usually players of games or retrievers of balls, and it is not advisable to roughhouse with them, even as puppies. Recall can take longer because their natural inclination is to work independently of people and make their own decisions. This doesn't mean they can't be trained, only that these are the issues that will need more dedicated work.

Guarding Breeds

As well as the flock guards, we have breeds whose original purpose was guarding people, especially when those people were unpopular e.g. tax collectors or bailiffs, or habitually carried sufficient wealth to be worth robbing. There were dogs bred to run with fast carriages to guard against highwaymen, dogs that accompanied people on their rounds, dogs that came out on exercise with horses, but most of all, dogs that protected people who might otherwise be in danger from other people. These dogs were more athletic than the molossors, but of course their protective function would have been much reduced if they chased an attacker to any kind of distance,

Guard dog.

because then the person that they were supposed to protect would be at the mercy of any others. These dogs therefore had a strong desire to stand and fight rather than pursue, and even though their initial function is largely in the past, they retain their instincts to warn with eager barking, and to drive perceived threat away. They bond strongly to their own people, and tend to have one preferred member of the family to whom they are distinctly attached. There is as a result a tendency to develop separation anxiety if the wrong circumstances present while the dog is at a vulnerable stage of development. Several of these extreme guarding types have smooth coats and are by tradition docked and with trimmed ears.

Though these last two cosmetic alterations are illegal in many countries now including UK, it is worth understanding the original reasons for this, which was to give the victim little or nothing to get hold of while trying to fight off the dog. Additionally, the facial expressions of some of these breeds is difficult to see, often because of black and tan markings or black masks, and in the case of the boxer, little mobility of facial muscles. Other people-guards have a wolfish appearance with pricked ears, longish muzzle and bushy tail, which intimidates at a subliminal level, for many humans retain an instinctive fear of the wolf even if they have never seen one. All of the guarding breeds have a tendency to maintain strong eye contact, which makes them seem threatening to other dogs as well as humans. Because of the need to guard their own person, these breeds naturally stay close, and return quickly if they have moved away from their handler. They bark readily, are quick to take offence, and if not thoroughly socialised have the potential towards developing man-aggression to a greater degree than most other breeds.

Herding breeds
Everyone knows the Border collie, the herding dog par excellence, hero of countless films and children's stories, hyper-intelligent and beautiful with it. There are many breeds that do a herder's job, but few that can work with the precision and willingness of the Border collie. Outside the flock environment, this breed excels at a huge variety of other tasks, and has performed astonishing feats of learning under scientific conditions. Herding breeds are broadly task-oriented: they don't want to think about whether a task is worth doing because their whole raison d'etre is to obey orders. Some herders, however, are expected to work on their own initiative, for instance by crossing rough country alone to find and bring back livestock that doesn't want to come, such as feral cattle, and of necessity they do not employ the finesse of a dog more suited to working flocks that need a less feisty approach. While individual dogs can alter their approach to most situations, inevitably different areas favoured different types of dog, and so the bold cattle-herder did not generally find employment with downland

Herding dog par excellence.
Photo: D. Morgan.

sheep. Some herding tasks have become obsolete, such as the droving dogs taking great herds to distant markets and then finding their way home alone, finding their own food too, money (so the tales say) fastened to their collars, for few would dare tackle them. While it is sometimes hard to separate romance from truth, some of the breeds themselves still exist, and some of them retain this readiness to use their initiative. Pragmatism has ever been applied to the working dog, and so, for instance, the very biddable herding Border collie was crossed into the more independent droving Bearded collie to create a more versatile animal, and nowadays when these breeds are kept in separate categories by show enthusiasts, a disallowed colour appears from time to time to indicate that mixed ancestry. We may consider that this is not the only time something like this has happened, and so our various herding dogs might not be so far apart in their recent past, which again will affect behaviour.

"Herding" means different tasks in different areas, different countries and with different livestock, but broadly it does mean working under human direction at least some of the time, and, critically in training terms, working towards the human side of the arrangement. Outlying animals are brought to the herdsman, and herding types are more likely to stay with their owners, respond well to recall training and be mellow about being given orders, than breeds that are programmed to do everything themselves. Equally and less well-known is their desire for occupation, which they will find for themselves and in ways generally not liked by people, if their owners do not provide sufficient daily exercise and mental challenge for them. The desire to herd can be particularly alarming when directed towards other animals or children, especially as the process of herding includes an inborn nip, as anyone who has been "heeled" by a corgi or bitten on the bottom by a collie will testify. We cannot take that nip out of the dog, so we need to establish in early puppyhood that it is unacceptable, and ensure that it has no chance to develop into a full-grown habit. The nip does not mean that the dog is bad or vicious: it means it is a herding dog. The nip is preceded by the stare, and some herding breeds if not taken in hand early on will show a marked tendency to sink, stare, run at and nip humans, other dogs, other animals, even poultry. All too readily, they can extend the herding behaviour to moving vehicles or cyclists. As this is a genetic behaviour, performing the sequence gives huge reward, and encourages repetition at every opportunity, so if herding breeds are our pleasure, we need to commit to interrupting this behaviour whenever it shows the slightest inappropriate beginning, and replacing it with a more acceptable substitute.

Alert Dogs

Watchdogs could be indoor or outdoor. While the perceived picture is of a huge fierce-looking dog chained outside, to bark and warn of strangers approaching, there were also smaller types such as temple dogs, whose task was to notify monks or nuns that people were on their way who might need food and shelter. Equally, temple dogs needed to be prepared to guard, because temples tend to be isolated places often containing treasures, and which are occupied by peaceful people, so presenting a potential target for robbers. Alert dogs bark readily and do not stop easily without training, because their job was to keep on barking no matter how much strangers swore and threw things at them. Traditionally allowed to run loose rather than being chained in the way outdoor guards often were, they also needed the will to bite if necessary, and although most alert dogs are smaller than true guarding types, they are feisty, and quick to scale up their reactivity to running and snapping at people. Their job was not to drive off or hold down like the bigger guarding breeds, but to alert the people of the settlement and then let them take over. They still, however, needed the belligerence to impede those of evil intent by grabbing a foot or barking in their faces until reinforcements arrived. Alert dogs are generally very happy with human company and prefer it to dog relationships; they are intelligent and need mental occupation as well as physical exercise. Being a different type entirely from the herding breeds, their default mode is "bark at it" and so owners should aim at controlling the bark right from puppyhood. This does not mean suppressing the bark – that would be downright cruel, because the bark is very much part of the alert dogs' genetic makeup. It does mean acknowledging the warning bark and then limiting it by teaching "shush", rather than letting the dog bark unchecked. Equally it means teaching an alternative and more acceptable behaviour when visitors call, the telephone rings and so on, and never leaving the dog to bark at passers-by or wildlife it sees through the window, nor leaving it unattended for a barkfest in the garden. Alert dogs also have the will to go in and make contact, usually to hands, heels or even faces if someone is seated or bending, which is a behaviour that should not be allowed to develop. Grabbing at or using feet near this type of dog may be enough to stir the genetic programming into life, and they should never be encouraged to grip and pull at clothing.

Draught Breeds

Several specific draught breeds of dog exist, which can be broadly subdivided into the farm dog types, such as the Bernese Mountain dogs, and sled dogs such as the husky. In days gone by, a large dog was cheaper to acquire and keep than a pony, because dogs had litters of puppies, while ponies only produced one foal at a time. The dog could also be worked at a younger age, didn't need shoeing, and could draw small carts very effectively. Aside from specific draught breeds, which are celebrated nowadays at country shows, pulling decorated carts and looking smart and happy, prior to the early 20th century law which made using dogs for draught work illegal in UK, any dog could be and was harnessed and used to draw. It was generally a short and miserable life: many of them starved to death, and it was said that dog teams could be followed by the blood trail left by their feet. So the draught dog history in UK and elsewhere was an unhappy one, and a far cry from the modern concept of specific breeds of dogs giving cheery demonstrations in show rings (it is still legal to use draught dogs on private land). Similarly, although the various husky types are what we now think of as sled dogs, during the 19th century Alaskan Gold Rush, any type of dog was taken to the Arctic and used in a dog team, and the ones that survived would be bred from. The husky type was the greatest survivor for obvious reasons, but in fact purity of breed was not maintained at this time, and some interesting characteristics remain as a result, such as a susceptibility to the drug Ivermectin, which is shared by huskies and border collies, among others. We need to be aware of this, because latent mental characteristics can emerge in husky types which are at odds with the main perception, whereas the big breeds that helped peasant farmers to transport their goods are pretty consistent in their mentality.

Draught dogs used on farms would also have other functions, being used to manage all kinds of livestock and also warn when strangers approach, as farm dogs still do, whatever their origins, today. They were people-oriented rather than dog-oriented, because few farms could support more than one big dog at a time. Husky types by contrast simply ran in front of the sled, needing a totally different set of skills and obviously a different physique. Therefore modern husky types are still understood to have little desire to recall and a great need to run and pull. People are of less interest to most of them than other huskies, and they are not always tolerant of other breeds, nor even their own if outside their particular group. While the farm dog had to be benign towards livestock, the husky is known as a committed chaser and would-be killer, and if the farm dog would be content to stay on the farm, huskies have to be strongly confined, and are great escapers.

All this shows us that while the function may be broadly the same, the mindset is not, for these two types of draught dogs are very different in character, and this is something that cannot be changed. The husky types need a very particular kind of owner, one who is aware of their needs and prepared to fulfil them, especially their huge exercise requirements, while the farm dog types are more flexible in outlook and far better as general pets, though their guarding abilities should not be underrated.

Hunting Breeds

Where many working breeds are task-oriented, hunting breeds are very much results-oriented. Hunting is the process that leads up to a catch, and although any dog can and will hunt, true prey drive relates to the catch, and is seen at its purest in hunting breeds, that is, the scent-hunting and the sight-hunting dogs. Once this has been seen, no more will there be any doubt in the observer about real prey drive, and the chasing of balls and ragging of toys presented by other breed types, and often described as "prey drive" by their trainers, has absolutely nothing to do with it. We humans have used hunting breeds from time immemorial to catch our food and to find and kill predators. To do this, two distinct types of hound have been created, and only hunting dogs may be truly awarded the compliment of being called "hounds".

Scenting Hounds

In densely-wooded country, rugged hills, or where there is thick ground cover, we need a hound that can follow the scent of the prey animal until either the human hunters or the hounds themselves can catch it. Scent is pretty much a mystery to us humans: "There's nowt so queer as scent" said Surtees, through the mouthpiece of his famous hunting man John Jorrocks. Scent can be on the ground, caught in vegetation, or in the air, and seasoned hunters can tell a lot by watching whether hounds scent upwards or at ground level. Scent rises in certain atmospheric conditions, and falls in others, is moved about by wind, held by moisture, and disperses with time. Because we know so little about scent, and all dogs are born knowing a great deal about it, using dogs to hunt betokens a totally different relationship from using them for other canine tasks, where the humans are very much the driving force. Hunting dogs know far more about their job than we humans do: they lead and we follow. Hounds have to be independent enough to work on their own, but controllable enough to stop or return if bidden. Some breeds of hound are "low-scenting" or "deep-scenting", which means that they are capable of finding and following scent that is hours old. Allegedly, bloodhounds of old used to be considered capable of following scent that was days old; it would be interesting to find out if they still could.

Scenting hounds are customarily used in packs, for so capricious is scent that several noses tend to produce better results than one. To aid people following them through woodland and other tricky country, they were bred to bay (bark) as they ran, and from there grew a whole genre of hunting traditions where the cry of the hounds was as important as their scenting ability "match'd in voice like bells" as Shakespeare wrote. Indeed, the sound of hounds hunting in full cry touches a far-off race memory in most of us, and is thrilling even to modern mankind.

Therefore with scenting hounds, we have a dog that has been bred to follow scent to the exclusion of any distraction, to work as part of a team of dogs, and to make a specific noise while it is doing that. We can take the hound out of the hunt, but we can never take the hunt out of the hound. If we opt to own a scenting hound as a pet, we need to be aware that it will always find scent compelling, and far more interesting than anyone or anything else. When the nose switches on, the ears switch off; the hound has been bred for centuries to hunt without allowing anything to distract it, and that includes the owner trying to get it to return. We also need to know that, being a pack animal, it will prefer its own kind to any human, which is distinct from most other types of dog. The owner has a tricky balancing act with this, as the dog will naturally be drawn to canine company. In a two or more dog household, it will bond by nature to the other dog or dogs rather than to its human, but if kept alone, will tend to be very vocal when left, as it tries to contact other dogs. Traditionally kept kennelled outside in groups, hounds can be rather awkward as pets, for they need plenty of space, tend to be clumsy and boisterous, noisy, and needing careful management if they are not to put themselves at risk by running off after scent. They have tremendous stamina and require a great deal of exercise. On the plus side, their long history of working with people means that they are people-friendly, kindly dogs which easily accept human guidance as long as it is nothing to do with avoiding following scent or telling the world that they have been left alone. The history of hounds being kept and worked in packs means that they are accustomed to behaving the way their humans direct them, and because historically their job is done once they have either killed or brought their quarry to bay, they are generally quite happy to have the human part of the arrangement take hold of the quarry afterwards. This is, it has to be said, the result of ruthless selection, for any hound that showed aggression towards any other hound or any human would not be bred from, and so the further a hound is from working ancestry, the more chance there is for a touchier temperament to sneak into the gene pool. But generally, scenting hounds that are worked to animal quarry are exceptionally nice-natured, and it is incredibly rare to find one that does not adore people and want to be with them – as long as there is no scent to follow or pack to run with.

Man Hunters

A very few breeds of hound were developed to hunt people, and these by tradition were used in ones, twos (couples) or threes (leashes). The bloodhound

is the best-known of these, but there are others. This background is critically important from a behavioural point of view, because such hounds have little "packing" instinct, and although breed enthusiasts have worked hard to breed out unwanted temperament issues, they are not genetically as biddable as true pack hounds. They were – and are, where they follow their traditional job – worked on leads, so historically did not need to comply with the level of discipline displayed by other hounds. Where bloodhounds are used in packs to track one or more human volunteers and are then followed on horseback as a recreation, they are a little different from other hunting pack hounds. Many have been crossbred with other hounds, notably the black and tan Dumfriesshire foxhound, in order to instil a desire to work as a pack, and also to improve the general health and physique, which is comparatively poor in the show variety. Most bloodhound packs field a mixture of pure and crossbred hounds for this reason. It is often noticeable to the knowledgeable observer that, while some of these hounds are truly following scent, others are bowling along happily following their packmates and not hunting at all. Bloodhound voices are incredible: loud, deep and sonorous, they are thrilling to hear. When they catch up with their human quarry, the only danger is of being licked and nuzzled; however in the days when bloodhounds were used to find escaped criminals, slaves and so on, their reputation was far from gentle, and they were much feared.

Sighthounds

As the name suggests, these hounds hunt by sight; it is less well-known that they are more than capable of following scent too, and then switching from scent to sight-hunting to course (run down) their prey. Some are sprinters (e.g. greyhounds) some are stayers (e.g. salukis) but all of them rely upon their exceptional eyesight and speed to catch their quarry. They are traditionally worked solo, apart from Borzois which were used in groups of three to hunt wolves, but singly on smaller quarry. Nowadays there is quite a fashion to work sighthounds in groups, but unless the quarry is as formidable as a wolf, coyote or one of the larger deer, a single sighthound should be capable of bringing it to hand. From a behaviour point of view, it means that we have a highly efficient and committed hunter with a prey drive that makes most pack hounds look like lapdogs. This is not in any way a criticism of either but simply making the point that sighthounds don't rely on other dogs. They are not team players. They can – and they know they can – do the job themselves. What is more, they can't afford the time-lag where the scenthound by comparison follows scent until it catches up with its quarry. Instead they need a hair-trigger reaction to any opportunity, or they risk losing their prey. This means that as far as they are concerned, we can tag along or not, but they don't need us and they won't wait.

Where pack hounds are effusively friendly, sighthounds are most often described as "aloof". They tend to be one-person dogs, and while utterly charming to their immediate humans, they couldn't care less if they never met another person or – crucially – another dog. Traditionally, sighthounds lived with their people, whether in desert tent or baronial hall, Borzois again being something of an exception as they tended to be kept kennelled before the Russian Revolution, which almost wiped them out in their native land. So most sighthounds have an element of "guard" in them, and while known for their sweet natures towards people, they can give warning to strangers – and when a hound of that calibre warns, people would do well to take heed. So far as dogs are concerned, sighthounds like other sighthounds and don't seem to regard any other canine as worthy of their attention unless a specific relationship has developed. They don't look for trouble, and their first line of defence is usually running away, but they can give a good account of themselves if forced to, and are astonishingly fast to react if they must.

With eyesight that can detect movement a very long way away, and can make the most of any light available so that they appear to be able to see just as keenly in the dark, plus the speed to be somewhere else every quickly, sighthounds present their own training challenges, particularly as they are not programmed to return until they have either caught or lost whatever they were chasing. Because they are so very results-oriented, they have little patience for any training that seems pointless to them, which is why the more obedience-competition sit-stand-down-heel obeying orders for its own sake type of training will not appeal. They can be trained to a very high standard, but they need to see a reason and get a result. If pressurised, they will run away or down tools; they are smart dogs and will not fall for any trickery after the first time. They are also unforgiving, and masters at the art of passive resistance. While quiet in the matter of barking – they only ever bark for a very good reason – they do enjoy a good recreational howl. Sighthounds may appear nervous, but in fact what they are is sensitive: they read us well, and also their environment, because of their hunters' attunement to the natural world. Small changes are very important to sighthounds, which means that we need to manage their home life carefully to get the best out of them. This should not be seen as "giving in" to them, because it is all about understanding the raw material, rather than being a matter for human egos. Anyone egocentric would do well to stay away from sighthounds.

Gundogs

Dogs that assist humans in the finding and collecting of shot game are dogs of great endurance, capable of working long cold wet days and covering miles of unfriendly terrain. They are tough dogs with a huge work ethic, and need to be kept busy. For them, the task is all, and while some types work more under human direction than others, they are very much people-oriented dogs. Their main tasks are to find game, flush it when directed and not before, and to retrieve it once it has been shot. They should be eager to take direction, but also capable of using their initiative once sent for a retrieve, which may not always be where the human side of the partnership thinks it is. Ignoring the exciting smells of fresh game all around, once sent on a retrieve, the dog should only search for shot game; despite the inevitable smell of blood, the dog is expected to retrieve game to its owner without eating it or damaging it further. A soft mouth is vital for a gundog.

Most retrieving types are expected to be silent while working, which requirement varies from country to country. In UK all should be silent except one, the exception being the Sussex spaniel, the breed standard of which approves giving voice while hunting in cover, but only to the flush, so that the Guns know there is about to be the chance of a shot. Random babbling noise is not allowed, and the dedicated people who work this rare breed are very keen to maintain that standard. In other countries, gundogs are allowed to make a noise while working, but apart from as above, the merest squeak is an eliminating fault in UK Field Trials, and much frowned upon in the general shooting environment.

Gundogs adore water, and most take any opportunity to get into it, even in the depths of winter. While desirable in a working gundog, this can be challenging in a pet environment. It is unreasonable to expect such water-

Sussex Spaniel.

Gundog. Photo: F. Sechiari.

loving breeds to stay out of it, so exercise and house layout should bear this in mind – if we don't want a soaking wet muddy dog in the home, we either keep away from water on our walks or have a suitable place for the dog to dry off when we get back. While strong swimmers, gundogs can get into trouble in fast water, or else strike out for the horizon if taken to the beach, and owners need to be aware of this. The Labrador, probably the world's most popular retriever, did not start life as a gundog, but as a breed that helped men working on boats, and its affinity for water and swimming capability has survived in the breed to the extent that there are many stories of prodigious feats of swimming. Labrador owners in particular should therefore be very careful about the swimming opportunities they give their dogs, so as not to put them at risk.

Within this type, we expect to find a dog that is eager to find scent and follow it, thence to flush whatever creature it finds. Gundogs tend to be "mouthy" dogs because of the retrieve instinct, and as puppies especially, they can be extreme about needing something in their mouths. If not directed, this can spill over into grabbing hands and clothing, often quite roughly. Early bite inhibition training is very important for this type of dog. They can also be invasive of personal space with both dogs and people, which if not controlled may develop into body-slamming into either. Gundog programming is to work reasonably close to their person, but if not managed properly, they can be overcome by the need to find game and so disappear after it. They need people, need to interact with them, and are eager to oblige once they have been shown what is wanted and properly rewarded for it. Some gundog types are known as "velcro dogs" because they need strong and frequent physical contact with their owners; if you are an aloof type yourself and find needy dogs irritating, don't get one of these. If we do not use gundogs for their traditional tasks, we need to find other occupation for them that satisfies their need to seek out and retrieve.

HPRs, Pointers and Setters

HPR stands for Hunt-Point-Retrieve, and encompasses a variety of European gundogs, most of which are naturals at the Hunt and Point, but usually have to be taught to retrieve with more care. Pointers and setters are not required to retrieve at all, although many will. These dogs were developed to range across large areas of country finding game, particularly birds, by scent, and then to hold the game down by assuming a characteristic posture until the guns are within range. These dogs then flush on command. Ground game (animals) is often indicated by a different posture in the point, and these dogs are expected to hold their point for as long as required. They are also widely used in falconry for the same purpose, but when working with birds of prey, the dogs' entire job is to find and flush; they must never retrieve. This makes the task unrewarding for dogs with a strong retrieve instinct, which should be taken into account when choosing a breed for this work.

Pointers, setters and HPRs are dogs of great endurance, needing a lot of exercise, but unlike the retrievers, with far less inbuilt desire to return, because in their task, people go to them. They have excellent noses and a natural desire to find game. Apart from the desire to point and the controllability of the flush, they are not naturally as biddable as the retrieving types. They like people and other dogs, but as their work needs independence, they do not need either. Their exercise needs are more physical than cerebral, which means that any mental work has to be very rewarding if they are to attempt it, and is more tiring for them than it is for other gundog breeds.

Spitz Types

The spitz breeds' hunting function is very independent. These dogs are expected to find game in large areas of forest, to track it and then bring it to bay or tree it. Then they stand and bark to guide the hunter to it. Thus we have a dog with a powerful scenting ability, great endurance, an independent nature and the ability to bark literally for hours. Worked as individuals, they are not inclined to need the company of other dogs, and much prefer their own immediate group of people. Translate this to the pet environment and you have a dog that requires a lot of exercise, needs work to teach the recall as its nature wants it to hunt by scent and expect its people to catch up with it, and will be very noisy. All of this can be controlled, but will take more effort than with less driven breeds. Some spitz types are used for herding, especially reindeer; and this adds an extra dimension of challenge anywhere there are animals that might present a herding opportunity. Unlike the border collie, whose job it is to herd towards the flockmaster, this type of herder moves stock from one place to another, and so does not have the extreme desire to work towards people in the way the collie has. This is significant when training recall.

Terriers

True terriers fall into two broad categories. The proper terrier function is as a vermin dog capable of finding, and bolting or killing, a variety of animals both above and especially below ground. Regardless of the laws of any land, that is the purpose of the terrier, and though laws change and the main terrier function has either been diluted or banned completely in many countries, this is what the terrier instinctively wants to do. The sheer raw courage required to go into tight tunnels and confront a well-armed foe in the dark, often one advantaged by size and dentition, should never be underestimated. If a terrier encounters foe that does not bolt when met, the terrier is required to bark continually in order to hold the prey at bay while its handlers dig down to it and despatch whatever it has in front of it. Therefore we have a bold and tenacious dog with a loud voice, which is easily capable of barking for hours, has a natural desire to pursue scent, wants to go down holes to take the fight to anything, and holds its ground without quitting even if injured. What we also need to realise is that terriers love to do this and get an enormous thrill from it. We cannot force a dog to do what terriers do – they really want to do it. The occasional terrier that does not fulfil its working destiny does not get bred from. This is in regard to working stock, because show terriers not only are not required to work, they are bred to show criteria which makes most of them the wrong size and shape for working. Ghosts of their original job still motivate them, but the show terriers seldom have that fierceness that is a vital requirement for their working cousins; however they are still capable of finding pleasure in combat, and of barking at anything that might be prey. So whether a terrier may be bred for the show ring or the fox earth, its tendencies are to take the fight to anything and everything that might present an opportunity regardless of size, and to make a lot of noise. The latter trait is lacking in the Bedlington, which was traditionally a silent worker, though possessed of a deep bark in other situations. An old saying goes that if two Bedlingtons are quiet, it is because one is trying to kill the other.

There are several terrier breeds that are too large to work underground, such as the Kerry Blue and the Airedale, and purists say that they should not be considered terriers at all, but while these polarised arguments will never cease, for our purposes, which are behavioural, these bigger terriers very much retain the terrier mindset. Terriers do not back down, so where some breeds in fearful situations will shut down or run away, terriers that are afraid will take the fight towards whatever it is they find threatening. It is vital to understand this. Their combative nature is very much a part of their characters, and in no way a fault or an exception. They are sensitive dogs and clever too, capable of figuring most situations out, and the majority of terrier breeds are very trainable when not working. Once we are at one with the terrier mind, we can fulfil their needs with more acceptable behaviour, and control the amount of barking that they are capable of producing, while keeping them out of trouble. Correctly motivated, there isn't much that a terrier can't learn.

Fighting Breeds

There is nothing new about organised dog-fighting, and many more breeds than seem obvious have a historical background of being used to fight each other. The molossor breeds still have to prove their courage in some countries by being matched in fights, and only the most savage and strong are bred from in those environments. Some of the larger breeds of terrier, notably the Kerry Blue, the Wheaten and the Bedlington, have fighting antecedents; more surprisingly perhaps, so has the bantamweight Chihuahua, which is not a terrier at all. In UK we have the collective "bull breeds" where the bulldog of long ago, a more athletic creature than the modern version, was crossed with fighting terrier breeds, some now extinct, to create the smaller and more agile "bull-and-terrier" which term was shortened to "bull terrier" in due course. These feisty breeds travelled over much of the world courtesy of their performance in the main (fighting arena), and while once English bull terriers and Staffordshire bull terriers dominated, the evolution of the pit bull terrier eclipsed them as the fighting breed of choice. In some countries, whether legally or not, these dogs are still fought, along with a number of other breeds, some of which are illegal to import into the UK, such as the Dogo Argentina, because of their fighting heritage. Behavioural characteristics are sharply split between those dogs that had to be handled even in the thick of a fight, which includes the bull breeds, and those that could barely be handled even out of it, which covers most of the molossors. Hence the bull breeds usually have to be badly maltreated before they will turn on a human, but the molossors in those countries where they are still fought are readily antagonistic towards strange people, and indeed even their own at times. Bull breeds are known to be people-friendly to a marked degree, and because of their high pain threshold, are especially forgiving of careless handling, hence very good with children. All fighting breeds have this high pain threshold, and a marked endorphin release as a pain response to parallel it. Behaviourally, the instinct to back off when another dog assumes a submissive posture has been bred out of most of them, and the desire instead to follow through and kill has been enhanced. They are foursquare dogs with a low centre of gravity so that they hold the ground and are not easy to knock over. They have immense jaw power, and bite well above their weight. Bite tests conducted in the USA are well-documented, and not surprisingly the molossors score the highest, but the bull breeds have an astonishingly powerful bite to weight ratio. Laws in UK that ban ownership of certain breeds are based on this potential rather than what the individual dog actually does, which is understandable taken in that context, because if something goes wrong, then it goes tragically wrong in a very short time. However, laws are not necessarily just, and justice is not necessarily the law; these laws are overdue to be upgraded and one hopes for the better where individual cases are concerned.

While it is necessary to acknowledge the laws concerning dogs (and dog-fighting has been illegal in UK since 1835) we here are concerned with behaviour, and it is very important to be aware of the genetic bias that dogs with fighting ancestry have towards – unsurprisingly – fighting other dogs. This does not mean that these dogs will fight, but it does mean that they are genetically predisposed to it, and if that particular switch is thrown, there is no going back. Fighting breeds can go all their lives without so much as raising a lip to other dogs; they are delightful companions to people, they are naturally tolerant and benevolent towards humans, very tactile and with a huge sense of fun. They don't like other dogs. Rehoming organisations that specialise in this type of dog can be very economical with the truth in this regard, making much of what wonderful family dogs the bull breeds are, and how great they are with children, but never mentioning any caveats about other dogs, and this is unforgivably irresponsible. Once that attribute has been absorbed into the potential owner's understanding and the resulting responsibilities accepted, there is no reason to dispute the type's value as a family pet, and countless people have grown up happily with them and would not have any other.

Toy Breeds

Lapdogs, small breeds, those considered to be ladies' or old people's companions have been around for centuries. To begin with, they fulfilled several additional functions to that of being company, for they killed rats and mice that appeared plentifully in dwellings, provided warmth, barked at strangers, and had spirit enough (if not size) to defend their owners if under threat at a time when even grand houses were not all that secure. Therefore we see a feisty little dog, quick enough to snap up rodents, alert enough to give a warning to undesirables, and very fond of human company. I admit I was guilty of underestimating lapdogs in general, until I came to study them. I found the level of natural empathy that these small dogs have for their people was far in excess of anything I had expected, and that the term "companion" meant a lot more in this context than simply being small, appealing creatures with soft coats and a tolerance of being held and cuddled on laps. Lapdogs tend to have infantile appeal through being bred to have big round eyes set in round faces, similar to a human infant, which does them no good at all in the way some people see them as baby substitutes – which, sadly, they often are. In this way, they so often fulfil human neediness to the detriment of their own requirements, and this is replicated even nowadays in the fashion for small dogs being kept as "handbag dogs". But small companion dogs are still very much dogs, and if only given the chance, they can be so much more than a sop to human loneliness. They are quick, bold, talkative, and will very much enjoy running about out of doors, following scents and getting muddy, just like any other dog. Their huge advantage as a pet is their level of empathy with people: they really do like us, want to be with us, and will fit in with however we feel at the time. Behaviourally, as long as their basic needs are met, they enjoy doing things with us, have lively minds and are quick to pick up training, though they can be vocal if not given guidance and sufficient occupation.

Intelligence

One of the amusing – and often exasperating – aspects of researching into different breeds is trying to get useful information from those who breed, show or work them. Of course we all get involved in different breeds and types because we have an innate preference for them, but that all too often makes people "breed blind". When I first became involved in studying dog behaviour and investigated an unfamiliar breed, I would ask the breeder or owner what the dog was like to train. I would invariably get a nonsense answer on the lines of "they know their own minds" well, yes, don't they all, but what were they like to train? If I persisted, I found that everyone described their breed or type as "intelligent". This too, to put it politely, was a misnomer. There is no doubt that some breeds are far more intelligent than others, and while this at first may seem just the kind of dog we all want, we should beware of the demands made by a highly intelligent dog every bit as much as the potential frustrations brought about by those breeds that are less bright. In fact, the latter are much easier to own as long as we make due allowance for their mental capacity and take care to break down training into chunks small enough for them to manage.

But how do we define intelligence, especially in an animal? Pat Parelli, the famous horse trainer, says that, "People are intelligent, but animals are smart. Every one of us has been outsmarted at some time by an animal." True enough, and we need to see "smart" as the fast use of natural instincts to bring about a desired result, where "intelligent" is more about problem-solving. "Smart" links cause and effect very quickly, often giving a result that people do not want, but intelligence anticipates, producing sometimes fascinating results, and even on occasion responses that bring us perilously close to challenging that scientific "certainty" that animals cannot think in the abstract.

There is a study on canine intelligence from some years ago that has passed into scientific "factoid", that is, one of those theories that "everybody knows" is "true", and while the original study no longer exists, there is a table of canine intelligence by breed that is widely available to dog enthusiasts as a result of the conclusions reached by the original researcher. The actual study, though, simply involved contacting a sample of around two hundred dog trainers in America, and asking them for a list of breeds that were likely to obey obedience commands the first time they were told, and those that would not. Unsurprisingly, task-driven dogs were top of the list, and results-driven dogs at the bottom. Classifying intelligence as a willingness to obey pointless commands indicates the limitations of the study.

So how might we observers of dog behaviour do better? One way is to refer back to the dogs' original tasks, considering how much initiative they need to perform them and which types might fail by showing too much enterprise. It isn't infallible, but it does give a good starting-point. Biddability does not necessarily indicate intelligence, and truculence is not purely the attitude of the mentally-challenged dog. Most of us know highly intelligent people who are not at all co-operative. While at the top of the scientist's list was the universally brilliant Border collie, which I believe most researchers as well as dog trainers would agree is an extraordinarily intelligent – and smart – breed, those dogs lower down the list have in my opinion been underestimated. It is a human failing to categorise something or someone as "stupid" far too readily. Umpteen times I have heard people describe their dog as "stupid" when what is actually going on is that the human has not understood the dog's communication, or the dog has no incentive to obey the human and therefore does not.

So when we choose a breed to share our lives, we need to be aware what true intelligence is, so that we know whether we want a canine Einstein or a less demanding animal. A dog that can problem-solve and anticipate can easily stay one step ahead of its owner. Fast learners learn quickly, whether we want them to learn those things or not, and dogs never forget what has worked for them, so we need to keep our training mistakes to a minimum. We should be clear about how much time we are prepared to devote not just to training, but to providing mental stimulation for the lifetime of the dog. Sadly, breeders and breed enthusiasts are often unreliable at providing this information, so we need to revert to our own experience, observation and common sense.

Lifestyle and the Dog

Given the foregoing, we can see how important it is to know how a dog's genes impel it before we commit to owning this breed or that one. While people are usually careful about a dog's physical appearance, it is far less likely that their choice includes researching its behavioural tendencies. With mixed breeds, it is a lottery, especially if those breeds are very different. For instance, a cross between two or more gundogs is going to be fairly predictable in nature, but a cross between a gundog and a molossor far less so. Once we are aware of a dog's inborn needs and drives, we hold the key to training it for best results most easily obtained. In some cases, we do best to find a trainer who concentrates on and has in-depth knowledge of our particular type of dog, because intelligent trainers understand that different training methods suit different dogs. As far as unwanted behaviour goes, we can see more clearly what is likely to happen and how to pre-empt it if we are already aware of what the dog would prefer to do if left to its own inclinations. We move dogs into our own world and then have expectations of them that are often unrealistic and sometimes unreasonable too; behavioural "problems" are almost always problems of our own making, either environmentally or genetically. Knowing the dog is one of the most important foundations on which to base our training.

Chapter Three

Training that Works

Motivational Training and Why Some Methods are Undesirable

THERE ARE TWO main levels of dog training: training dogs to live in harmony with us and by our rules in our world, and training dogs for specific tasks so that they can work for us: hunting, herding, police and military work, assistance work and so on. For the latter tasks, we choose dogs that already have the inborn desire to perform whatever is the essence of those particular jobs, and fine-tune them with training. We do not have to consider motivation, only structure. Oddly, we do not do this so much with our companion dogs, most people choosing their pet for its looks rather than how it will fit in with their lifestyles.

There are of course many dogs that are not trained at all, and live perfectly serene lives close to humans but not actively involved with them, such as street dogs found all over the world. This last group is apt to meet an early and probably unpleasant death from traffic accidents or when local committees instigate stray dog purges, but until then, they pretty much manage their lives on the edges of human habitation, any that are antagonistic to people or take a too-keen interest in livestock being killed early on. They are not dogs inclined to interact with people, though occasionally individuals waylay a tourist who eventually takes them home at great expense, to live "happily ever after" in a more constrained environment. I wonder how they really feel about that? We shall never know.

I mention this last aspect because it is only relatively recently that we have come to ask so much more of our pet dogs. It is only in the last century or thereabouts that so many dogs were considered purely companions: even ladies' lapdogs were supposed to keep vermin down inside the house, and also to offer a guarding voice even if too small to do much about an actual attack. Where dogs were always very much dogs, they can now be expected to be entertainment, companionship or a human substitute to a degree seldom seen in days gone by. This has contributed to a great deal of tension and misunderstanding between dogs and people in the pet environment, but as a result, we are beginning to understand dogs better, because we have to find out what has gone wrong when something does, and how best to manage it when we do.

First we need to acknowledge that many of the ways we want dogs to behave are alien to the ways they are programmed to behave. This is crucial to our understanding of why a dog might be "stubborn", "independent", "naughty" or even "bad". Of course dogs are none of those things – they are simply being dogs. We take them into complicated areas we call our homes, expecting them not to soil indoors when "indoors" is a concept not easily understood by dogs, we expect them to know whether we want them on or off the furniture, we leave them alone for long spells and expect them to be quiet, we surround them with food and smelly items and expect them not to eat the food or chew the smellies, we speak a different language but expect them to understand what we want if we shout, we put strings round their necks and expect them not to pull against them, we hurt and frighten them and expect them to forgive us. All of this in a society where dogs are supposed to endure physical contact they don't like from people they find unpleasant, come when they are summoned even if they are doing something really interesting, live with other dogs they don't like or other animals they want to eat, and to behave better than a human of the same mental age. And most of us have no idea how lucky we are that dogs are so co-operative that they will learn these things if only we make it plain to them what we actually want instead of expecting them magically to know it all.

Training has come a long way in a short time, and it is inevitable that residues of previous training methods remain even though modern training is far more effective. We humans are a very punishment-oriented species; the message to our dogs used to be "do what I want or it's going to hurt". This worked up to a point, and was also the way many people raised their children and ran their workplace. What it did result in was a lot of "wastage" i.e. dogs that did not comply. Therefore punishment was increased often to the point of abuse, and if that still did not produce the desired result, for most dogs that meant the abrupt end of their lives. That one person could take on another's canine "failure" and make a fine dog of it was never seen as a lack in the previous training methods, but instead as a secret skill of the new trainer, or else the dog seeing sense at the eleventh hour. That many dogs were killed which could have been good dogs in other hands or for the want of some patience was not seen as a waste. Genetics being what it is, the upshot of these harsh methods was that surviving dogs that were bred from passed on more compliant natures to their offspring, so this crude system of culling did indeed provide a "better" dog. Late developers did not live to perpetuate their genes, and nor did the recalcitrant. Where people such as myself who enjoy getting into a dog's mind and unravelling its troubles see this as an appalling loss of potentially good dogs, it is undeniable that in the short term, this ruthless eradication of undesirable characteristics was directly responsible for the majority of nice-natured biddable pet dogs that we see today.

But times change, and nowadays we as a society are more tolerant of canine foibles, to the point when many of us put up with a level of misery directly related to dog-ownership that is as unreasonable as the killing of those dogs in times past who didn't obey even when we hurt them. Also there is more pressure on dogs, which, instead of living outside in kennels or being confined to the scullery and garden, are sharing our homes with us on a much closer level. In my childhood, dogs were turned out each day to stray until their owners came home again; some dogs and most cats in UK still live this way, and my family was considered quite strange because our dogs were confined in our garden, and taken out for walks. Dogs allowed to stray, while being a confounded nuisance to the neighbours, and being very much at risk of being run over, shot, poisoned or stolen, did at least socialise themselves with other dogs, and found plenty of exercise and occupation. So we very seldom had to deal with such issues as separation anxiety, destructiveness, aggression or the problems of ageing, because dogs seldom reached old age and aggressive dogs died early. There was usually someone at home all day, so dogs did not get bored or lonely, therefore there was no separation anxiety and no need for destructiveness. All this has changed, and while I would be the first to say that in today's society it is inappropriate to let animals stray, it did create a rough kind of natural selection so that certain behaviours did not occur in any measurable degree. Add that to the training-or-death methods already mentioned, and we can see that a hundred years ago we had a different type of dog, which lived in a harder but less demanding society. I am not saying for one moment that it was better, just that it existed.

Dogs now are more appreciated as individuals, and I believe that we have the opportunity to be far more enlightened for the most part in how we keep them. But we have a number of stumbling-blocks to overcome with the modern dog, and before we start to look at training, it is time well spent to look at the dogs themselves.

A good breeder.

The largest number of dogs we see now are pet dogs, bought to be family companions, child substitutes, company, competition dogs, emotional props, show dogs, or if they are really lucky, just because we like dogs and want one to live with us. Where do we source pet dogs? Many pet dogs are bred by puppy-farmers, breeding large numbers of puppies for profit, quite often from dubious parentage in that they have had neither physical or mental health checks and the puppies have little or no opportunity to learn and socialise (see Chapter Seven). The puppies are advertised on the Internet, in local papers, in shops and markets and by notices outside the gate. These are not necessarily badly-reared puppies, though many puppy-farmed puppies are sickly or have genetic illnesses that would not be found in a quality litter. It is a far bigger risk to buy a puppy from these sources than to buy from a breeder who has the interests of the breed and their own puppies at heart. But good breeders choose their puppy owners carefully, and will turn down some people because they feel they will not offer a suitable home. Most such people do not then go home and change their lifestyle to be more dog-friendly – they go to a puppy-farmer. This all has an impact on future training.

Training Terms

Let's have a quick run through what is meant with well-known training terms, because sometimes trainers advertise that they only use this or that method, when a closer look indicates that perhaps they are not following quite the methodology that they indicate. All training/behaviour modification comes under the heading of either Classical Conditioning or Operant Conditioning, terms which might make your eyes glaze a bit, but which are easily explained, so resist the desire to turn the page and miss this bit, because it is the foundation of how to get dogs to do what we want.

Classical Conditioning

This is the "Pavlov's Dogs" term, where long ago the scientist Pavlov found that ringing a bell immediately before feeding a group of dogs would result in the sound being associated with food to the degree that the dogs' mouths would water when they heard the bell even if it was not a normal feeding time. Classical conditioning is essentially passive, involuntary and out of the conscious control of the animal. There is therefore relatively little classical conditioning we can use in everyday dog training. However where a certain set of circumstances has caused a dog to react in a manner we don't want, we can classically condition a change of attitude by pairing that circumstance with a reward. For instance, the dog goes in the garden and barks at the neighbour's dog, which barks back and starts a lot of noise that nobody (apart from the dogs) finds pleasant. In a series of steps, we re-programme our own dog to turn to us for a reward whenever it hears the neighbour's dog barking, so that from "next door's dog barks = I bark" we get "next door's dog barks = I go to my owner for a reward". Our dog becomes classically conditioned to pair the sound of the other dog barking with going to us, expecting and getting a reward. To achieve this, the reward of the new behaviour must vastly exceed the reward of the old behaviour, and we have to understand that the reprogramming takes time. If we allow the old behaviour to re-establish, then we have to start from the beginning again.

Operant Conditioning

This is what we customarily use for training our dogs, and the difference between it and classical conditioning is that the animal has a choice. It voluntarily produces the behaviour, and it is our job to see that our training method results in the behaviour we actually want. Bad timing is the downfall of operant conditioning, but fortunately it is usually possible to correct if we inadvertently train the wrong response. For instance, if we run to the door every time the bell rings, we can easily accidentally "train" the dog to run to the door with us, because its rewards are the excitement of running with us, and then lots of attention when it jumps all over the visitor. Attention, even of the uncomfortable sort where the dog gets shouted at (What fun! Now everybody is barking) is still rewarding, and in little time we create a dog that runs to the door barking, jumps all over the visitor, gets screamed at and becomes even more giddy, and develops into an excitable nuisance every time the doorbell rings. We re-train that by linking the doorbell ringing with a preferred behaviour, such as the dog being sent to its bed and being given a treat, so that when visitors arrive, the dog goes to its bed by choice and waits for its treat. Only then does the visitor come in, and the dog gets a second reward of quiet attention.

Positive Reinforcement or R+

R+ means adding something good

This means that the dog receives a reward for performing the wanted action. The dog mentioned above is told "bed" when the doorbell rings and once on its bed, it gets a treat. Thus the word, the action and the reward associate in the dog's mind. It is clear what is wanted of it and the dog is rewarded adequately for performing the action. Once the sequence is fixed, the food reward can be faded out until it appears randomly, then may not given at all, or only very rarely. The message is: " Do that and you can have this pleasant result". In this specific case, once the dog is on its bed and the visitor comes in, the dog may progress to being allowed to greet them in a controlled manner, such as on a lead, and so the food reward is superseded by the dog being allowed to interact with the guest – which is what it really wanted to do and so is an even better reward. If the dog becomes over-excited in its greeting, it has to go back to its bed until it is calm, and so learns impulse control. This is how we can manipulate behaviour with a sequence that is easily understood by the dog. Positive Reinforcement increases the frequency of the behaviour, and also motivates dogs to use their initiative in response to their handler.

For R+ to work properly, the reward for doing what is wanted should exceed the reward of doing what is not wanted, which can be quite tricky at times. This is why R+ works best when dogs have not yet learned the unwanted behaviour, because a lot of behaviours that the dog would choose to do are more rewarding than the behaviours we want from them. There are some situations where we simply cannot produce any reward on a scale to match the reward the dog will get from doing what we don't want, and in these cases we are better to use management. The alternative would be a severe aversive, which is a real hot potato in ideology terms. We'll look at this option in more depth further on.

Negative Reinforcement or R-

R- means removing something unpleasant

Negative Reinforcement involves the removal of a negative experience in order to encourage a certain behaviour. For instance, the dog tries to barge through the door as the person opens it, so the owner closes the door and tells the dog to sit. The dog sits and the owner opens the door, but if the dog runs forward, the door is closed before it can get through it. The dog learns that it has to sit until called through the opened door. In stages, the dog finds that it can only go through the door if it sits first, which causes the closed door to be opened, and then it waits until it is called through. By removing the negative – the closed door – once the dog produces the wanted behaviour – sitting – the dog is rewarded by being called to go through the doorway. Negative Reinforcement increases the frequency of the desired behaviour.

Positive Punishment or P+

P+ means adding something unpleasant

Old-style training was mostly positive punishment. Punishment does not have to hurt the dog: frightening it or making it uncomfortable is still punishment. For instance, each time the dog jumps up, it is hit with a rolled-up newspaper. This shows it that jumping up has uncomfortable consequences, but does not give it any alternative guidance on what we would like instead. The message is: "Life will get unpleasant every time you do that". Positive Punishment decreases the frequency of the behaviour. But by failing to show the dog an acceptable alternative behaviour, we do not necessarily succeed, as the dog may develop another unwanted behaviour instead. This is shown by the huge number of dogs that produce the same unwanted behaviour all their lives, despite being punished when they do so. Some dogs respond to P+ by refusing to volunteer any behaviour in case it is "wrong" and therefore results in punishment.

Negative Punishment or P-

P- means removing something pleasant or rewarding

This relies on knowing what the dog wants. For example, if a dog is attention-seeking by barking, the owner leaves the room each time it barks, counts to ten and re-enters. The dog will link the barking with the owner leaving, which is not what the dog wants. If the owner is consistent, the dog will stop barking for attention. However as it still wants attention, it should get appropriate attention as the reward for stopping barking. Negative Punishment decreases the frequency of the behaviour.

Motivational Training

Successful training incorporates each of these, but to different degrees. Usually people want to train largely by R+ and P+ but best results are attained by using all of them. This at first may seem odd, as survival has to train by negatives: we don't normally get too many chances at escaping from tigers. But what we want from our dogs is a lot more than survival; in fact the range of behaviours we expect from them is often counter-productive to surviving. We expect them to walk on leads when they would prefer to move about freely, to stay in a restricted area when their nature is to roam, to spend long periods of time alone when they are social creatures, to endure treatments, scents and sounds that cause them actual discomfort, and to suppress many of their natural drives. The highest motivator of all is the environment: if we give the dog the environment it needs, it is far more likely to respond by displaying the behaviour we want. And what dogs need most of all is to feel safe. If we become their "safe place" to go to, if we shield them from what they perceive to be dangers (not necessarily what we think is dangerous) if we arrange their lives so that with us they have enough to eat and drink, a secure comfortable place to sleep undisturbed, sufficient exercise and mental stimulus, if we are the greatest feature for good in their lives – they will find our presence rewarding. From this, we train them to do what we want by making the results of this more pleasurable than the alternatives. Sometimes it is a close-run thing between what we want the dog to do, and what the dog would do if we weren't calling the shots. Therefore we seek to make the desired behaviour more rewarding than the undesirable one.

Rewards and Bribes

People often resist changing to reward-based training because they think it shows weakness in themselves. They feel that a dog should obey them without any kind of reward, just because they are wonderful humans, utterly superior to dogs. Bribery, so offensive to our culture, is almost a term of insult. Fancy having to bribe a dog to get it to do something! So we have to let go of thoughts like this, and look at matters from the dog's point of view. Why should it please you when it can perfectly well and with a lot less effort please itself?

I frequently come across the comment that dogs should obey you because they love you. Anyone with teenagers knows that love is not a sufficient incentive for obedience. Whether dogs do love us, or love us in the way we think or hope or would like them to, is a moot point in any case. For sure, the dog that feels safe with us and unsafe away from us is much easier to

Border collie – task oriented. Photo: D. Morgan

train than the confident dog, which tends to work with us rather than for us. Other people think that the dog should do what we want because we are human and therefore better: we pay the bills, take them to the vet, supply their food and exercise, and own the house. This idea is very satisfying to the human ego, but the dog may well not agree: we are different but not better. Dogs have no comprehension of how dependent on us they are, and how could they know, when in their experience there has always been some form of food and territory? We hold all the resources, so dogs acknowledge that doing what we want can be advantageous but as for thinking we are "better", we should disabuse ourselves of that notion early on.

But many human cultures make the world go round, and in some of them, bribery is perfectly acceptable. So it is with dogs. We begin training them with bribery: "If you do this, I'll give you that" and develop the idea with reward: "thank you for doing that – here, have this". Dogs do not think the worse of us for capturing their attention and guiding their responses by offering something pleasant. Indeed, they quickly become extremely co-operative if doing what we want is also made worth their while. And when you think of it, although we might or might not be repelled by bribery, all of us work better for reward, not just at that moment (you can go home early from the office) but in the future too (here is your annual bonus). If the dog produces a behaviour and is rewarded for it, the dog will repeat that behaviour expecting another reward. Does that mean we have to reward it every time? Not after the behaviour has become fixed in the dog's mind as an appropriate response to a given cue or situation. This is where our cunning human minds are able to exploit the dog, because nobody ever got hooked on a vending machine, but gambling is highly addictive. When reward becomes random, the dog is motivated more, not less. This is how we fine-tune behaviour. For instance initially we reward every recall. Then we only reward the faster recalls. We vary the reward so the dog never knows quite what it is going to get, or whether it will get something this time. And from that, we get a dog that races back to us when we call it, to find out whether this time the reward will be extra-special. To humans, the annual bonus is a long way off in a new job, but the instant reward for a task well done has an immediate incentive effect. After we learn to "trust" the system that rewards good work with a hefty bonus at the end of the year, we are more willing to work where there is a gap between that and our reward. Dogs can make this progression to a certain degree once they have established that reward exists "soon" for co-operation "now" but to start with, reward has to be instantaneous and appropriate.

Different dogs find different things rewarding. Food is a great motivator for many, but certainly not all, though many dog-owners would find this surprising. Then we have to consider the quality of a food reward, which has to be better than or different from the dog's usual fare. When it can get that in its bowl for doing nothing, where is the incentive to work for it? In extreme cases, a dog may have to have all its food given in the form of rewards and occupational toys, but even this will only work with food-oriented dogs and with hungry dogs. So many times people take a dog out to train it after feeding, but hungry dogs are much more attentive, and find food a great deal more rewarding. Only dogs that are real gannets will work for food rewards if they have just been fed.

For other dogs, play is a reward, so a minute or so of a tug game or chasing a ball may be more useful than the standard titbit. Dogs that like to chase may also enjoy running after a furry toy on a flirt pole. Some dogs like physical affection and others prefer not to be touched: many dogs respond to a warm, kindly voice, but for others, particularly those which are often fussed and spoken to, it is no reward at all, because again, they can get as much as they want without working for it. Some of course can never get enough in the way of affection. Rewards should be varied in order to maintain the dog's eagerness to earn them, and reward is all about whatever that dog finds rewarding, not what the person thinks it should like, or what someone else's dog likes. Reward reinforces learned behaviour too: I reward my dogs for something every time we go out, to keep them interested in me and what I am doing. This means they always have an eye out for me instead of mooching off to make their own fun. It doesn't matter how old or how well-behaved they are, they still get randomly rewarded for doing something that I want them to do, and they never know quite what I have for them or when I might choose to give it.

Task or Result?

Some breeds are task-oriented, meaning that the task itself is what rewards them, and so they are eager to interact with us in the hope of getting another job to do. Border collies are past masters at this, and will learn a huge range of skills just for the sake of being able to do something new. Many other breeds are results-oriented, and do what we want in order to get a result that they find rewarding, for instance a hunting dog that will go to some discomfort in pushing through thorny undergrowth in order to eject a prey species that it can then try to catch. Note that the opportunity to hunt with the prospect of catching is the reward here, not the finding of quarry. Is the hunt the reward, or the catch? Few hunting dogs will hunt if they know from experience that a catch is unlikely, but all the while there is a chance of catching, they will try. Dogs used to find game and flush it to the gun, however, are task-oriented, and it is the act of searching that is most motivating for them. This is important for training purposes, because while a task-driven dog will always try because the task is the reward, the results-driven dog will not try if the result is unattainable. Hunting dogs would not

Lurcher – results oriented.

last long if they did not have the ability to "abort the mission" in the face of failure, and instead save their energies for those situations that are likely to bring about success. This is not a character flaw but a survival success. When one of these dogs refuses to participate because the likely result has no reward for them, we can only bow to their superior wisdom. Then we need to activate ours to find a way of producing a reward worth working for.

As an aside, people too divide into "Task" and "Results" for motivation. This reflects in our chosen pastimes as well as our choice of dog. While trainers should be able to change their methods to suit the dog in front of them, the dog we actually choose to live with should be the one we feel most comfortable with mentally, and is another important matter to take into account when we are deciding what kind of dog to get.

Reward-Only Training

While reward is crucially important, the way we train dogs and the situations we train dogs for means that we cannot get the results we want if we only use rewards, any more than we can if we only use punishment-based methods. Trainers of wild animals, particularly sea mammals, point to their success using only positive reinforcement and ignoring unwanted behaviour, because we can hardly punish such creatures, but their situation is quite different from that of keeping domestic dogs. Those undomesticated animals do not live in our houses, mix with our children, get exercised on our streets and most of all are not required to do anything they would not choose to do naturally. So where, for instance, we are shown sea mammals responding to food rewards, and this is often held up as the best way to train any animal or bird as a result, it is conveniently glossing over the fact that these creatures are being rewarded for something they do anyway. Put very simplistically, dolphin leaps, dolphin gets a fish and a bell is rung, easily progresses to the bell being rung, dolphin leaps, dolphin gets a fish. The dolphin can leap as much as it wants to, but it only gets a fish if it leaps when the bell is rung. If the dolphin wants a fish, the sequence unfolds as the human trainer plans, but if it doesn't want a fish, it will not leap no matter how often the bell is rung, unless it feels like leaping at that moment anyway. Trainers of sea mammals recognise those times when their charges are not in the required state of mind to put on a display, and they change the programme as a result. The fee-paying public knows no different, and the mammals do not get the chance to let their trainers down by refusing to perform.

The relationship with our dogs is far more complex. We very often want our dogs to do something they are not in the mood to do (leave that scent and come here), would not do naturally (keep quiet while that other dog is barking), don't particularly like doing (stay still for the vet to stick a needle in) or is actively unrewarding (don't scavenge that food). Dogs have to do what we want when we want and there is no time off for good behaviour; their lives are way different from that of a sea mammal that only has to jump for a fish, and only then if it wants to. Pure reward works remarkably well for a huge variety of creatures, but it only works for producing natural behaviour in response to a specific cue, and only when it doesn't actually matter if the behaviour is not produced, because there will be times when it won't be. There are even courses for dog trainers where they can work with chickens, which are very food-motivated and learn quickly to respond to a cue for a food reward. This sharpens up our timing, because reward has to come at the right time if the correct behaviour is to be captured. But even these carefully-reared chickens need downtime, and are only allowed to work for a certain length of time before being rested.

Pure reward works very well with dogs, but not all dogs and not in every circumstance. When we hear about "positive training" and "reward-based training" for dogs, it is as well that we understand the parameters involved, for there are so many ways to misunderstand what we are doing. Withholding of a reward still works on the non-reward part of the quadrant, and any aversive, no matter how mild, is still on the "punishment" side.

Timing

Good timing makes good training. Animals are adept at timing, for survival depends upon it. Humans are more variable, some of us being very good indeed while others never quite manage the knack. Just as we have to train our dogs within their capabilities, so we have to manage our own, and most of us are able to improve our timing even though some may never be as slick as others.

Reward (and indeed punishment) must follow the desired (or undesirable) action as quickly as possible, because the dog associates what it gets from us with the last action it took. If someone shouts at a dog as it returns from running off and disobeying recall, the dog assumes that it is the act of returning that is being punished, not the previous disobedience in running off. Therefore this creates a dog that is ready to return but is now afraid to do so. But if the dog is welcomed back, then recall is still rewarding and no matter what it has done previously, it is always happy to come back. As coming back is what we want it to do, that is what we should reward. Always reward what we DO want, not what we DON'T want – therefore we want the dog to come back, and that is what we reward. When we are training a dog to be quiet, we need to time the reward with the "quiet" not the bark, and often there is only a tiny instant to begin with in which we can do so. But if we fumble our reward and give it to the dog when it barks again, we have inadvertently trained the dog to bark as a response to the command for quiet. Therefore we need to have the reward ready in our hand, to give to the dog at precisely the right time, and it is better not to reward if we fluff it and miss the moment, than to reward the opposite of what we want. There is also a result of mistiming that we call "fallout" which is when an unwanted side-effect happens as a result of an external occurrence which coincides with a training specific. This is most destructive with aversion training, for example when an aversive action is applied to a dog (such as jerking it hard with the lead) at exactly the same time as a passing dog gets close to it. Such a dog then links the sudden pain in its neck to the appearance of the other dog, and may well become reactive when it sees that dog again, or another dog of the same breed type, because it is anticipating pain. Mistiming has inadvertently taught the dog to be more reactive. Similarly if a reward had been applied as the dog lunged and barked at another dog, then the "fallout" would be the dog being more likely to lunge and bark when it met other dogs, whereas the right time to reward would have been when it was quiet and relaxed again after the strange dog had passed by.

Clicker Training

Clicker-training is a very useful method of showing the dog that it has performed the right behaviour and will get a reward. The "click" must always be followed by a reward, and timing is crucial. Not everybody has the timing skills to teach dogs this way, and some dogs that are not food, play or toy-oriented are difficult to clicker-train because rewarding them

Do I have to? Photo: F. Sechiari.

is not easy in this context. For those with the ability and those dogs which are easily rewarded, clicker-training can be immensely successful. Many books and DVDs exist on clicker-training which explain its use in detail (see Appendix i).

Interrupters

Sometimes the dog has so successfully blocked us out mentally while it produces or is about to produce an unwanted action, that we need to use some kind of interrupter to bring its focus back to us. This can be verbal, such as in using a sharp "Oi!" or physical, such as a nudge with your leg against the dog. Interrupters do not have to be loud or frightening: their job is to bring the dog's attention back, not to scare or hurt it. Interrupters should be followed instantly with action that identifies with the dog's redirection. For instance, if the dog is about to roll in fox muck, the interrupter gives us a split second in which to get the dog back on the lead, distract with a toy, push it away from the offending pile or divert its attention any other way we know will work. Interrupters should not be expected to work on their own and must be accompanied with instant follow-up guidance.

NILIF

This stands for "Nothing In Life Is Free", which sounds every bit as depressing as it is. It is another outmoded behaviour modification method from the days of dominance theory, but it still persists in a few training scenarios and with some trainers. NILIF is a type of passive bullying, where the dog is required to perform some deed before it is allowed any interaction with its owner, and is never allowed to initiate interaction itself. For example, the dog that comes up for attention is refused it, instead only getting attention when the owner decides to give it some and so calls it over. It must then do something such as "sit" before it is given attention. NILIF dogs have to grow accustomed to being ignored except when their owner deigns to interact with them. Before they are awarded something pleasant, such as food or a walk or game, they have to perform their specified action. While it is reasonable and indeed sensible to teach a dog manners in that it should not knock us flying when we go to put its lead on or its food bowl down, NILIF lends itself to unpleasant extensions to the point of mental abuse, such as making the dog sit for ten minutes watching its bowl before it is "released" to eat. It is possible that the initial concept of NILIF was more benign but it quickly became all about the great god human dictating to the dog its every interactive move. The result is that many dogs experiencing it go into a form of protective depression, shutting down and abandoning any attempt at interaction with their humans. This is a survival response to extreme stress and can take a long time to reverse if the dog changes homes or the owner changes ethos. More sensitive dogs can retreat into this very quickly, and at first owners think that the dog is "better" because it is no longer doing whatever it was doing before that annoyed them. It takes a while to realise that actually the dog is not doing anything with its owners at all, and those events that previously brought joy into its life, such as being caressed, eating meals and going on walks, are too stressful to be fun any more. Aside from being a miserable way to live together, the bond between dog and owner is weakened or lost, which means that some responses we really want, such as a good recall, no longer happen because the owner is not worth returning to and no pleasure to be with. If the owner is not a safe place, then the dog has no security, and insecure dogs may develop all sorts of issues, from digestive and skin problems to obsessive-compulsive behaviours.

Flooding

This is a method of altering a dog's response to something it is reactive over, which consists of exposing it to the trigger to an extreme degree. It has been used on humans too, notably for phobia treatment, and it is manifestly unsuccessful. However it is another way that suits the human mindset, and old- style trainers can be very reluctant to let it go. In humans, for instance, arachnophobia (fear of spiders) was sometimes treated by putting the patient in a small room full of spiders. The idea was that, having been exposed to the feared situation and learned that nothing hurt them, they learned not to fear spiders. Understanding of how the mind works in this area has moved on considerably, and flooding is no longer used on people, but it is still recommended here and there in the dog world. For instance, if a dog is afraid of small white dogs because once when it was at a vulnerable age it was attacked by a small white dog, the flooding principle would be to expose it to as many small white dogs as possible. The idea would be to teach it that small white dogs are not dangerous. But of course, this dog already knows that small white dogs can be dangerous, and it is not prepared to allow any small white dog an opening to hurt it again. According to its genetic legacy, it will either shut down completely – which will be regarded as "success" because the dog is "calm" – or it will react more and more violently and at a greater distance each time when it sees small white dogs. Flooding makes fear worse not better, and has the potential to create serious long-term psychological issues. It should be firmly confined to the collection of "methods we used to use until we knew better".

Bad Dog

It is said that "there are no bad dogs, only bad owners" which sentiment is really demoralising to people who have tried to be good owners but have a dog whose behaviour is causing them great unhappiness. It would be better if we changed this to: "there are no bad dogs, only misunderstood dogs". We humans have to step forward and take the responsibility for understanding the dog, because the dog is not mentally equipped to understand us. Understanding the dog is crucial to getting the best out of it. When we say our dogs are "bad" "naughty" "stubborn" "spiteful" we are tempted to rectify their perceived wilful evil by punishing them. Punishing a dog may stop it doing whatever it is doing at that moment, but it does not teach the dog what we do want, nor does it build a good bond between us. Dogs do what works for them, and what seems to be beneficial to them at that time. They do not do anything out of "malice aforethought" or revenge. Words may just seem to be words, but using the right words makes all the difference to our attitude towards the dog, and once we realise that it is not plotting to irritate us, but doing something because it has no idea of what we would prefer it to do, we mentally become an instructor, a guide and mentor, rather than a gaoler and punisher. This affects our whole attitude towards the dog, which in turn affects the dog's responses towards us. Incidentally it also affects our body-language, which our dogs find very important.

Predatory Sequence

This is a scientific interpretation of how dogs go about catching prey, and it is useful for determining reward, noting that for some breeds there is more than one reward to be found in the sequence. With some variation in words depending on the source we study, e.g. Coppinger, the sequence is: Find, Stalk, Chase, Catch, Kill, Dissect, Eat. Every dog has a built-in "stop" in this sequence which differs from breed task to breed task. For instance, a Border collie comes high in "find" because one of its tasks is to hunt out and find sheep on the hill or in the snow. Border collies make magnificent search-and-rescue dogs because they love to "find". But a collie that preferred the far end of the sequence would be no use for sheep; it needs to stalk and demonstrate a controlled "chase" when rounding up, not a desire for mutton. Some collies go as far as "catch" by getting hold of recalcitrant sheep, but these behaviours need to be under strict control and must never be allowed to get any further along the sequence. Police dogs need to be big on the chase and catch, but must be tractable enough to stop the sequence there, which is why certain breeds have been tried for such work and found wanting, though very good in other ways.

"Find" has its reward in searching and finding something. For instance spaniels love to "find" so much that they can easily be induced to search for something like a tennis ball or a retrieve dummy, will readily go into cover without checking by scent first if there is anything in there, and can be seen repeatedly "hunting" a completely bare stretch of grass in the ring at any country show that has a gundog display as part of the entertainment. This does not mean that the spaniel is stupid – dogs are never stupid, only misunderstood – simply that the reward of searching, even for something that could not possibly be there, hits a high spot for a spaniel. A terrier, by contrast, is all about "kill" and does not waste its energies by pounding the beat. Terriers seek out quarry with their incredible sense of smell, and once found, will do their all to get to and deal with their quarry in the shortest time possible. Once we find out by breed task where the dog we are training finds most reward, we know not only how best to motivate it, but also which buttons are best left unpressed unless we can deal with the consequences.

Latent Learning

This occurs after the initial experience from which we want the dog to learn, and after the brain has had some downtime to process it. We know from our own learning processes that some things take time to sink in, or that we can puzzle over something, go to sleep, and miraculously everything seems understandable when we wake up again. Therefore when we teach the dog something new, we should not overteach it by constant repetition – instead we should catch the behaviour with a great deal of reward once we get it for the first time, and then stop. It is human nature to persist, to go on and on until the animal is bored silly, to prove one success wasn't a fluke or to try and get perfection, but that way only turns the dog off when training sessions loom. Besides, brains can only work the way they are designed to work, and no amount of human schedules, goals or wishful thinking can change this ancient and effective process. Instead, we should let latent learning do the job for us once we have the basic response we want, and then use subsequent sessions to fine-tune the exercise. How much downtime does a dog need? This depends on the dog, but most have processed the information thoroughly by the following day.

Extinction Burst
This is not what happens when somebody finally gets to the end of their tether with a dog's behaviour! The extinction burst occurs when a behaviour that has always had a specific and desired outcome for a dog suddenly stops giving that result because we are working on behaviour modification. The dog reacts in an accelerated and often violent manner, trying to change the cause and effect back to the way that has always worked before. We perform this behaviour too. If our computer freezes, most of us will click the mouse again (and again). If the light doesn't come on, we flick the switch again. If the car won't start, we turn the key again. And the dog will click our mouse, press our switch and turn our key, often in an escalating display of frustration, trying to get us to do something that we always did before. This is when people tend to quit on behaviour modification if they have not been warned of it, because they say the dog has become much worse. But we need to hold our nerve and uphold the new system, because once a dog has exhausted its extinction burst, the new behaviour will replace the unwanted old one. However, it only takes one incident where the owner allows the old reward to reappear for the new behaviour to vanish and leave us back with the old unwanted one again, because a random reward is far more compelling than a regular one, and to have the "jackpot" turn up after a run of "failures" is a huge reinforcer. Sometimes dogs are smart enough to know they have to behave this way with one person and that way with another; a certain terrier I know pulls like a train when the owner takes her out, but walks demurely to heel without being told when I pick up the lead. This is because her owner is inconsistent about heel training, whereas I never tolerate dogs pulling. The dog does not "love" me more than her owner; she is simply astute enough to do what works, and when I have the lead, nobody goes anywhere until it is slack.

Standards
Your dog needs to fit in with your life, not mine or anybody else's. Consistency is essential when training, so make sure that everyone who lives with the dog is committed to the same standards before you ever get the dog. For instance, if the dog is not to be allowed on the beds, everyone needs to be capable of shutting bedroom doors, and if the dog is forbidden to beg at the table, then nobody should ever feed the dog from the table. Dogs can become bitterly insecure if varying standards are applied, though some clever dogs will quickly figure that they can greed food off some family

members but not others. When setting ground rules, whatever you want is fine, and nothing is wrong. I do raise my eyebrows when I hear of trainers who say that dogs shouldn't be allowed to sleep on the bed with the owner, or must spend some time every day shut away from the family. Whatever goes for you is absolutely okay as long as it is not abusive. Be aware that if you wish to take your dog into other people's houses, or to the office, or to stay in hotels, you will need to set ground rules for the strictest situations, but if your dog is never going anywhere else, then your own home rules are perfectly fine.

Out in the world, however, you need to train in socially acceptable behaviour, not only to avoid legal action against you if your dog scares or hurts someone, but because we are all ambassadors for dogdom whenever we take our dogs out. Plenty of people are afraid of dogs or hate them for other reasons, and this is how we end up with draconian restrictions on where we can take our dogs as well as people trying to pass laws which make dog-ownership ever more difficult. So by taking out dogs that know how to behave around people and other dogs, we are being responsible as well as protecting ourselves and our dogs. Dogs need to be able to pass people without jumping all over them, be pleasant around other dogs, stay to heel unless invited to interact, ignore livestock, poultry and cats, and if offlead, recall when required. "Out in the world" does include your garden in that dogs should not be allowed to bark constantly, charge the fence or do anything that might cause upset or risk to neighbours, tradespeople or passers-by. All of this can be trained, but not all of it can be trained in the traditional village hall environment. Trainers who do address these issues as part of their curriculum or even as an optional extension of their class lessons are well worth finding.

Training Classes
Training classes vary widely in effectiveness, and it is wise to look around before committing to a series of classes. Most trainers do not offer a "drop in and drop out" option, as there would be less incentive for people to keep attending week after week, especially after a long day at work and what seems like the whole world wanting a piece of us. So we pay upfront for a course of lessons, which makes it an expensive mistake if the classes turn out to be unsuitable for our dogs.

"No time lost that is spent in reconnaissance" goes the Army saying. We can start by word of mouth, especially if it comes from people whose dogs are well-behaved. We can check out local advertisements and explore websites, remembering that even the best training class can be too far away, but the most conveniently-placed one might not offer the best training. Once we have narrowed down the options, we can learn a lot by going along by ourselves and without a dog. Most trainers will not object to this; a few may charge a small fee. If the latter, pay up with good grace and see it as an investment. While we watch the classes, we should be thinking:

1. Is this what I want my dog to learn?
2. Is this the way I want my dog to be taught?
3. Do I like the way the instructors teach?
4. Are all the clients getting the same amount of attention?
5. Do I want my dog to look like these dogs while it is being taught?

These considerations are far more important than the instructors having qualifications, but nothing is more important than the twin attributes of teaching skills and experience. Many instructors are very highly qualified, but by itself this is neither good nor bad. It is possible to gain some qualifications, yes, even up to Master's degree level, without having owned a single dog. Some others might have been training for thirty years but don't have thirty years of experience: they have one year's experience thirty times. Some courses promote outdated methods, so the diploma at the end only tells you that the instructor has completed the course, not how good the course was in the first place, and some courses are completed over a few weekends and are very basic indeed. Some instructors are very able dog trainers but poor communicators with people, and dog training is really about teaching owners to train their dogs. Other trainers make a fine job of some breeds and are completely at sea with others. It isn't enough for the instructor to own an immaculate team of task-oriented dogs if they expect to train a results-oriented dog in the same way, because it plain doesn't happen. So when you watch the class, see how the dogs most like yours are being handled. The instructor doesn't have to be an all-rounder if they can train your kind of dog. Meanwhile, you need to have a clear idea of what you want your dog to learn. For instance, a lot of classes are based on competitive obedience, so the dogs march round close at heel, sit every time the owner stops, perform "finishes" after each recall, and do "sit-stand-down-stand" type exercises as well as long "down-stays". These are great if competitive obedience is for you and, crucially, the breed of dog you own, but you might not want your dog to do many, or any, of these things in real life. Most people simply want a dog that walks nicely on the lead, comes when it is called, and keeps its feet on the floor when meeting and greeting. Dogs that aren't task-oriented get bored and mulish if asked to do exercises that are pointless to them. (Why should I sit? You'll only ask me to stand. Then you'll ask me to sit again). This is a great way for your dog to lose trust in you, especially if punitive methods are used in class, such as dogs being pushed and pulled into position. However, if you have a task-oriented dog, it will be thrilled at having all these different exercises to do, with rewards for getting it faster, straighter, more in keeping with the discipline's standards (Hey! We're playing Sit!). This is why we need to be very sure what we want from our dogs, and very sure that what we want is reasonable for the dog.

Dogs do what works for them, and like what they find rewarding. If the exercises themselves are unrewarding for the dog, don't expect the dog to change just because we want a dog that does those things. Sometimes the best reward we are able to offer won't be good enough.

Specialist Training

If we have a dog that needs to work in a particular discipline, then we need to be even more careful of the classes we attend. A working gundog, for instance, is best to go straight to gundog classes. There it will get a sound foundation of everything a gundog needs to do, and the owner will get the same on the way they need to do them. As an example, it is no good devising your own unique assortment of whistle-signals only to find out that the conventional gundog instructions by whistle are different. However, gundog training, while focusing on calmness and obedience, does not equip the dog for living outside the work environment as it might have to if also a pet. The shooting season lasts the season, but the dog is a pet all year round, and if it is a nuisance to take anywhere, then some pet dog training is required too. We only have to spend time watching certain gundogs interacting with other gundogs on shoot days, or misbehaving in the lodge at lunchtime, to see gaps in the training of some of them. Show dogs are best to go to Ringcraft classes right from the start, because conventional training classes

Fast recall. Photo: F. Sechiari.

place a lot of emphasis on the "sit" and that's the last thing we want Show dogs to do. But again, they still need everyday manners, and so often are not taught them, behaving beautifully inside the ring and being a liability outside it. So – specialist work means specialist training, otherwise the dog and owner can have to unlearn a lot of previous work, which is a miserable experience, but dogs still need good manners. Dogs are pretty bright for the most part, though, and once the favoured discipline has been learned, they are perfectly capable of taking in a different set of activities. A different collar and lead arrangement is often all it takes for a dog to know that today it is going to be at a show or that tonight is Agility night. So train first of all for the main discipline, and once the dog is foot-perfect in that, we can if we wish teach it another set of tasks. But alongside this, we still need to train basic niceties that apply in the wider world of our society, which is the one the dog has to survive in too.

Rewards

Reward-based training is not always what even the trainers themselves think it is. It isn't just a matter of posting food down a dog's throat – some dogs are unmotivated by food unless they are starving. Tug games are used in some classes, but not all dogs like playing tug, and some owners have disabilities or injuries that preclude this as a reward method. Some dogs like toys and others are totally indifferent to them. To get an idea of what motivates our own dog, we need – again – to think about their original breed tasks, and we also need to look carefully at what our dog is doing when we offer it a conventional reward. If the dog takes the titbit eagerly, glows with anticipation when it sees the tugger, likes to parade with the toy in its mouth – this is what your dog finds rewarding. Some dogs love a fuss and a kindly-spoken "good dog", others wouldn't do anything for that. Some dogs don't like being fussed at all, or only enjoy being touched by their owner, seeing it as a liberty and looking very affronted if other people try to touch them. Other dogs prefer to walk round the perimeter (patrolling), follow a scent, or chase a rag on a string. Dogs created to find "results" rewarding rather than "tasks" need to have a "result" at the end of completing their task – so let the whippet catch the rag, let the beagle find a "jackpot" of treats at the end of the scent, and if you have a friend who will be a "find" for your mastiff when it checks the perimeter of the training area, you will have a very happy mastiff. Note that the mastiff only has to "find" and then it can get a fuss or a treat after it has indicated the "find" in any way you prefer, such as one "woof" or by sitting.

Old-fashioned training expects the dog to carry out commands without reward, and many successful old-style trainers can get hot under the collar at the very thought of the dog having any kind of reward except that of pleasing the owner. They will tell us that dogs love to please, and indeed some dogs do; other dogs couldn't care less. It doesn't mean that the second kinds of dogs can't be trained; it means that they need different motivation if they are to carry out exercises that, to a dog, are utterly pointless. It's the difference between "What can I do for you O noble owner" and "What's in it for me?". This is nothing to do with the dog respecting, liking or loving you: it is the nature of the particular beast in front of you. The dog can only be what its genes make it: it is we who have to change our methods to suit the mindset of that dog. Old-fashioned training has its successes, but it has its failures too, and a high percentage of dogs in the old days would be discarded as "useless" or "untrainable". Assuming a healthy dog, gearing the reward to something the dog finds rewarding is far more likely to get us the results we want. But we do need to go with reality, and there are circumstances where management is a far better method than training. It takes a lot of pressure off dog and owner, too.

Teaching Methods

People need rewards too. The best rewards come when our dogs learn the behaviours we want from them, though there is a subtler reward in class training because somebody always has a more difficult dog than ours. I can recall an ex-military trainer of the old-fashioned sort, who claimed all dogs could be trained by the same methods, being run ragged by a beagle. That same beagle could have so easily been trained by reward-based methods, but the trainer only knew one way to train. Some modern trainers think that all dogs can be motivated by food, and are flummoxed when they come across one that isn't interested. Good trainers adapt their methods to suit each dog and, crucially, each owner. Not every owner has the precise timing required for clicker-training, or the ability to read canine body-language at the speed the dog produces it. This does not mean that they are any way inferior as owners, simply that the teacher has to teach in a different way. Teaching is a vastly underrated skill, and if we can find an instructor who can not only do but also teach, we have someone worth giving our business to. Because the instructor trains us to train our dogs, he or she must be approachable, a great communicator, and able to present what needs to be learned in a way that the individual learns best. This is particularly important when people come from an old-fashioned-training mindset, and need to be coaxed gently away from prong collars, choke chains, leash "pops" and shouting at the dog, without being made to feel embarrassed. Every dog and every owner should leave a training session in a happier frame of mind than they started it: there is no room in good teaching for anyone ever to feel diminished or demoralised. Trainers should set "homework" to be carried out between sessions, because it is unrealistic to expect dog and owner to train as a unit if they only train once a week in a class environment. So often we see a dog gazing at its owner in amazement because training is never apparent in their everyday relationship. Teaching needs incredible patience sometimes, but that is what we are paying for; we should never train where we are reluctant to ask questions or for something to be explained again because we aren't sure. It should be obvious that the trainer is on the side of dogs and owners and wants them to succeed and be happy with each other.

Another great benefit of group training is the support given to the human side of the team with social interaction, competitions, fun activities, certificates to mark progress and so on. Training can be very lonely, especially when we hit a plateau where our dogs do not seem able or willing to progress, and at times we all need to take a few steps back or to the side before we can go forward again. To be in an empathetic group with an encouraging teacher can be hugely supportive, especially if we have to go home to a disinterested family, or are given gratuitous "advice" from all sides on what we really should be doing. Good trainers can put matters into proportion for us, and will have a supply of anecdotes to make us feel less fraught and encourage us to keep on with what we are doing. The option of progressing up through grades or working towards awards such as the Good Citizen Scheme is helpful for goal-oriented people too, but we should never lose a sense of proportion when reaching for our own targets. We must give careful thought to whether we are about to put too much pressure on our dogs by going just one stage further.

Allocated Time

We don't have to be maths wizards to work out how much time the class instructor is able to give to each of us when we train as a group. It isn't more than a few minutes, so we need to get the maximum out of those minutes. We can still learn by watching what the instructor is doing with other dogs, but only if there is a good explanation given each time, and a thorough summing-up at the end, with time for questions. Good instructors start the session with a recap on the previous one and a brief description of what is going to be done this time, so that everybody can prepare mentally for what lies ahead. All of this ticks minutes away from the time we have spent with us as individuals. If one person/dog combination needs extra input, this can all too easily strip time from the better-behaved dogs, which have paid the same money and are deserving of the same amount of attention. After all, the chances are that the less needy dogs are that way because the owners have worked hard on them between classes. So good classes include at least one competent assistant who can either give one-to-one help to the individuals who have hit a problem, or else take over the class while the instructor helps the difficult dog. You do not want to experience, as I once did, an extremely dog-aggressive dog being part of a class of twelve, where eleven of us were crammed and idle in one side of the village hall while the instructor worked on the other side with a single dog.

One to One

This gives us maximum time value, and enables a lot of ground to be covered in one lesson. It is very tiring for owner, dog and yes, instructor too, to work this way, so instructors may not stick to a precise time schedule if one or more of the arrangement is getting too tired to learn any more (or teach). While a class includes plenty of time for handler and dog to relax and allow latent learning, the pace of a one-to-one session has to be managed very carefully if it is not to overwhelm those involved. For basic training, the class environment is adequate, but for anything behavioural, we are always better to work one-to-one. A good instructor will be able to progress a dog and handler very quickly up the scale, setting suitable "homework" between sessions so that, although the cost is much higher one-to-one, it works out over time to be only a little more than a set of class lessons. One-to-one can also be tailored to the specific environment that the dog needs help with, and I find it very useful to be able to take dog and owner for a walk and introduce modification strategies in the real world as the walk unfolds.

Other Dogs

Watching the other dogs in a class is so revealing. Do they look alert, keen, happy and compliant? Do they look worried, bored, resentful, scared? What do they do when another dog comes near? Does the instructor allow dogs to lunge at other dogs, bark incessantly, mug the owner for treats, jump up at any passing human? Are dogs expected to sit or lie on a cold hard floor for long spells? You would be amazed at the difference in learning that is achievable by keeping dogs from lunging at others, distracting the barkers (it's harder to bark when lying down and they can't bark at all with a toy in their mouths) treating only as a reward (rather than mindlessly stuffing food down a dog), insisting on "four on the floor", and asking owners to bring a blanket for their dog to sit or lie on can make a huge difference in a dog's willingness to comply. Class discipline is important; it needn't be overt, but good standards must be applied the whole time, and not just while a dog is performing an exercise. So often we see a car park in a chaos of lunging, barking dogs that then drag the handler into the hall (except for the dog that has to be dragged in) and at the other end of the lesson, the dogs drag their owners back out of the door again (except for the dog that has to be dragged out). Some owners can do denial very well, and I have long lost count at the number of times I have had to "bark" at an owner whose dog is about to empty itself in the hall. Before a class, dogs should be emptied out and not fed: hungry dogs pay attention. The hall environment can be stressful and dogs may need to empty out again from sheer excitement; some dogs also want to mark every vertical surface. The instructor should make it plain that any dog that needs to "go" should be taken outside, any dog prone to marking should be prevented from doing so, and any owner who ignores the signs will not only have to clean up, but pay a "fine" into the Christmas party kitty.

The Venue

It gets harder to find the old-style village hall that is available for dog-training, as Health and Safety considerations can sometimes be used as an excuse to forbid dogs or else to introduce regulations so difficult to comply with that the venue becomes unusable. Acoustics can be overwhelming in some halls, which can panic sensitive dogs and make the instructor difficult to hear. Then there is the floor surface to consider, which should be non-slip and easy to mop. The big pluses of village halls are that they offer shelter from the weather, have facilities such as cloakrooms and kitchens so can offer a tea break, and are generally easy for parking, but they have their limitations as dog-training venues. Ideally we should train outdoors, as outdoors is where we encounter most of our challenges and distractions. Outdoors is also better for puppies, who can pee and poo from excitement remarkably often over a short time. But outdoors can be cold, hot, muddy, windy or wet, which is pretty miserable for everybody, and even dogs designed to work in the most extreme weather will not be able to concentrate as well as they could if they were more comfortable. Owners too will get fed up. One compromise is to have the use of a Dutch barn or similar building in wet weather; it still lets some of the weather in but is nowhere near as unhappy a circumstance as being outside without any cover at all. Indoor riding schools can sometimes be hired for dog training, but should be checked first in case the surface is dusty when stirred up, which will be harmful to the dogs as well as any owners with breathing difficulties. There are cleaning considerations too, as no rider wants to fall off into something nasty left by the dog-training session. Purpose-built indoor dog-training buildings are becoming more popular, but again these need to be inspected before hiring; one near me stinks to high heaven from the solvents used in its construction and cleaning, which is distressing enough to a human nose, never mind a dog's. Venues should have plenty of parking, and lavatory facilities are a boon, because owners get nervous too. A short tea break helps to consolidate human latent learning and allows owners to socialise, so facilities that allow this are very useful too.

Gadgets

There is a plethora of gadgets to "help" with dog training, and very little need for most of them. A few can be helpful during a transitory period of behaviour modification, but unfortunately the human mind is geared to a quick fix, and so many people, trainers too, use a gadget and never progress any further.

Body Harnesses

These are a handy way of attaching a lead to a dog that has previous neck or windpipe damage – often caused by other gadgets. Dogs that have been made headshy are usually also happy to wear a harness. Where the dog is using its strength against its owner when being walked, a harness used correctly gives extra control. They vary a great deal in quality so care must be taken to get a comfortable fit, and they should also be checked daily to make sure that they have not rubbed sore patches, or twisted in use. Stitching, buckles and clips should also be checked frequently. For control purposes while the dog is being retrained to walk properly, the harness should have its lead attachment on the chest, with two leads or a double-ended lead, one attached to the harness and one on the collar. This works in the same way as double reins on a horse, and is not difficult to use. The dog is walked primarily on the collar with the handler holding both leads, but if it attempts to lunge at something or drag the handler, the harness lead comes into play to guide the dog back to face the handler, whereas a harness with a lead attachment on the back will not help with control and indeed allows the dog to pull like a freight train. If the dog is on a harness because of physical damage or mental trauma rather than being a works-in-progress behaviourally, then the placing of the lead attachment is not so important assuming the dog already walks nicely. Harnesses are useful devices, and many people prefer to walk their dogs on one. Some harness companies make individual pieces so that worn straps can be replaced, and the fit can be altered to suit each dog.

Face Harnesses and Headcollars

These come in a variety of types, the basic idea being to tighten on or twist the dog's head if it pulls but remain slack if it does not, thus encouraging the dog to walk nicely because it is uncomfortable when it does not. Like body harnesses, these enable people to have a degree of control over a dog that lunges or pulls. They must be carefully fitted, as otherwise some designs ride up into the dog's eyes, or can twist and rub. They are no substitute for correct training – and it is ludicrously easy to teach a dog to walk on a slack lead – but do tend to be used by many people as a permanent device rather than a temporary aid. There is a danger with certain types of dog for the face harness to actually damage or risk breaking the neck, if the dog tries to take off after something and the gadget whips its head round at speed. Not all dogs have the right shaped heads for face harness, which at least has the bonus of nudging their owners to use a better method.

Muzzles

Muzzles also vary very much in type, from the cloth ones that hold the mouth shut to the box type which allow the mouth to open. No muzzle is perfect for every situation; those that hold the mouth shut endanger the dog that gets loose because it cannot eat, drink or pant, while the box type allows all of this but the dog can still bite, albeit not as effectively. Muzzles are mostly used to stop dogs from biting in situations such as the veterinary surgery or where there is extreme man- or dog-aggression. They are also used to protect dogs during mating where one or both is known or suspected to be a biter at this time, during racing to prevent dogs attacking each other from frustration because they cannot grab the lure, or to prevent dogs from scavenging. Some people use muzzles on dogs that would be likely to chase wild animals or livestock, but this is only a partial solution, as a muzzled dog can still chase and frighten livestock into abortion or death, and can still batter an animal it catches up with instead of effecting a clean kill. All told, the muzzle should be a transient device in most cases while the root causes of the behaviour are dealt with. They are not suitable for separation anxiety or self-mutilation as these are stress-related activities and wearing a muzzle would exacerbate the stress, so causing other unwanted behaviour to develop. The only value of a muzzle in a long-term situation is where a dog is severely aggressive, in that the sight of it does encourage people to keep their dogs away and refrain from touching the dog themselves. On the other hand, it is tempting for owners to use the muzzle in order to put the dog into situations it can't handle, rather than going down the long road to rehabilitation. A muzzle is better than a bite, but it should be used carefully with a view to addressing whatever is causing the dog to do whatever it is being muzzled for. Dogs need to be carefully habituated to wearing a muzzle, with plenty of reward for each step. Initially, a little pate or peanut butter spread on the inside at the end of the muzzle will encourage them to put their noses in, and the owner should build up very slowly to the muzzle being fastened, and then to the dog wearing it for short spells. Dogs should not be left alone with a muzzle on, as there is a risk of injury, especially to toes and dew-claws where a dog tries to scrape the muzzle off. Dog faces are soft, and muzzles can easily rub them sore, so care needs to be taken to avoid this. Some dog face shapes do not suit a muzzle at all, notably the squashed-nose types.

Extending Leads
These are dreadful devices in the wrong hands, and in the wrong hands is where they mostly are. The extending lead is usually the badge of the person who can't be bothered to train their dog, and while it is an individual choice to live with a trained or untrained dog, it is a racing certainty that most dogs on extending leads are trouble to every dog and most people they meet. The very thin cord cannot be seen by other dogs, so unless the handler is polite enough to reel their dog in when others approach, and keep it on a short lead until they have passed by, there is a real risk of injury to other dogs if they run into the lead. There are types of extending lead that have a wide

tape instead of the thin cord, and this is much safer if one of these devices has to be used, because at least it can then be seen that the dog is attached to the owner.

The extending lead teaches dogs to pull, because they run to the end of the lead and then lean into it. There is danger to the dog on the lead if any of the clips or fixtures break, and it runs into danger; there have been some horrible accidents where people have been complacent about the dog being on the lead and therefore "safe", and the dog has jumped off a bridge or run into the road. I have been riding along the road and had a dog, complete with extending lead, run under the horse, which could have resulted in an almighty mishap. Luckily the horse behaved beautifully and disaster was averted. Many handlers do not realise that it is important to reel their dog in and walk it on a short lead whenever other dogs are about, and of those who do, a proportion reel the dog out again as soon as they have passed, which usually results in their dog going round behind the other dog and running into its hindquarters, often with malice aforethought. There was a certain dog rescue that rehomed ex-racing greyhounds and told owners to keep them on extending leads, the result being a scattering of accidents where dogs had lunged into a run – greyhounds are a lot more powerful than they look – pulled the plastic handle out of the owner's hand, then panicked at the rattling and bouncing of the handle behind them, and just kept going. Yet greyhounds in training walk beautifully on a hound collar and lead.

The extending lead can be operated correctly while a dog is being exercised from an invalid buggy or by someone with limited mobility, which is probably its only justifiable use. For those dogs undergoing remedial training in recall, a horse lunge line is a far better and safer option because it is stronger and much easier both for the handler to hold and others to see.

Choke Chains and Half-Choke Collars

The severity of these depends on the handler at one end and the dog at the other. They do not stop dogs from pulling or lunging, though they can easily cause deep bruising and trauma to neck and throat. Sometimes dogs release endorphins as a response to the pain and so continue to pull because the pain has actually become rewarding; others appear deadened to the pain the way a horse can ignore a severe hand on the reins. These collars tempt handlers to jerk at the leash to bring the dog back to heel; people can walk their dogs this way for years without actually ever reaching the conclusion that the collar isn't helping. If a dog walks nicely, these collars aren't needed: if it pulls, hauls or jumps around on the end of the lead, the collars won't work.

Dogs in competitive obedience are sometimes trained to walk to heel offlead by the use of a chain choke collar. The handler pulls up the collar as the dog goes into the ring, and that is the signal for the dog to walk very close to the handler for the duration of the exercise. Whatever we think about this, competitive obedience bears no resemblance to what ordinary people want from their dogs, and there is no reason for pet owners to emulate this particular practice.

Citronella Collars

The citronella collar is activated by the dog barking, and squirts a blast of citronella oil into the dog's face. It is often seen as a humane device, but in fact is arguably less humane than a shock collar, which at least delivers a shock on the instant that is then over with. Citronella collars squirt out a scent that is as foul to the delicate scent receptors of dogs as something like raw sewage is to us. The collar punishes not just the bark at the time, but continues to punish the dog until the scent clears, and so the dog is unable to link cause with effect. By the time the smell has gone, the dog may well have forgotten what triggered the initial blast. Another unfortunate effect is that if two dogs are in close proximity, one may trigger the other's collar by barking, so punishing the dog for something it has not done. Far worse is that the collar-wearing dog may start to associate the aversive experience with the other dog, and behold, we have the start of an aggression problem.

Prong Collars

Prong collars are a step up in punishment from choke collars in that they drive metal prongs into the dog's neck if it puts its weight into the collar. They are capable of causing a lot of physical damage in a short time, and don't work any better than choke chains for the same reasons. They are illegal in some countries, including UK.

Electric Shock Collars

These apply an electric shock to the neck in the same way that the dog gets shocked from approaching a buried electrical fence (see Chapter Four), but the difference is that the shock is delivered by the trainer. There are graded degrees of shock from the mild pulse to very strong, and some of these collars can be set to emit a warning note before the shock. In some countries these are illegal, and in others are commonly used for basic training. Their drawbacks are chiefly in the hand that holds the transmitter: where they are available for anyone to buy, there is enormous potential for abuse from people who lose their tempers, do not understand or want to understand why a dog is behaving as it is, or actively enjoy hurting another being. The only justifiable use of such a device would be for very narrow purposes, namely of stopping stock-chasing, or teaching dogs to avoid creatures such as snakes, skunks or porcupines. Even then, it takes such exquisite timing that the average dog-owner, and a good many trainers, would simply not be able to operate the device properly. It is likely that these will be illegal in UK before long.

Other Shock Devices

To my sorrow, I find that there are "shock mats" which people use to stop a dog getting onto furniture, going into certain places, and even going to the door. There is absolutely no justification for using this device when there are kind reward-based ways to train a dog to go to its bed when the doorbell rings, and there are doors and baby-gates which stop dogs from accessing parts of the house where they are not wanted. If the dog can jump one gate, put one on top of the other. If the dog can open the door, put a bolt high up where the dog can't reach.

Slip Leads

The slip lead has an incorporated loop at the collar end, so that instead of being clipped to the collar, it is dropped over the dog's head. The device tightens if the dog pulls in the same way a choke chain will, but is milder because it is made of rope, fabric or leather, which means it loosens as soon as the dog stops pulling. However, if the dog pulls or the handler jerks the lead, it can still cause damage. Once a dog has been trained to walk on a slack lead, a proportion of handlers find this a better choice that a clip-on lead, especially with the types of working dogs that do their job without a collar on. I use these all the time because they are less fiddly to get on and off a dog, and it is easy to teach a dog to put its own lead on by holding the loop out with a titbit the other side. Slip leads are a real boon for arthritic or damaged hands, and I also find them helpful for re-training when a dog has learned to snatch a titbit and run away, because we can get the lead on the dog as it reaches for its treat, and it barely notices.

Gadgets vary in value, and most say more about the trainer than they ever do about the dog. At best they should be seen as aids to progress, except as above where they assist people who are not as agile or dextrous as once they were, or else indicate that dogs and people should keep away from a troubled dog.

Mind Exercise Games

It is generally understood that dogs need regular and sufficient physical exercise to keep their bodies fit, ideally in two or more walks each day. Every bit as important is the mental exercise they get when out and about. But mental exercise does not have to stop when dogs get home. By working together, owner and dog build a strong bond, and this is every bit as attainable with pet dogs solving mind games as it is with working dogs fulfilling traditional tasks under the guidance of their handlers. Mind games are especially useful when installing recall, as they add considerably to the dog's impression that the owner is an interesting person to be around. Far too many dogs find their owners boring because most interaction centres on them stopping the dog doing pleasant things rather than finding fun things to do together. Mental exercise is also useful when either dog or owner is convalescing, when the dog is too young to be walked far but is brimming over with energy, or if dog or owner are at the other end of their lives and long walks are no longer achievable. On those rare occasions when the weather is truly unwalkable apart from hygiene breaks, mind games save the day. They should not be seen as a long-term substitute for proper exercise, which every able-bodied dog needs to take outside its home environs every single day, but as additions to the dog's quality of life as well as a relationship-strengthener between dog and owner. Many mind games are ideal for children to organise and participate in: even small children can be a great help at preparing puzzle boxes and laying scent trails. Thus the child feels thoroughly involved with the dog and their relationship is built in a positive way. Nevertheless, children should always be supervised when with dogs until they are old enough to take proper responsibility.

While there are mind games that can be bought, such as the Nina Ottosson range of interactive toys, there are plenty of alternatives that cost little to make. In multi-dog households, mind games should be played with one dog at a time, the others to be in a separate area with something pleasant to occupy them.

Task-oriented dogs will be much keener on these games than results-oriented dogs, and some dogs, notably sighthounds and mastiff types, will not work for anything other than an easy result at first, so make the game easy and the rewards high and quickly accessed to begin with. Help the dog as much as it needs: this is not cheating and the dog cannot get anything "wrong" because the games are not "win" and "lose". They are for occupation and bonding, which is why, tempting though it is to set the dog up with some games and let it get on with them, we should really play these together.

Here is a list of favourite games, but our own imagination is the limit.

Save all your cardboard centres from paper rolls, and a lot of newspaper.

Wrap a small strong-smelling treat in crumpled newspaper and hide it in the middle of a cardboard tube. Make the game more difficult by adding more newspaper to fill the tube.

Place one small piece of biscuit in a plastic bottle for the dog to roll around until the treat falls out. Use a suitably-sized bottle so there is no risk of injury to the dog. Make a small hole in the other end of the bottle so that a dog cannot get its tongue trapped by creating a vacuum.

Russian Doll boxes – start with one treat hidden in one screw of paper in one open box. Progress to adding extra screws of paper without treats so that the box is filled with paper, then by degrees make the box more difficult to get open, then place a box inside a larger box filled with paper and one treat, then add more boxes and more treats.

Scatter some tiny pieces of food around the garden so that he or she has to hunt for it. The dog will not know when it has found the last piece so will continue to hunt for some time.

Fill a large plastic container with water, put a ball on the top or a dog toy that floats. Let the dog splash around with this.

Scent-trailing in the garden. Fill a spray bottle with water and add one very smelly treat e.g. a piece of liver, sausage or cheese. Shake well and start to lay a trail at ground level, easy at first (a squirt every stride) and as he or she gets better at tracking, extend the space between squirts. Add a tiny treat every few paces to begin with, and a "jackpot" of several really special treats at the end. Once the trail is laid, take him or her out on a lead to the start of the trail, give a command e.g. "Find it" and work round the trail together. As he or she gets the idea, they can progress to doing this off-lead, the trail can be made more difficult and the treats fewer.

Show him or her a treat and hide it under a paper or plastic cup so that they can see, and then let him/her knock the cup over and get the treat. Progress to two and then three cups but only one which has a treat under it. Then put him/her out of the room and line up three cups quite a way from each other and let him/her find the treat. Note that they cannot get this wrong – they may sniff out the treat or just randomly knock the cups over. It's okay whatever he/she does, as the objective is to make them think. If he or she needs you to help them, that's fine – the important thing is that you are doing this together and deepening your bond – which all builds confidence.

Take a bun baking tray and some tennis balls. Put a tennis ball in each bun space and put a tiny treat under one ball. Let the dog find the treat by removing the tennis balls.

The same exercise with a larger container e.g. a washing-up bowl, cardboard box or laundry basket and a number of tennis balls.

Training Treats

When using treats for training, we must be sure that they are really worth working for. They do not have to be big – the size of a little finger nail is sufficient – but they do need to be strongly scented. Pet shop treats seldom fulfil a dog the way tiny pieces of meat or cheese will, and few dogs will work for mere kibble. And we should take care to adjust the dog's other food to allow for the extra food given in training, because nobody wants a fat dog.

Cost/Benefit

All training involves a cost/benefit analysis. Training by reward involves more work on behalf of the owner in the initial stages, the benefits being in the future because the training is more likely to "stick" in the face of temptation, and most importantly, the dog will trust the owner. The more dogs trust owners, the more likely they are to produce desired behaviour even in the face of considerable temptation, and the more they are likely to return to their owners no matter what the circumstances. But to achieve this, the handler needs to be acutely aware of the way the dog wants to react, the way it is feeling at that particular moment, the immediate or potential effects of the environment, and how to avoid or pre-empt unwanted behaviour. The best training is benevolently manipulative on the part of the owner in order to instil habitual responses on the part of the dog. Obedience is a habit: disobedience too, and if dogs never get the chance to practice unwanted behaviour – and find they like it – they will never develop habits that are difficult and in some cases impossible to eradicate.

Chapter Four

Sex and the Single Dog

How Reproductive Hormones Affect Behaviour

THE NORMAL state of the dog is sexually entire. This is the design specification, the successful model, the healthy dog, and dogs of either gender can remain entire for the whole of their lives without causing problems to themselves, their owners or other dogs. This can come as a shock to many of us, subjected as we are to a continuous stream of pro-neutering pressure. There are good reasons for neutering and good reasons for leaving the dog as Nature made it: we will be looking closely at each from the point of view of how it affects the dog's behaviour. This is especially important nowadays when the usual professionals to whom we go for help with our dogs – trainers, veterinary practices, books, television shows about dogs, large dog charities, the canine press – very often have absolutely zero experience of an entire dog or bitch. And as so often, people don't know what they don't know, or don't care what they don't know, or have a vested interest in promoting certain practices, and for any of these reasons may continue to repeat received wisdom as if it is first-hand experience. So strong is the pressure to neuter all dogs that complete strangers will ask us when we are having our dog neutered, and if we say we aren't, will deliver a speech on why we should, based on no experience whatsoever. It would come as a surprise to them that in some countries, neutering except for lifesaving medical reasons is illegal. For the moment, in UK we do still have

A much-wanted litter of working border collies. Photo: D. Morgan

a choice, although many large agencies here are pushing to have it made very difficult indeed to keep an entire dog or bitch. In USA, the everyday term for neutering is "fixed", thus subliminally implying that the animal, entire as designed, is somehow faulty. We humans are uncomfortable about much that is normal for dogs. Many of us are acutely edgy about the concept of our pets as sexual beings. Subconsciously, there are those of us who feel that anything concerned with breeding dogs should be kept behind closed doors, and the fact that every dog in existence was bred from two parents is something better not thought about. People want their dogs to be as asexual as fluffy toys, which is why any normal, unremarkable and harmless sexual indications on the part of the dog can cause reactions in its owners that are out of all proportion to whatever has actually happened. As for more visible sexuality, well, that is just beyond the pale. Therefore we can find common ideas that are not reasonable if examined closely, but are easily manipulated by those with a different agenda from genuine dog welfare. It does not take a huge leap in attitude before we dog owners are pressurised into thinking all dogs should be neutered, and that this is actually for the dog's benefit. One rather gets the impression that some people will not be satisfied until all dogs are created in petri dishes and have no sexual differences at all.

There is nothing wrong or faulty about entire dogs of either gender: it's a system that has worked for millennia. There is nothing wrong with dogs of either gender being neutered at the right time for the right reasons.

However, we neuter dogs mainly for our convenience: there is little other good reason to do so. Let's look at this more closely.

Male Dogs

Pro-neutering propaganda makes the normal male dog appear to be an insatiable sexual monster, scaling high defences to get to bitches, fighting every other male he meets, running off on walks and being a generally uncontrollable mass of raging testosterone. Every behavioural problem he displays is directly related to his gonads, and will miraculously be cured upon the removal of said items. Neutering, we are told, will make this dog happy. Not doing so will inevitably result in a really miserable one-track-minded pet making a life's work of creating vast numbers of unwanted puppies. Once he has experienced the delights of the boudoir, he will be fixated on this to the extinction of all other matters. The normal dog is entire, but clearly this is a design fault because he cannot possibly be anything except a rampant blur of lust until surgical intervention turns him into a proper dog. You may be interested to know that this is utter nonsense.

Wandering Star

All dogs will escape and travel if they are not confined within their home area. Good fences don't just make good neighbours: they make good dogs as well. The dog of either gender is a roaming beast by nature, so we fence it in to keep it safe, and replace the interest and exercise it would get roaming free by giving it plenty of exercise and occupation while under our control. This is one of our biggest responsibilities as dog owners: we cannot deprive a dog of such a basic need and replace it with nothing. We have the Internet, our friends, our jobs and hobbies, telephones, books, music players – so many ways of entertaining ourselves and keeping ourselves occupied. Anyone who has been confined at home through illness or accident will tell you how quickly we go stir-crazy, even with all these things at our disposal. The dog has nothing like that: instead it has us, and it is up to us to give our dog adequate physical exercise and mental stimulation. We should also be clear in our understanding that no matter how interesting we make our dogs' lives, they will still want to stray if they possibly can. That is old, young, male, female, neutered or entire, the dog is still a roamer by need and instinct. Therefore, removing its sexual organs will not cause this to change.

Electric Shock Fencing

Here we have a system, presently legal in UK, where the dog wears a specially-made collar which delivers an electric shock if it approaches a buried wire at the perimeter of wherever the owners wish to confine it. There is usually a warning sound before the device shocks the dog, which gives it the chance to retreat from the boundary. To begin with, the boundary is also marked visually in some way, such as by flags in the ground, but the dog has to experience electric shocks before it "learns" the limits of the device. Thus it is teaching a behaviour by an example of P+.

This is not an appropriate barrier method for dogs, though many people like it because it cannot be seen and so does not change the view; also, because they personally are not shocking the dog, it does not seem so punishing. There are, however, several difficulties from the canine perspective. The incentive to brave the shock and leave if something sufficiently tempting comes by (a rabbit, a bitch on heat) can be strong enough for the dog to cross the boundary, but the prospect of the shock can prevent the dog from returning. Other dogs can enter and leave without restriction, and may attack the resident dog. In countries where dog-eating wild animals such as boar, coyote or bear roam the area, these can enter and terrorise or kill the dog. People can enter, some of whom may be of malicious intent and might torment, injure or steal the dog, or lure it over the boundary for the "fun" of seeing it shocked. Operationally, the device can malfunction, especially at the collar end, and there have been cases where dogs have been burned by the collars. The throat is a vulnerable area, and there may well be long-term health implications from electric shocks in the vicinity of the thyroid. Mentally, the dog is ill equipped for "enemies" that it cannot see or scent, and if the sound warning is not activated, the shock can appear random, thus frightening the dog and potentially giving rise to behaviour problems such as shutting down, or repetitive comforting actions such as, tail-chasing or self-mutilation. One famous dog behaviourist, Sarah Whitehead, in her book *Clever Dog* (Harper Collins 2012) mentions a dog that refused to leave its bed in the house and became completely shut down because the noise from someone pressing the button on the electric gates was the same as the warning note that preceded the electric shock from the hidden wire.

Part of taking on a dog is adapting our homes to their needs, and this includes proper fencing. We do not have to fence our entire property: it is sufficient to create an inner area from which the dog cannot escape, and which will keep it safe from people and animals that might cause it harm. If people accessing the home have a tendency to leave gates open, then we need to provide an inside gate that can be bolted or locked, just as we would with a small child, to ensure it cannot wander into danger, and nothing dangerous can accost it.

Fighting

The aspect of dogs fighting other dogs is dealt with more fully in Chapter Six, but neutering does not prevent dogs fighting, and due to the low social confidence that follows it, can actually increase a propensity to fight. Bitch fights are far more likely to end in severe injury or even death than fights between male dogs, regardless of whether the combatants are neutered or not. It is normal dog behaviour for males to scrap with males, and females with females; female dogs may snap at males who are over-familiar, but properly-socialised male dogs should never lift a lip to a female. While normal fighting is a behaviour we do not want, and is easily managed in the majority of cases, many dogs will go their whole lives without fighting or even looking as if they might. Most exceptions are due to genetic manipulation that favours fighting, grave under-socialising or the wrong kind of socialising, keeping incompatible dogs in close confinement, or early neutering, which we'll look at shortly.

Running Off

This is a simple training issue: properly-trained dogs do not run off during exercise. Almost all adolescents will try it, but once they are mature, as long as they have been properly trained and kept, they don't run off. If they are inadequately trained, frightened of their owners or bored with their lifestyles, any dog will run off, neutered or not. Neutering does not prevent dogs from running off.

Scent Marking

One of the most abhorrent behaviours to people is that of dogs which constantly scent-mark, anointing any reachable surface with urine. This is the behaviour that gets dogs banned from shops, cafes and numerous other places where we would like to be able to take them, and the fastest way I know of getting dogs banned from places where they previously were welcome. While "cocking a leg" is seen as a male behaviour, both dogs and bitches will scent-mark, neutered or unneutered, though the behaviour first appears at adolescence and is most obvious in the male. Some bitches will lift a leg and urine-mark with almost as much accuracy as a male, while others will never attempt this. A few males, especially of larger breeds, will never lift a leg to mark at all, preferring to stretch out and urinate like a horse instead. But most male dogs will exhibit this behaviour with great enthusiasm, and often to an irritating degree in that they only go for a few yards at a time before repeating the process. Behaviourally it is interesting in that it is the insecure dog that squirts everything and anything; secure dogs only mark where they want to convey specific information.

For our own convenience and also because whenever we take out a dog we are representing the whole dog-owning community, it is essential to take charge of marking behaviour and control it right from the start. We can easily put it on cue with a suitable command, restrict it to certain areas (mine are only allowed to mark when off-lead) or simply be vigilant and keep our dog away from tempting vertical surfaces. Most dogs give a fair bit of warning before they mark by sweeping the sides of their faces against the surface about to be watered, and turning back and forth until the angle is just right, and most people ignore what is about to happen until appraised by the outraged roar of a shopkeeper or stallholder that the crime has been committed. Although a stream of urine in the wrong place is not life-threatening, it creates a huge level of annoyance, and so allowing it should be considered every bit as irresponsible as the creation of unwanted puppies. Where one dog has marked, others will want to, so there is the potential for an escalating level of offensiveness. It is a simple behaviour to control by keeping the dog on a lead in risky places, away from upright surfaces, and watching out for any signs of its wanting to mark. Having said that, we need to be aware that marking is important communication to dogs, and so it should be permitted in areas where it will cause no offence, namely in outdoor environments such as fields and woods. Dogs should not be allowed to mark other people's gardens, fences or other property, nor any animal feed or bedding such as hay, straw or shavings.

Checking out and "replying" to scent-marks in suitable places is a big part of dog social life, so where no upset would be caused, they should be allowed to do it, and again it is simple to put this on cue so that the dog knows when it can go ahead and read the weemails. Watching your dog gives fascinating information about the "tags" left by others, for instance the chittering and drooling that tells you a bitch in the area is coming into season, or the posturing and raking-up of soil that leads to your dog's scent reply. Dogs have scent-glands in their pads, so the soil-scraper is effectively underlining a bold statement by kicking up the surface leading to its "comment". Pheromones in urine and faeces give a lot of information to dogs, who can tell the name, rank, number, sexual status and all manner of other information just from sniffing. It might seem revolting to us, but it is important to the dog.

Humping

This is not always about sex, although so many people will panic and insist the dog is neutered at once if it displays this behaviour, because our society finds it embarrassing, and very much because many people dislike the idea of their pet being a normal animal instead of a soft cuddly toy. Tiny puppies hump each other as a part of exploring adult behaviour (see Chapter Seven) and dogs of both sexes, neutered or unneutered, will hump as a stress-reliever, because repetitive action offers comfort by releasing endorphins. Dogs quickly learn that humping is a great attention-getter, and so display the behaviour even more. Wrongly-socialised dogs will attempt to hump other dogs because they become over-excited and haven't learned correct greeting protocol. It is high on our list of unwanted behaviours, but it is a part of normal development and we can easily make it an established behaviour instead of a passing phase by handling the issue badly. Dogs have to live in our society, so they need to be taught impulse control with humping, but with the overall understanding from us that it is normal and that it is usually a temporary phase. The dog that attempts to hump another should be lifted off and removed from the other dog's vicinity at once, before the other dog has a chance either to reprimand it or to submit. This should be done without speaking, because scolding just adds to the excitement and attention-getting. Instead, the humper learns that this behaviour results in an immediate end to canine interaction, and being made to wait beside its owner until it calms down. To begin with, the dog may try again and again, but it will learn quickly that such behaviour results in the end of its fun, and so acquire better manners.

Dogs humping people is absolutely not on. Any attempt at this should result in the dog being bodily removed from the person and if circumstances permit, given a ten-second time-out. If not, the dog should be put in a "down". This does not mean any kind of forced "down" but simply the command and the owner's refusal to accept any other reaction. The behaviour should never be rewarded by laughter or more attention: the dog must understand that doing this is totally unacceptable. This does not mean "telling it off". This is not a time for verbals, which equal attention as far as the dog is concerned. Instead, the owner must take charge right away and prevent the behaviour. If a dog is going through this phase, the owner can very quickly learn "that look" and pre-empt the dog by putting it on-lead, in a "down" or else removing it to a suitable distance. Once more I stress that this should be done in silence, and the owner should resist any form of positive punishment. The message to get across is that this is not allowed, that the dog should lie down instead, and all will be well. Calmness and the lie-down should then be rewarded.

During this phase, the dog can be given an acceptable outlet at home by redirecting it to a suitable item such as a cushion or a large soft toy kept for the purpose. Thus when the dog gets "that look" in the home, it can be shown its cushion and left to perform its behaviour on its bed, or in another room if the focus of the excitement is a visitor. After the evening meal can also be a prime time for humping, as the dog finds it relaxing and pleasant, so by simply redirecting the action to an item and a place that is less embarrassing to us, we bring it under control. At the same time, we need to look at causes for the behaviour if a dog that is past adolescence is performing it. Some dogs are highly-sexed, but for most it is a behaviour showing a need for comfort, so we should look at the wider picture and see what has happened in the dog's life that might have created this need. We humans can be remarkably dense at times in recognising what are, to dogs, massive changes in their lives, so we have to investigate thoroughly in order to find out what may be upsetting our dog. Reviewing the lifestyle of the dog may indicate where changes are needed, for instance with more exercise or mind work. Most dogs cease humping behaviour once the hormonal turmoil of adolescence has passed, but it may reappear in either sex at times of uncertainty or insecurity. In these cases, it is best dealt with by addressing the root causes (often there will be more than one) and the behaviour itself will disappear once this has been done.

Over-Sexed and Over Here

Some breeds and some individuals have a much higher sex-drive than others, and if this behaviour presents to the point that the dog is making its own and its owner's life a misery, such a dog is a suitable candidate for neutering once it is mature. Most adolescents go through a hypersexual stage, but they grow out of it quite naturally as their hormones settle. It is said that an adolescent male dog has higher testosterone levels than a working stud dog, but the great thing about adolescence is that they all grow out of it unless they are neutered during it, which can lead to more in the way of unwanted behaviour because the dog has no chance to establish correct adult hormone levels. A normal mature male dog will be keen to mate when the occasion arises, but part of essential survival programming is the ability to recognise when it is not a good idea, and back off. They do not become obsessed with the idea in the way those who know little about normal males think they do. A male dog should always be prepared to take "no" for an answer, whether that "no" comes from the bitch, another male dog, or his owner. We hear about dogs that won't stop whining or howling when there is a receptive bitch in the area, and supposing these dogs are properly fed and exercised, it is up to the owners whether this is a sufficient nuisance to castrate, but be warned – a lot of neutered male dogs will still whine or howl too. This is a time when more exercise, more mind-games at home, and the temporary use of a veterinary calming agent can be an alternative to surgery that might not work anyway – and we can't stick them back on once they have been removed. Your vet will have a variety of non-drug calmers available: Bach Flower Remedy Mimulus helps many dogs (anecdotally I heard that one lady was so impressed that she gave her husband some as well) Skullcap and Valerian herbal mix is very well thought of, and then there are preparations such as Zylkene, for which you need a prescription at present. Veterinary science is ever evolving, so by the time you read this, there may be other remedies to try: a bitch is only receptive for a few days each time she comes into heat, but if your dog finds this mega-stressful, then these are useful alternatives to neutering. It would be a shame to have a dog castrated when you didn't want to, and then find the bitch has moved home and is no longer within your dog's radar.

Unwanted Puppies

It is extremely irritating for responsible owners to be told that we should neuter our dogs to prevent unwanted puppies. There is no earthly reason to suppose that an entire dog is going to be allowed to mate without the connivance of his owner and that of the bitch(es) he covers. Properly-kept dogs do not create unwanted puppies. They might create very much wanted ones, or they might never mate at all. An entire male that never mates is not a miserable unfulfilled dog – there is a lot more than sex in a well-kept dog's life.

Will It Change Him?

Sometimes people are asked if they will allow their male dog to mate a bitch as a one-off. This is rather flattering, as it implies that someone else has recognised the quality of our dog, and that he is good enough to put over a well-loved bitch for a much-wanted litter. Alternatively, someone might be wanting to make a quick buck out of breeding a litter, and ours is the nearest dog of the breed they want. It won't make a hap'orth of difference as far as the dogs are concerned, but might twang your conscience more for the latter case than the former. But what of our dog? Will he then become obsessed by sex, where he has previously been ignorant or else only mildly interested? Will this one instance ruin your dog as a pet? One thing for sure: there is no undoing it once it's done.

Putting a dog and bitch together needs a fair bit of skill: it might seem as if it only goes flawlessly when you don't want it, the way it used to happen on street corners when I was a child. It certainly isn't a matter of shutting them in a shed and letting them get on with it: dog and bitch risk severe injury that way. I am not, in general, in favour of breeding as a one-off unless the dog and bitch concerned really are of exceptional quality and will add something to the breed that it would be a crime to lose. That, in all honesty, rules out most pet dogs. Whether the dog will change or not in terms of looking for sexual opportunities in the future is an individual matter and also dependent on breed, where some are much keener than others whether bred from or not. My own stud was so mellow that I could call him away from a receptive bitch, and he would refuse to mate if I was not present, even if I was only in the next room or had gone to the car to get something. This was not anything I had trained, but just a part of his own obliging personality. Others can be very different, and honestly, if stud work is not going to be a career, I would recommend that the average male pet dog remains in blissful ignorance. Another reason to neuter, as you are not planning to breed? Be aware that many castrated male dogs can still mate and tie; the vet or the dog rescue society will very seldom explain this. It is not a good thing to happen, as it might introduce infection to either dog, and also, because it is not a complete process, the tie may go on for longer than is usual. And as a normal tie can last easily for forty minutes, most dog owners can run out of polite conversation while they wait for their dogs to part company.

Vasectomy

It is sometimes suggested that male dogs that are not wanted for breeding could be vasectomised, therefore developing correctly with the right hormone levels, and with no risk of creating unwanted litters. There would still be the possibility of such dogs mating, however, and so little if anything to be gained that could not be achieved with proper management.

The Bitch and Seasons

We have already touched on many sexual aspects shared by dog and bitch, for instance in the matters of straying, humping, aggression and scent-marking. Specific to the female is the oestrus season, sometimes called the "heat". This perfectly normal development is frequently made out to be the most horrific experience for owner and dog, not to mention every male dog within miles, and the very people who describe the process with the most drama are the ones who have never experienced a bitch's behaviour when in season. Even respected professionals such as some vets can promulgate received wisdom as if it is fact. To hear some "experts" you would think nuclear war is preferable to allowing a bitch to come on heat. So let's look at what really happens.

Preliminaries

Most bitches give plenty of warning before they go into heat, and for several weeks prior will scent-mark more often when out, to leave any passing males information that something interesting is about to happen. Males for their part will inhale the scent with approval, running it over a scent receptor in the roof of their mouths (Jacobson's organ) as well as over their tongue and flews, displaying a typical "chittering" rapid jaw movement and probably some drooling too. This does not mean that a dog will suddenly charge off on an uncontrollable mission to find a bitch that is coming on heat in three weeks' time, but he may well look up at his owner with the canine equivalent of a conspiratorial wink and maybe a telepathic suggestion that "you should smell this!" We will notice behavioural changes in our pre-oestrus bitch, which will depend on her individual character. Serious ones can become skittish, secretive ones more communicative, ditsy types even more scatty – any change in everyday behaviour should have the owner checking the calendar. Female hormones make fur softer and shinier, and bitches that hunt for a living can become even more predatory or else lose their concentration and often their quarry. Bitches that live with other dogs might cause observable changes in group dynamics, for the bitch that is about to come in season becomes more important in status, which sometimes tempts lesser characters to take on stronger ones. Where there are uneasy relationships between individuals in a group of dogs, the wise owner becomes more vigilant, and separates them when unsupervised if there is any perceived risk of a fight. Within a well-adjusted group, nothing much changes at all.

The Season Starts

Individual bitches have individual cycle patterns, so this is a description that fits most, but owners should allow for minor differences. The season begins with "showing colour" that is, a red fluid drips from the bitch's vulva, and this is counted as day one. Some bitches are very clean and owners have to be quick to notice the change, while others are more lavish and spots of red can be seen in their bedding and on floors. The very first season does not set a pattern for those following, and bitches may produce much less fluid on subsequent seasons than they do on their first, but in any case it is not a vast amount, just some spotting, contrary to hair-raising reports that imply we will be wading through great pools of blood. During the next week, the bitch's vulva swells dramatically. Many text books state that the fluid changes to straw-coloured after the first ten days, but this has not happened with any of mine, nor with any bitch belonging to friends; ours all show red throughout the heat. Ovulation normally occurs between ten and fourteen days, and these are the optimum times to have the bitch mated if you are breeding, and to be very careful if you are not. However, bitches are individuals; some may mate outside these times, and bring forth a normal litter, so personally I am very careful throughout the season. Normal seasons last for twenty-one days, after which the bitch's vulva will cease to drop fluid, and will shrink back to its normal dimensions, which latter may take another two to three weeks.

Some bitches are very particular about their partners, and it can be exasperating when having chosen exactly the right stud dog from our point of view, the bitch wants nothing to do with him. Others are much less fussy. We need to understand that any creature which is not sexually available for long stretches of time will be correspondingly more needy when the time is right, and at ovulation, many bitches are extremely keen to mate. Because bitches ovulate a number of eggs at a time, it is possible for them to mate with a series of dogs and conceive pups by all of them. This is a great way of widening the gene pool in terms of Mother Nature, but not what we want if we are managing breeding for a particular series of attributes. It is not necessary for a bitch to mate at all in her life, and she won't need counselling because of it. Most bitches distract easily enough during even the few days where they are most receptive, so as long as they have plenty of exercise and occupation while being kept away from male dogs, they manage well. Hormonal changes can make some more clingy and others more independent than normal; however this should not be misinterpreted as "suffering". It is part of the normal cycle.

A bitch will come into her season pattern depending on breed, with more primitive breeds cycling later and less frequently. We are told that bitches cycle every six months, and many do, but just as many delay a first season until over a year old, cycle annually, and with a longer receptive phase. All of this is normal, and no bitch has ever read a textbook. I have had bitches that cycled every ten months, every thirteen months, every eight months and so on, with seasons that last three weeks or four, and each is within normal parameters. Large breeds and sighthound types may only cycle a few times in their lives, and I knew a deerhound that did not have her first season until she was four, which is not unusual. Others cycle every six months very promptly. Anything more frequent than six-monthly seasons may be seen as outside the norm, and once such bitches are mature, assuming they are not intended for breeding, most owners would have those spayed because such animals get no break from the whole process.

False Pregnancy

Whether or not a bitch has been mated, it is normal for her body to "assume" that she has been, and to prepare for pregnancy. In unmated bitches, this creates the condition known as "false pregnancy", which again is a natural process and not the devil's invention that some dog professionals make it out to be. Put simply, her hormones make her appear pregnant, and can be very convincing. Her abdomen may thicken at the tuck-up above the hindlegs, her nipples may stand proud, and her tendons and muscles may slacken. It is this latter process that makes many working dog people take their bitch out of serious activity until the false pregnancy is over, because extreme stress on limbs and muscles, such as a coursing or racing dog might experience, has the potential to cause injury.

Bitches show differing degrees of false pregnancy. With some it is barely noticeable, while with others even an experienced breeder may pause and wonder if she could have been mated by accident. Sixty-three days after the mating is when a pregnant bitch would give birth, and the bitch in false pregnancy will have a body preparing for birth at around the same time. She may even come into milk. Owners should resist any tendencies to touch or squeeze her mammaries. In cases of extreme milk production, I have found homeopathic Pulsatilla to reduce this almost to nothing over a very few days, and a small amount of milk can safely be ignored; it will dry up in its own time.

Milk or not, many bitches will become broody, and take to nursing soft toys. They may make nests in quiet dark places, and spend a lot of time hidden away. This is not abnormal, and the dog is not sad; it's her hormones talking. Again, some professionals make a really big deal about this stage, to the point of recommending forcible removal of the surrogate puppies, and even giving veterinary drugs to the bitch. Many owners feel concern and imagine the dog to be miserable, but she is not. She is going through a perfectly normal process which quite probably has its roots in the time when far-off dog ancestors would assist in the suckling of litters when food may have been in short supply and so one bitch could not provide enough milk for her young. Other wild canids are known to share suckling duties with maiden bitches in group environments, so there is every reason for our own domestic dogs to have retained this aspect of their breeding responses. Where there are several pet dogs kept together, they will usually come into season concurrently, emulating their wild relatives. It is a well-known practice for breeders who want a particular bitch to come on heat to kennel her next door to a bitch already in season; it usually brings the other bitch into heat as well.

Popular Misunderstandings

Although the false pregnancy is a natural part of the season, many people treat it as an illness, and it is shockingly common in veterinary circles for owners to be pressurised into having their bitches spayed because it is made out to be an aberrant condition instead of the perfectly normal one that it is. People think that the bitch is feeling woebegone when she dens up with her imaginary litter, but this is anthropomorphism. She is different, but she is not unhappy. She is in a hormone-led world of motherhood, which runs its course quickly; soon the phantom "puppies" are weaned, and the bitch returns to her anoestrus state.

Risks and Difficulties

Just as there are risks attached to neutering, especially before development is complete, there are risks attached to keeping dogs of either gender entire, and if we choose to do so, we need to be aware of them. For the male dog, there is little overall risk except that owners have a duty to ensure that no unwanted litters are bred. This is very simple to achieve by responsible management. In physical health terms, I suggest exploring research listed at the end of this chapter, which addresses the different issues in detail. A dog cannot get cancer in anatomy it doesn't have, but testicular cancer is not all that common and if it does occur is easily dealt with because it is contained. Prostate cancer is statistically more likely to occur in neutered males, while benign prostate swellings can occur in neutered and intact dogs, with the bias towards affecting the intact; again it is easily treated. Incorrect development of joints and long bones due to early neutering, because it is hormones that cap-off the bones at the right stage of development, has been implicated in cruciate ligament injuries because the stresses on the joints are therefore unnatural, and it is thought that bone cancers are more likely in some neutered males. However, this must all be seen against a background of percentages in order to get it in proportion.

For bitches, again there is no possibility of getting cancer in organs that have been removed. Pyometra, which is a condition where pus builds in the uterus, is life-threatening, and again cannot usually occur when the uterus has been removed, though there is a rare condition called "stump pyometra" where infection builds in the remaining tissue. Pro-spaying people mention pyometra as if it is inevitable, but while we should always acknowledge its seriousness, it is not a common condition in properly-kept bitches. We who do keep our bitches whole must be vigilant about this condition, just as we need to ensure that they do not breed unless we want them to. Mammary cancer is touted as being another inevitability in the intact bitch, but statistics show that it occurs just as readily in spayed bitches, along with benign tumours. Scientifically, it is very difficult to prove a negative: we cannot say with any credibility that something might or might not have occurred if something else might or might not have been done; we only know what has or has not happened. The false pregnancy means watching out for mastitis if the bitch is very milky, a rare occurrence but possible nevertheless. If a bitch is especially possessive of her surrogate "puppies" we need to make sure that she is kept away from any people, especially children, who may try to take her toys or force their attention on her when she would rather, in the style of the best Hollywood screen sirens, be left alone.

Exercise

Quite the most difficult part of the season, unless we have our own land, is exercising the bitch during it. She must be exercised for her health, mental and physical, but it is sensible to keep her away from other dogs, and if her recall is not reliable, she will have to be kept on the lead. We may have to change our exercise schedule in order to take advantage of times when few dogs are about. If we live in an area where people let dogs roam free, then our exercising really is compromised, and if we cannot drive to a safer area, it is likely that we would be better off to have our bitch spayed once she is adult.

Hormones and Development

Hormones have a huge part to play in the physical and mental development of our dogs, and adolescence in any mammal is a tricky period. Because we live so closely with our dogs, we can find their adolescent behaviour really trying, as our sweet obedient puppy appears to have been abducted by space aliens, and a stroppy monster left in its place. This is the age when a huge number of dogs come into rescue (see Chapter Six) because it is so hard to see our way out of the upsurge in challenging behaviour. This is when people with no knowledge of natural development push owners into having their dogs neutered, but neutering now prevents the dog from progressing into correct physical and mental adulthood. Physically, hormones switch off growth at the right time, which is why dogs neutered before or during adolescence have a taller narrower build and different head shape from the correct version. This is important because it places different stresses on limbs and joints, which has been implicated in certain types of illness such as bone cancer and cruciate ligament failure mentioned earlier. There are studies mentioned at the end of this chapter which cover these and other physical changes from early neutering, but we are looking primarily at behaviour, and in behavioural terms, neutering in adolescence is catastrophic. Hormones play a huge part in mental development, and we are still learning about their full importance. The dog is a co-operative species, which is why it works with mankind in so many different ways. But co-operation as a mindset is not present in infancy: the infant of necessity is selfish, because that is its key to its survival. Adolescence is a time when great changes are not just physical: the brain changes as well, in people, in dogs and in other social species too. After adolescence we find the ability to co-operate is fully installed, which is why training really can be fine-tuned in the adult dog, though we are wise if we lay the foundations early in puppyhood. During adolescence, the animal is incapable of much in the way of co-operative learning, which is why training usually takes a back seat and we often struggle even to maintain the standards we had in the puppy. Post-adolescence gives almost a feeling of relief as we get our obliging, pleasant dog back from Planet Zog, and if you have had teenage children, you may have noticed something similar. But neuter the dog in the midst of this hormonal re-wiring, and the upgrade cannot take place properly, because its hormonal balance has been destroyed and its mindset cannot develop further. This creates a type of dog we know all too well: the teenage thug in the adult body. Puppy amnesty is past, but the dog's brain holds onto its puppy behaviour, and this is the dog that goes barrelling into other dogs and either terrifies them or gets a hiding from them, but never learns from it. This is the dog that is far harder to train, the dog that goes into Rescue and comes out with separation anxiety, destructiveness, noisiness, neediness, but not as a passing phase because it cannot develop beyond this stage without the right levels of hormones. While entire dogs can display these traits too, they have the option of being helped out of them because their mental development is complete, but with early and pubertal neuters, we can only progress so far.

Neutering Pre-Adolescents

Continuing onwards from the above, there is a regrettable tendency with certain dog rescues and some veterinary practices, to neuter pre-pubertal puppies. Some organisations even neuter puppies that are only a few

Entire working Basset hound.

Neutered pet Basset hound.

weeks old. I understand that in veterinary terms the operation is much easier to perform on very young puppies; however it may be interpreted as unethical in that the puppies have no chance to develop normally, mentally or physically, whereas the puppy neutered in adolescence, while still potentially troubled and troublesome, at least has been exposed to some level of hormonal development. Very early neuters are easily recognised by their body-shape, which is weak and "shelly" compared to the correctly-developed animal. Some vets are of the opinion that very early neuters are more disposed to allergy and immune system issues, and behaviourally they are likely always to be puppyish. This last does appeal to certain types of owner, but such dogs may always have issues with other dogs.

Neutering at Maturity

Not everybody is prepared to keep unneutered dogs, or has a lifestyle that allows this, because there is an extra responsibility, and that cannot always be extended to other members of the family. Moreover, neutering gives us the freedom to keep mixed genders if we want more than one dog, for although this can be done with entire dogs and bitches too, nobody who actually does it will pretend it is easy at season times. However, as mentioned earlier, we need to be aware that neutered males can still mate and tie even though there will be no pups from the union. Neutering at or after maturity makes all the difference to having a healthy dog afterwards. There can still be problems, but so can there be with entire dogs too. It's useful to know what we are letting ourselves in for in either case. Again, we here are looking from a behavioural point of view: there are also other physical issues worth researching which impact on behaviour too.

Urinary Incontinence

Particularly with bitches, neutering can lead to urinary incontinence. Sometimes this is due to the way the operation itself is conducted, but more usually it is a lack of sphincter competence due to the drop in hormones. It is a very difficult condition to live with both for bitch and owner. The bitch may or may not be disturbed by constant leaking; some become very distressed and others don't appear to notice. What they are affected by is the change in lifestyle if they have been used to accompanying their owner almost everywhere; incontinence is very isolating and a dog that leaks is not welcome in many social human situations. If the dog is kept outside in a kennel and run, as many working dogs are, neither dog nor owner may notice the issue at all, but this assumes that the dog has plenty of company and occupation. Modern equipment for human incontinence in the way of sheets and covers that wick moisture away from the surface and hold it until laundering, are very useful with house dogs, but even so, access to some rooms may have to be limited, and the dog used to sleeping with its owner may have to give up that arrangement. Nappies for dogs are not a healthy solution because they create a warm moist environment that is ideal for bacteria to flourish, which has the potential to create even more problems for the dog. Urinary tract infections are subtle in their symptoms, and there is often not even a temperature, but the dog may present symptoms that are eccentric or even resemble dementia. There are various veterinary drugs that can be tried as well as herbal and homeopathic remedies, or a combination of these, so it is useful to try whatever is available, particularly as some dogs can react quite badly to some of the drugs, and again this reaction is usually seen behaviourally, with the dog appearing either depressed or aggressive. Other dogs of course do well on them without any apparent character change.

Other Dogs

Dogs have a "respect" hierarchy regarding whole or neutered animals, because to the normal dog, the neutered animal, especially the early neuter, smells, looks and acts differently. In the world of animals, "different" is unwelcome, and so some neutered dogs can have problems with entire dogs of either sex. Well-socialised and confident dogs of any neuter status usually ignore other dogs with which they do not want to mix, but issues arise when dog-to-dog manners are compromised by lack of social skills between one or more animals. It is sometimes suggested that, because a bitch is only in season at certain times, that between seasons she is the same as a spayed bitch, but she very much is not. Hormonal input continues whether she is on heat or not, and so her scent is quite different from that of the spayed bitch. Whole bitches are top of the survival tree, especially when they are about to come into season, then entire dogs, spayed bitches, and finally, neutered male dogs are bottom of the status heap and gain the least respect from other dogs. Personal observation indicates, however, that a male dog that has been castrated towards the latter part of his life, say at about nine or ten years old, appears to maintain his "entire dog status" among others to the extent that bitches will flirt with him and earlier-neutered males walk wide of him. It would be interesting to find out whether this is physical and due to sufficient testosterone remaining in his system from other sources, or if it is purely behavioural in that he is used to commanding respect, which is one of those responses that you often get just because you expect it.

Fat and Furry

Another major effect of neutering is that dogs put weight on more easily, which, while it can be managed by strict dietary control means that the dog may always be genuinely hungry (as opposed to always being ready to eat, which is quite different) which again has its effect on behaviour. Managing other people can be demanding, though, particularly if we are trying to keep our dog's weight to a sensible level while other family members are sabotaging our efforts by giving secret food treats.

The dog may be more likely to scavenge, or simply be anxious and unhappy because it has stomach ache. Coat changes are commonplace following neutering, and nothing can be done to avoid it. Commonly, the coat alters in texture and becomes woolly and heavier than previously. This can become a welfare issue if the dog is of a heavy-coated breed, is living in a warm climate, or is required to work. Consultation with a professional groomer who knows how to manage such a coat by thinning, as distinct from one who merely clips it, is the way to manage this. Of course, the dog can no longer be shown, but show dogs are rarely neutered anyway.

Working Dogs

Working dogs in hunting, shooting, guarding and pastoral tasks are seldom neutered; what a tragedy for the breed as well as the owners if the best workers could not be bred from. This is why the standards are so high in general for such types of dog, or for the working varieties anyway. "Form follows function", and in most cases, only the best are bred from. But there are other activities that come under the heading of "work" where dogs are routinely neutered, such as any branch of assistance dog, and most bitches in search and rescue categories. Assistance dogs lead a highly unnatural life in most disciplines, though not all. Many are trained to ignore other dogs totally and always, to only eliminate in one place,

Working dogs are seldom neutered. Photo: F. Sechiari.

and are never permitted to behave in any way like a normal dog, such as by enjoying scents they encounter outside. Some agencies insist on prepubertal neutering, though anecdotally it appears that there is a high failure rate in training terms afterwards, which is unsurprising given that such dogs have no chance of adult co-operative mental development. However, there are no official figures to support this, and it would be cultural dynamite to pursue by research. While some branches of assistance work allow the dog "downtime" to be spent as a dog would like rather than as people like to think they like (chasing a ball does not compare in pleasure and fulfilment terms with snuffling out scents) others are kept well in physical terms only, their behavioural needs rarely being addressed at all. It is arguable that prepubertal neutering and an artificial lifestyle is justifiable within the context of using dogs to help badly damaged humans to lead a fuller life, and that is a debate for a different arena. Purely on behavioural grounds and within the mores of canine welfare, large and uncomfortable questions are raised.

Dogs that work in such areas as Search and Rescue, or drugs and explosives detection, are often in a situation where the males are left entire but the bitches are neutered because they are not worked while in season. This does mean that some very good dogs cannot be bred from. In behavioural terms, as long as the dogs are mature before their neutering, it is unlikely to make any difference to their work. For guarding, police and military work, it is usually the practice to use entire male dogs only, though some agencies will use bitches. The discerning behaviour student notes that a bitch on heat will distract most male dogs whether they are entire or not, but is unlikely to be a distraction to another bitch.

Neutering is surgery that is "sold" to the dog owner as a benefit to the dog, but in truth, we neuter for human reasons not canine ones. Those reasons, however, are often good ones regarding keeping dogs within human society. It is a choice, not an imperative, and keeping whole dogs suits some of us better than having them neutered, while for others, having the dog neutered is the only way we can keep dogs at all. There is no "right" or "wrong" about neutering except for the age at which it is done; otherwise there are problems and advantages with either condition. As long as the choice we make is an informed one, and we are fully aware of the effects of either course of action, we are able to take the best decision for our own particular circumstances.

Some Modern Studies on Neutering

Sanborn, Laura J.M.S. of Rutgers University, *Long-Term Health Risks and Benefits Associated with Spay / Neuter in Dogs* 2007.

Zink, Christine, DVM, PhD, DACVP *Early Spay-Neuter Considerations for the Canine Athlete* 2005. Nolen, R. Scott *Rottweiler Study Links Ovaries With Exceptional Longevity* JAVMA 2010.

Retaining ovaries may be a key to prolonged life in women and dogs DVM Newsmagazine; December 2000.

Hines, Ron DVM PhD article on early neutering.

Articles in public domain by vets Richard Allport, Steve Dean, Mark Elliott and Nick Thompson.

Chapter Five

Food for Thought

*How Behaviour is Affected by Nutrition
and Feeding Practices*

S TUDIES IN NUTRITION for humans and its effects on health have come on immeasurably, albeit rather confusingly at times, when we find constant conflicting advice on whether something is a wonder food, should be taken in moderation, or will see us off in short order. What scientists do agree on, however, is that a varied diet of fresh food is good for us. So why then do some animal health professionals promote feeding exactly the same processed food, day in day out, to our dogs?

It is one of those cases where you can't serve Dog and Mammon. Where money is concerned, morality and even common sense is usually a casualty, so we need to conduct our own research on what we should feed our dogs, because we cannot always trust professionals. In fact, professionals cannot trust each other either, especially where canine nutrition lectures are given to veterinary students by representatives of companies that make commercial pet food, or such companies invest appreciable sums of money to ally themselves with respected canine organisations. Nowadays there are many vets who have progressed beyond this early indoctrination and studied nutrition by the simple method of feeding their own animals and observing the results, and apart from a very few occasions when severe illness affects an individual animal's ability to process certain foods, no health professional to my knowledge has ever gone back to commercial food after feeding fresh. Nowadays there is a lot of information in the public domain about suitable food for dogs, and a reading list appears at the end of this chapter for those who would like to research further. Because this is a book on behaviour, we are only going to look briefly at physical differences where they impinge on mental health; the books and other research listed are there for anyone who would like to explore onwards by themselves.

While the link between food and behaviour in people is generally accepted, it can take quite a leap of understanding to extrapolate this to dogs. There is a perception that animals can eat any old rubbish and stay healthy, a centuries-long history of dogs being fed on bread, slops and scraps (that grand saying "fit as a butcher's dog" indicates how few dogs ate meat with any kind of regularity) and only recently even in the developed world has there been enough meat to spare to give to dogs. Dogs that were able to roam had the chance of adding to their diet by scavenging, or perhaps catching prey. Dogs in any case tended not to live long lives as once they could not work, they were rarely kept longer out of sentiment. Veterinary care was rudimentary, and there was a general air of animals being considered expendable in many homes, though not all. Even nowadays, many people will boast of how cheap the dog food they use is, or get whatever is on "special offer", with no conscious understanding that good quality food equals good health.

Owner Appeal

It is people who buy commercial dog food, so manufacturers obviously make their food to have person-appeal rather than dog-appeal. Some foods are made in a variety of shapes and colours, though dogs couldn't care less about shape and colour in their food, and in any case have a different colour perception from ours. But the bowl of pretty shapes and colours looks lovely to the owner, who might otherwise feel as if a dog that has a bowl of brown nuggets every day might not be getting as good a meal as the one that has shapes and colours. Then there is the lovely meaty smell, so strong when a sack is opened, and so elusive by the time we get to the end of it. This is because the "smell", called "digest", is manufactured separately and sprayed onto the food last thing before packaging, and why all brands of dog food smell similar. The smell itself travels almost unchanged through the dog and creates unnaturally smelly excrement; while dog muck is never ashes of roses, what results from the additive-enriched commercial food is really vile to the human nose. If we are trying to retrain dogs that eat other dogs' muck (coprophagia) we begin to understand from this that dogs fed on commercial food expel muck that smells just like dinner, and so is more appealing to those dogs with depraved appetites. (see Chapter Six).

Balanced Diet

For those of us who take more of an interest in what our dogs eat, there is the seductive myth of the "balanced diet". Over decades, pet owners and especially dog owners have been subjected to the information that what our animals eat has to be scientifically balanced with the same amount of nutrition in every morsel. Any other way will, we are told, lead to ill health. Despite the fact that most of us feed ourselves and our families perfectly satisfactorily, the smiling scientist on the dog food sack or tin assures us that we don't know enough about nutrition to feed our dogs. And so even people with the confidence to feed their families organic this and homemade that are browbeaten into thinking that they are too stupid to feed their dogs. Dog food manufacturers collude with this by providing a series of specialist diets. And you thought you just had a dog. It is important that a dog has the full range of necessary nutrients, but it does not need exactly the same at every meal any more than we do. Feeding a good variety of suitable food over time will achieve this quite naturally and without difficulty.

Breed, Age and Illness Diets

We now have a bewildering choice of different foods according to the breed, size and age of our dogs. Food for purebred dogs, giant breeds, small breeds, puppies up to this or that age, old dogs, working dogs; find a category and someone will have designed a food especially for it. Some aspects of dogdom do benefit from a slightly adjusted diet, but this should be geared to the individual in front of us, rather than presenting as part of a blanket ideology. For instance, puppies do not need different food from adults once weaned – they just need more of it. Not one single mammal living as Nature intended eats anything different when young from the food it will have as an adult. Livestock to be fattened quickly has to have an artificial diet, but we don't want fat puppies – we want strong puppies. Veterinary surgeon Dr. Ian Billinghurst in his book *Grow Your Pups With Bones* states that healthy pups should only grow to seventy-five per cent of their potential, and as a man who has bred Great Danes, he knows about potential. Giant breeds should be allowed to grow slowly if they are to be healthy adults. We see "small breed" food, where pieces of food are much smaller than that marketed for other breeds. Dogs have teeth, and are more than capable of chewing up bones and hide: they do not need cute tiny pieces of kibble with the implication that their little mouths cannot manage normal-sized pieces. In fact, the harder a dog has to work for its food, the better its behaviour, because any dog only has so much chewing in it, and if it can address much of this need by diet, that is a lot kinder to our possessions. We see breed-specific foods, that pander to our pride in a purebred dog but are honestly unnecessary, because selective breeding may have changed the size and shape but it hasn't yet changed the digestion except where illness presents as a result of breeding from genetically poor stock. And we have a lot of people who come badly unstuck because they have a working breed as a pet, and think it should therefore have food especially for working dogs.

Real working dogs need more food when working, but they do not need different food. Even high-performance working dogs such as greyhounds do best on a simple diet of good quality fresh ingredients. Artificially high protein levels have the potential to cause poor health, especially those from starch-based foods, and that ill-health is often first seen in behavioural changes. Elderly dogs again do not need special food for geriatrics but a diet based on individual needs. Some may have a smaller appetite and so need to be fed small quantities more often, and less competent absorption due to age may invite the use of supplements or neutraceuticals. Other old dogs develop a voracious appetite and so need extra vegetables that fill them up without putting on weight rather than cereal starch, and different neutraceuticals to help them get the best from their food (see reading list at the end of this chapter).

Types of Food

We have quite a choice of food available now, some of which is very convenient to store and feed, some of which needs care and forward planning. Wet food, dried food, pouch food, all commercial foods are easy to buy under one roof and store in a cupboard. Fresh food needs planning ahead and ideally more freezer space to take advantage of bargains and unexpected but welcome offers of large quantities of meat or vegetables. There are now several good sources of raw food mixes, packaged and frozen ready to thaw out and feed, so this is a very helpful identification of a previous gap in

Something safe to chew.

the market. However, buyers must still take care to read ingredient lists thoroughly, as some manufacturers are rather flexible in their definitions and have allowed large quantities of processed starch, cereal and filler to sneak into their recipes. Some of these have been implicated in behavioural changes.

Dry food, while very convenient to store and feed, does create an added need for moisture in the dog, and so dry-fed dogs will need to drink a great deal more than those fed a more natural diet. There is often a significant amount of salt in both dry and wet commercial diets; while there are legislative restrictions on how much should be added, it is still more than a dog would come across when eating a more natural diet. Therefore the dog drinks more and needs to urinate more as a result. This needs to be bourn in mind when house-training, as a dog taking on extra liquid is going to need to get rid of it at some stage. If we must feed dry food, then changing the timings of the dog's meals can make all the difference to its elimination pattern. We should never restrict water; it is inhumane, and in some countries, illegal.

Ingredients

While there is legislation that controls what may and may not be put into dog food, it is very broad, and almost anything with a nodding acquaintance to animal or vegetable origin can and does end up in dog food. Some high-end better quality dog foods exist, with a minimum of ingredients and no artificial additives, chemicals and sugars, and these are rather expensive, but we feed less because there is less in the way of filler, and so incidentally less excrement as a result. If we are struggling to housetrain a dog, it is worth avoiding those cheap foods packed with indigestible ingredients, because the dog will not then need to move its bowels unnaturally frequently. One of the first things noticed by people changing to a fresh food diet is that the dog's output is markedly less in quantity. Dogs have very strong digestive juices and a short gut, so the throughput takes around twelve hours with a suitable diet. Reading the list of ingredients on dog food labels often reveals a high percentage of "filler" that ends up as excrement; we are in effect paying for muck, just as with some tinned foods we are paying for a large percentage of water and textured cellulose. Though the better dog foods appear to be more expensive, once we check the actual available food as distinct from the total quantity, we realise what a false economy it is to buy the cheaper alternatives. Label-reading is quite an art, however, and manufacturers are adept at hiding what total content of their food is cellulose, grape pomace, sugar beet pulp, cereals, sugars and other ingredients that we would not feed our dogs from choice, so we need to take our time and read those labels critically. There are some dog foods that are so high in sugars and colourings that many behaviourists will not take on a case until the dog has had a clear month off that food. Like us, some dogs can react violently to certain additives, and produce behaviour that goes away by itself once the food is changed. We cannot retrain a dog that is "high" on substances that affect the way its mind works because it is incapable of learning while in that state. There is anecdotal evidence that a diet high in maize interferes with serotonin production and uptake, which can cause significant issues with anxious types of dog. I have several times recommended a dietary change which has cost me the consultation, because once the dog was on decent food, its behavioural issues disappeared.

Refusing Food

This is another behaviour that really riles some of us. Providing food for the dog touches an emotional response in many people, so when the dog refuses to eat, it almost feels like a personal insult. Old-style training theories wove a whole pattern of reasons for why a dog would choose to offend us by refusing its food – the dog is being dominant, controlling, trying to decide what it wants to be fed. But there are only a few reasons why a dog would refuse food, and none of them are to do with its plans to take over the world starting with its own household.

It is commonly thought that all dogs are greedy and unselective eaters, so when a dog that is apparently healthy refuses to eat, it flummoxes us. First of all, we need to ensure that there is no physical reason behind this, so a trip to the vet is in order. A painful mouth can be the cause – teething puppies often go off their food – or some change in organ function where loss of appetite presents as an early symptom. Post-surgery or other trauma, a dog can feel that food is not worth the trouble, so may need some quiet company and possibly hand-feeding while it feels particularly vulnerable. Hand-feeding is sometimes considered "spoiling" but a bit of spoiling does not come amiss when feeling rotten, and it is a very intimate time to share with a dog. Feed out of an open hand, the way people do with horses, and do not offer more than a few mouthfuls at a time. Far from "giving in" to the dog, hand-feeding when it is feeling out of sorts is a very bonding experience.

There can be quite a few other health reasons for a dog refusing to eat, so we need to eliminate these causes before we focus on behaviour. Assuming a clean bill of health, does the dog refuse to eat anything, or will it still eat treats or leftovers from human meals? The dog is not being manipulative: it is communicating. It may simply not like the food it has been given. This is not an insult to us and should not be taken personally: we don't eat what we don't like either. Or it might not like the bowl it eats from. Plastics and polymers can leach chemicals into the food and change the taste and smell, metal bowls move and clatter, which can be very off-putting to a sensitive animal. Weighty toughened glass or ceramic bowls are more acceptable to dogs. Sometimes the problem is caused by location, because dogs need to feel safe when they eat. If other dogs are too close, or are allowed to threaten or even take this dog's food, it may be stressed to the point of refusing to eat. I am frequently presented with a situation where one dog intimidates another out of its food and the owner has no idea that it is possible, never mind necessary, to prevent this. If the family pounds past while the dog is eating, or the household is noisy and lively, this can easily be enough to put some dogs off their meal. While some dogs would continue eating under any circumstances, others are easily cowed into inappetance, sometimes by situations that seem unremarkable to us.

Dog food manufacturers often change the ingredients in their products according to whatever is cheap and readily available at the time, so the dog that has always eaten a certain brand and then starts to refuse it may be indicating that such a change has made the food unappealing to it. Or the food may have been badly stored, or contaminated, before you bought it. It may be that too much food is being offered: while some dogs will eat until they vomit, others will stop as soon as they are full. Some are stressed out by being given too much food because they think they have to guard it. Consider the size of your dog and how big its stomach is likely to be, and you can see how easy it is to overfeed. Look objectively at the dog: might it be too fat? Food with a high proportion of filler might mean that the dog has to eat a lot more food in bulk in order to fulfil its nutritional needs, and some dogs won't do that. A higher-quality food means that we feed a lot less in quantity, and the dog is more eager to eat. We also shovel up less muck too – who wants effectively to pay for bigger faeces? Growth stages make a difference too: while a growing puppy eats more than an adult dog, an elderly dog tends to want less. When the young dog reaches the end of its major growth spurt, it needs less food, but the older dog may need encouraging to eat sufficient to maintain its health. At both ends of the age scale, therefore, we need to monitor what and how our dogs eat, for it is a good stockman's way of keeping a check on overall health. Rather than being an example of awkwardness, a dog that refuses to eat is telling us something important. Rather than getting all high and mighty about it, we owners best address the issue by giving the dog food that it wants to eat. If you feel your own hackles rising at the dog having the nerve to want food it likes rather than the food it is given, pause and consider why you feel this way.

Removing Food

It is natural for dogs to carry their food away from their bowls and eat somewhere else, and while this is a lot more difficult with kibble than with raw meat and bones, many dogs still try. Others simply eat from their bowl, as we expect them to. The dog that moves its food may not be happy with where it is being fed, so if this can be changed then the behaviour will change also. However, some dogs just prefer to carry their food away regardless of where it is supplied. As few of us are fans of finding bits of dog food stashed around the house, it is quite in order to feed the dog in a crate, outside in a covered area, or in one room with the door closed or a gate across it. Once the dog has finished its meal, remove it from the feeding area by guile and treachery, such as in offering a titbit, shut it out, and check for stashed food. This is particularly important outside, as leftover food can encourage small scavengers, and some of these may carry unpleasant diseases or parasites, for instance slugs and lungworm or rats and leptospirosis. It might seem a faff to feed the dog where it wants to eat rather than bending it to our inexorable will, but it's a small issue to us and a big one to the dog. Those dogs that are calm when they eat will not risk digestive upsets or escalating nervous responses the way they might if tense and unhappy during what should be one of the high spots of the day as far as the dog is concerned. Where undesirable behaviour is rooted in insecurity, as so much of it is, feeding problems are quite often a big part of the cause.

Company

Most dogs like a degree of human company when they eat, and watching your dog with its food is a good stockman's way of assessing its wellbeing. Unless the dog has such deep-rooted food aggression that a desensitising programme is necessary, a trusted owner present while it eats gives it a sense of security. This does not mean a crowd of people coming and going, and should not be seen as a captive time for humans wanting meaningful discussions. The atmosphere should be calm and quiet. This is much appreciated by dogs, especially those that are feeling vulnerable for one reason or another.

Muzzle-Wiping

Most dogs have a ritual of muzzle-wiping after they have eaten, which is irritating to humans, who resent being used as a napkin and get annoyed when their soft furnishings develop grease smears. Even dry-fed dogs will often wipe their faces after a meal. This is an instinctive behaviour that comes from the days when primitive dogs fed on carcases. A dog can only lick upwards, and therefore cannot clean its lower jaw of flesh and fatty deposits. If it did not clean its face properly, it would risk flies and other creatures laying eggs or making a home in its muzzle. So with the modern dog, we should have a towel or some kitchen paper ready, and encourage it to come to us for face-wiping before it can choose something less appropriate.

Grazing fresh grass.

Condition Scoring

Many vet surgeries have posters showing the visual differences between underweight and overweight dogs, and the stages between, to help owners judge whether their dog is a healthy size. Sometimes the practice will sell commercial food specifically designed for overweight dogs, though in truth a healthy dog will lose or gain weight according to how much it is fed and how well it is exercised. Representatives of dog food companies that sell "diet" food have been known to insist to customers that the less food/ more walks system is a health risk, because the dog will not be getting the very precise amount of completely balanced nutrition it needs. This is an amusing and brave effort to increase sales of food we never realised was essential to the dog, but the concept does not stand contact with reality. Dogs are not precise and identical machines with precise and identical nutritional requirements, and as long as your dog is healthy, then it will gain or lose weight just like any other creature, according to its energy intake and output. We do not need to weigh our dogs to find if they are the right size, and nor is a heavy coat on the dog an excuse for us not knowing. Instead, we can run our hands over the dog and feel. Our fingertips and hands are so sensitive that we can detect a single grain of salt on a smooth surface; we can tell at once if our dogs are too fat or too thin by feeling them as well as by looking at them. The right weight shows a clear "waist" when viewed from above, and it should be easy to feel the ribs through the skin without pressing them. Very fit dogs have the last two ribs visible through the coat, but pet dogs do not have to be so fit, so one rib is fine. Some breeds such as salukis always "run up light" and such dogs are healthy even if you can see all their ribs plus the "pin bones" at the top of the pelvis. No dog is meant to be "cuddly" no matter how appealing a fat round dog may appear to those who like to hug them; they are not teddy bears but athletes, and every bit as nice to touch when they are at their correct weight. What has this to do with behaviour? Very fit lean dogs appear to be just that bit more sensitive to their surroundings, and can be quicker in their reactions for better or worse. The exercise regime that brought them to their peak then becomes a necessity. If fit dogs have come to the end of their working season, they need to be brought down from full fitness gradually rather than having their exercise dropped overnight. While working dog owners are largely aware of this, it may not seem so obvious with the pet dog that goes out running or hiking with its owner and then has a major drop in exercise as the year changes, weather worsens and daylight reduces, holidays end or work commitments escalate with a corresponding drop in physical work for the dog. Such dogs may become destructive or noisy as an outlet for their restless muscles. The solution is twofold: always plan in advance to raise or lower your dog's exercise, rather than picking it up and then dropping it as outside commitments dictate, and as you reduce the physical exercise, increase the mind work, especially by scenting games which are fulfilling as well as tiring for dogs.

Overweight dogs may experience low-level physical discomfort, both those past their youth, when arthritis threatens their joints, and those still growing, where too much pressure on immature growth plates can cause pain. Many instances of obsessive-compulsive foot or leg-chewing have their origins in painful joints. Giving painkillers or anti-inflammatories is not the solution, because masking pain without addressing the causes is detrimental to a dog's well-being. If diet has to be reduced, again this is better to address gradually, and in tandem with slightly rather than greatly increased exercise. Unfortunately we humans have an all-or-nothing tendency, and it is tempting for some to suddenly engage in a massive diet-and-exercise regime upon discovering that their dog's weight has crept up. Whatever privations we incur on ourselves, the dog should have its life changes made gradually; dogs have no concept of something that hurts being "good for them". Still on human behaviour – and so much unwanted dog behaviour stems directly from human behaviour – beware the people who will feel sorry for a dog on a diet, and ruin all your efforts by sneaking extra food into it. I once saw a whole roomful of dog behaviour trainers reduced to helpless laughter when somebody gave the definition of "a fussy feeder" as "a fat dog".

Hunger

Because dogs are opportunists, and most will take advantage of any available food source whether it needs it or not, it is quite difficult to tell when a dog is truly hungry. Those big eyes fixed on your plate or the worktop give every expression of starvation, even if the dog has only just eaten its own meal. Can we be sure that the dog is not hungry? How much does it matter if it is?

We should always train a hungry dog. Hungry dogs pay more attention, and their rewards are more rewarding to them. But a dog fed every day and that is not underweight is not going to be "hungry" to the point of distress. The dog has a short gut and a fast digestion, so is not designed to feel "full". Herbivores are pretty much always eating, because their food takes a lot more digesting to release its nutrients. Omnivores like us humans have a long gut and eat frequently, but dog design is for eating a big meal every day or so. Nowadays many people feed their dogs twice daily, and this is sensible with breeds that are prone to digestive upsets or even bloat (gastric torsion volvulus). Working dogs that cover long distances, such as foxhounds, or run hard in a series of instances over a short period of time such as coursing greyhounds, have for their health's sake to do this on empty stomachs, whereas gundogs that work a longer slower day can be given a small meal before they start and a lunchtime high-energy snack, with the main meal when work has finished, and, importantly, after at least an hour's rest so that the digestive system is ready for use. After exceptionally hard work, it is safer to give the dog a small meal, allow it to sleep, and then give the main part of the meal once it has rested, because exhausted dogs have a bigger need for recuperation than digestion. In very cold conditions and with endurance work, such as long runs with sled dogs in Arctic conditions, food is given warm, because the dog then does not have to expend vital energy in bringing food up to a digestible temperature. Such dogs are fed frequent high-protein "snacks" during their short rest periods, especially when competing in long-distance runs. This is specialist knowledge that most of our pet dogs will never need.

Starvation Days

Old kennelmen used to starve their dogs one day each week because it was supposed to be good for dogs to fast. We come across similar ideas in some branches of human medicine too. While illness and especially fever tends to make the patient want to fast, there are no health benefits to be gained by starving healthy animals (including people) who want to eat. The advantage of this old idea was strictly financial in that fifty-two days' worth of food a year was saved per animal. Some dregs of this concept still exist, but there is nothing to be gained except a hungry morose dog that does not understand why its owner has forgotten to feed it.

Neutered Dogs

Although Chapter Four covers most aspects of neutered dogs, there is one issue which is allied directly to feeding, and that is the increased tendency for neutered animals to gain weight. While easily managed with good stockmanship, there is no doubt that these dogs are actually left hungry if fed rations that keep their weight correct for their size. To an extent, we can ameliorate this by feeding extra green vegetables as "filler", because these provide bulk in the stomach but not weight gain, unlike cereal filler. But there is always the risk of the dog being hungry to the point that it becomes obsessed by scavenging, or develops unfortunate behaviour such as coprophagia. Some may become irritable or uncooperative because their hunger is driving them to the point where it is overriding all other concerns. With some working dogs, it can mean that they eat birds or animals that they should be retrieving, and I did hear of a deerstalking dog that, sent out to locate a shot deer that had run on, ate a significant amount of it before returning, looking rather rounded, to its owner. This was not a disobedient dog but an over-hungry one, though there is no doubt that such behaviour could easily become a habit. Therefore we have an extra commitment with the neutered dog, to make sure that it does not spend its days ravenous and yet still maintains a healthy weight.

Puppy Problems

The way a puppy is fed before it ever leaves the breeder can create problems that linger on well into its adult life. Puppies fed from a single bowl, who have had to fight their corner to get enough food, may be established food-guarders by the time they reach their new homes. This can mean that the hand that feeds it might get bitten, or that anyone or anything approaching the food bowl will be warned or even charged at, to make it retreat. Food is a primary resource and so we are all programmed to defend it; the puppy that has never enjoyed a peaceful meal has no concept of that being a possibility, and unfortunately we humans easily become upset when the puppy is behaving completely normally for any creature that thinks it is going to lose its food. While some puppies will lunge and snap, most will show an escalating level of warning, starting with lowering the head when someone comes near its food, then eating faster, then stopping eating, followed by showing the whites of its eyes, lip-licking, turning its head, growling, snarling, and finally the charge, closed-mouth punch, followed by an inhibited bite. If all these warnings are ignored, then the bites will become harder. But there is no need for this behaviour to develop to the point where a desensitising programme has to be engaged if we respect the puppy's need for its food as the driving force. The puppy is not being vicious: it is protecting its food in the only way it knows and, crucially, the way that has always worked for it during in its short life. It might look like a small thug but it is one very unhappy puppy. Most will reform this behaviour by themselves once they are quite sure that they do not need it, and remember what is only eight weeks to us is the whole of the puppy's life so far, and it has, at this stage, no idea that feeding times need not be stressful. Dogs do what works, but they also do not waste effort, and food-guarding puppies will almost always grow out of such behaviour quite naturally, as long as there is never any threat to them while they are eating. Any kind of slip-up on the human side of the arrangement, however, "proves" to the puppy that it is right to guard its food, and so the behaviour will reinforce to the point of needing active de-sensitising. So the easiest and most successful way to handle a food-guarding puppy is to see that it eats with no threat to its food in its own perception. The owner should stay in the room with it, but not near the food; instead, relax quietly with a newspaper or similar, until puppy has finished. No other people or animals should be allowed in, and this is not a time for making telephone calls, listening to music or playing electronic games – the atmosphere should be peaceful. When the puppy has finished its meal, it needs to be taken outside, and once it has completed its ablutions, can be left out briefly while the owner picks up the food bowl, leaving a tiny morsel of food in its place. This last is important because it satisfies the puppy's understanding that its food does not vanish while it is out, and it "changes the subject" because the edible item is so tiny that it can be eaten at once and there is nothing left to guard. If such a puppy is prone to guarding other items, such as chew toys or bones, then it should be offered something else just as or more desirable as a "swap", or else in extreme cases, lured out of the room with a treat that is not only desirable but very quick to eat, such as a piece of sausage or cheese. Then the owner can return to pick up the guarded item and take it away while the puppy is out of sight. While it is tempting to overpower the puppy physically and just pick up whatever it has, remember the puppy will grow, and you are putting in extra effort now to install the best possible behaviour in the future. By being tactful at the start, you will end up with a dog that is willing to let you take anything it has, because it knows that it will get something nice in return. Force begets force, and dogs understand force. If we manhandle a pup and rob it (remember we need to see these situations through the dog's eyes) one day it will rebel and use force against us – and pound for pound, dogs are much stronger and better armed than we are. They are hopeless against our intelligence, however, and trickery will always win the day. It doesn't betray the trust we want from them, either.

Further Reading

Billinghurst, Dr. Ian   *Give Your Dog A Bone*
                               Grow Your Pups With Bones

Drakeford J. and Elliott M.   *Essential Care for Dogs*
                               Essential Care in the Field

www.markelliott.co.uk
www.dogfoodadvisor.com

Chapter Six

The Rescue Dog

Typical Problems Explained –
What to Expect and Why the Dog isn't Grateful

DOGS COME into Rescue for a fairly short list of reasons: a change in owner's life circumstances, unrealistic expectations of dog ownership, a dog bought and discarded on a whim, medical reasons (human) such as allergies, medical reasons (dog) when the dog has an expensive health condition for which the owners are not prepared or able to pay the veterinary bills, and behaviour with which the owner cannot cope and does not seek guidance or else receives the wrong guidance. None of these are the "fault" of the dog, which can only ever behave like a dog and have the health and traits it has inherited, but all of these, even the most innocuous-sounding, can have a profound effect on the behaviour of the dog in its new home. Similarly, the human attitude may be questionable, such as with those who want the warm fuzzy feeling of having "rescued" a dog, which they then expect to show gratitude and adoration for the rest of its life. Others take on a rescue dog for sounder reasons, such as not wanting to deal with puppy-training and so preferring an adult that has all that turmoil behind it, or because they like managing behaviour issues and are confident of being able to help a dog readjust to the world it is in. Whatever the reasons, even the nicest dog comes out of Rescue with psychological and often physical "baggage" and the humans in their lives need to be able to deal with it, either by themselves or with the help of a suitable professional. One person's "terrible fault" is another's "normal dog"; I have known dogs sent in to Rescue because they caught rabbits, or barked at other dogs, or indulged in other perfectly unremarkable dog activities such as digging holes. Most unwanted behaviour can be easily managed with the help of the right professional and a healthy dose of common sense, but in many cases people do not want to commit any further time or effort. A few behavioural issues are very hard to manage indeed, even with the best of assistance, and sometimes all we have available to use are compromise, acceptance and management. Note that I am not suggesting people do not take dogs from Rescue, but that we must be realistic in our attitudes and expectations when we do. For instance, one Rescue I know uses the mantra "Don't get a dog from a puppy farm – take in a rescue instead". But that dog from Rescue quite probably originated from a puppy farm, and so still might have the same issues to overcome relating to ill-health, lack of socialisation and poor genetics. Therefore we should be practical with our expectations, and if we decide to take in a rescue dog, we need an idea of what is to come. It is immensely rewarding to be able to give a good home to a dog that had a bad one the first time round, but we do need to go into that commitment with our eyes wide open and a fair idea of what to expect. That way we can follow the mantra and "set ourselves up for success".

Foster Dogs

Ideally, a dog should go from its original owners to its new ones, but this isn't always or even often possible, because by the time most people have decided to part with the dog, they will have come to the end of their patience, or else having made the decision, they want to get rid of the dog as soon as possible to spare their own feelings. Foster homes are provided by some Rescues as a halfway house that is an alternative to kennelling, and often better in that the fosterer should have more time to study the dog and the experience to understand what they see. The dog lives in a home instead of in a kennel, so goes from one domestic environment to another, and fosterers usually have other dogs, sometimes cats too, and can see how the dog interacts with them. During its time in foster care, a dog can be assessed with children, a variety of adults, other dogs, and in different environments such as town or country, with livestock, on and off-lead, and so on. Few kennels have the staff or the time to conduct such an in-depth analysis of the dogs in their care, so good fosterers are really valuable as part of canine rehabilitation.

When a dog moves out of its original home to another, it typically goes through a "shut-down" period, sometimes called "the honeymoon period" where it is quiet and non-reactive as a defensive measure. Once it has learned the dynamics of the new home, it will start to behave more naturally, and then assessors begin to get a feel for the dog as it really is. Most dogs come out of the kennels environment totally shut down, so a dog assessed as quiet and well-behaved by the kennels may in fact present a different character once it has settled in its new home. Here again, the foster carer provides invaluable information because during its time in foster care, the dog should progress to showing its true self. Some owners provide accurate information about their dog when they hand it over, but many do not, either because they fear the Rescue will not take the dog if they know its true character, or because the owners themselves don't understand what is going on with the dog. The foster carer ideally finds all this out, and keeps the Rescue informed. As with any arrangement, carers vary in skill, some being extremely astute, and others simply taking on the overspill from the Rescue kennels without doing much else for the dog.

Rescue Kennels

There is nothing wrong with dogs being kept in kennels while they await their new owners, and indeed it is an efficient way of housing dogs in numbers. Depending on the kennel's owner, you can have those which have behaviourists working with the dogs, those that simply keep the dogs warm, fed and housed until new homes are found, and those which, while providing adequate care, are no more than second-hand dog dealers. We can get good dogs from any of these places, but some are more honest than others, some offer good back-up while others offer nothing, and some are risky places indeed to get a dog from. Many import dogs from abroad, and some of these dogs carry parasitic diseases such as leishmaniasis, which requires lifetime medication and risks making the parasite endemic in UK – totally immoral. Some even import dogs that are badly damaged physically from maltreatment or, more usually, traffic and other accidents, relying on sentimentality to encourage people to take on a poor crippled dog that may well be in constant pain all its life and therefore afraid of other dogs. Not only does this kind of dog face limited quality of life, but it will be highly likely to present behavioural problems. Because "throughput" is important to Rescue kennels, many are genuinely unaware of the problems they inflict on future owners. Their remit is to rehome as many dogs as possible, and the sick and crippled do attract a particular type of owner, who thinks love will overcome all difficulties.

Rescues tend to have an aggressive neutering policy, which again can cause more behavioural problems than it solves (see Chapter Four) though we can be sympathetic to the thoughts behind it, considering the numbers of unwanted dogs that they encounter. Most dogs, though, are wanted at the time of purchase, especially if bought as puppies: it's only later that people stop wanting them. Though unwanted litters do occur, these are a drop in the ocean compared to the quantities of adolescent dogs brought in to Rescue with behavioural issues, or elderly dogs dumped because they are becoming needful of veterinary care. Moreover, all the while puppy-farmers continue to churn out inferior dogs in genetic terms, badly-reared and sold without thought, the consequent behaviour issues matched with novice or unaware owners will continue to create discarded dogs.

Increasing the turnover in dogs rehomed often leads to some creative descriptions of the dogs, which is bad news for good but inexperienced potential owners. Sometimes the basis is genuine ignorance, where age and breed mix is made up by kennel staff who simply don't have the training to identify either. Sometimes wilful deception is the norm, where older dogs have a few years knocked off their real ages, and unpopular breed mixes or types are presented as something more acceptable to the public. Large organisations with national reputations are as guilty of this as small ones. In UK where pit bull types are illegal to keep except under very specific circumstances, and must never be rehomed, some dog rescues continue to present them as other crosses, and the unwary new owner does not realise they have been duped until either a representative of the law or an unfortunate incident brings the facts home to them.

Another area where some Rescues are found wanting is in the care required for dogs. It is quite common for people to be told that dogs need far less exercise than they actually do, for instance the "two twenty-minute walks a day" perpetrated by certain breed rescue groups. Sometimes people are told that a small type of dog is happy enough with a large garden and does not need regular walking at all. But appropriate exercise is often the key to unravelling behaviour issues, because it is so necessary to the dog both physically and psychologically. Leaving aside those few breeds which are so appallingly malformed that they cannot run or even breathe very well, the dog is an athlete. It has a need to run that lasts well into its dotage, and even very old dogs and hopelessly malformed breeds benefit from twice-daily exercise outside the home environs and within their physical capabilities. Movement dispels stress hormones, and the mental refreshment of going out into the world to check the weemails, and see what has passed where, is absolutely essential to a dog's wellbeing. They cannot watch TV, work the computer, play on electronic games pads, phone their friends or read. Boredom plays a big part in so many behavioural issues: often problems go away once the dog is getting proper exercise. Probably the single most difficult aspect of dog ownership for most of us very busy people is finding the time to build in those two hours or more of exercise each day, so we can see why some Rescues fudge it and pretend it isn't necessary, because they home more dogs that way – but home them to what? A dog that has a total of forty minutes of walking exercise a day is a miserable dog, even if it does spend the other twenty-three hours on a nice bed, and ten minutes eating.

This is not said to negate the fine work done by many Rescues but to point out that "rescue" does not finish when a dog leaves kennels or foster carer. I and many others make a living out of bored frustrated dogs whose needs are not met, often with loving, kind owners who are completely out of their depth when their dog does not behave the way they want. If only we could get the information out there that dogs really do need proper exercise, mental and physical, then the Rescues themselves would see far fewer "returns". Of course, some people feel it is a failure on their part when they take on a dog with problems that are too big for them to manage, and so the dog does not go back to Rescue at all – it has a one-way trip to the vet, or else is passed on to another home which has not undergone the checking procedure that most Rescues insist upon. These dogs drop out of the system quickly, because the kind of person who can genuinely manage them is difficult to find, and will have enough dogs of their own already. It is not "failure" if a dog's behavioural issues are too much for that particular home, but sadly we are a species attuned to seeing life in terms of "success" and "failure", which stops some people from asking for help or else returning the dog to the Rescue. Although many Rescues have contracts that insist the dog is returned to them if matters don't work out, or indeed maintain that the dog is always theirs and the new owners "adopt" it but do not own it, many people choose to ignore that because they fear loss of face, or that the dog will be euthanased if they hand it back. It is a moot point in any case whether these "contracts" are enforceable.

The Love Burden
When people consider getting a dog from Rescue, the word "love" turns up a lot. The Rescues want their charges to have "loving homes". The prospective owners have "so much love to give". Dogs are advertised as "lovable". What these dogs need is "love". The dogs need a family to "love". Every issue can be fixed given enough "love". Let's get real here, because dogs need clear pragmatic thinking on the part of their humans, and human love is, more often than not, a huge burden to them at a time when they don't need any more stress. Our kind of love all too often comes ringfenced with unrealistic expectations and baffling inconsistencies. So many dogs suffer because their owners want to "love" them. If only they would simply care for them instead.

It isn't wrong to love your dog – I love mine dearly. But they don't need it, and all too often we humans expect something back which is not in the power of the dog to give. The dog needs its natural requirements met in terms of appropriate exercise, healthy food in suitable quantities, quiet places where it can rest undisturbed, mental stimulation, physical occupation, and ideally an element of understanding of how its mind works. The dog needs to feel safe and comfortable. It does not need the uneasiness or neediness of human adoration, particularly when, as so often is the case, that comes instead of proper care. "Loving" a dog is no compensation for failing to exercise it, letting it get too fat, keeping it in conditions of discomfort and utter boredom, or expecting it to feed some human longing. "Loving" a dog

The love burden.

is not wrong, but if done it should be a free one-way offering that the dog can take or, crucially, leave. We should not love our dogs in the expectation of getting anything back, which is a tough call for most humans. So far as the dogs are concerned, they are simply not equipped for the insecurities and moving goalposts that make up human emotional needs. If they love us at all – and it is nice for us to imagine that they do – then they can only love us as dogs are capable of loving. If we offer them everything they need in terms of comfort and occupation, if we are straightforward and consistent with them, if we are their provider, most of all if we are their "safe place" then they will find us good to be with. If by contrast we make demands on them that they are totally unable to understand, never mind fulfil, we will have troubled dogs indeed, and many of those will then display what are behavioural problems in our eyes.

Coming from its previous background, about which we often know little, the rescue dog knows what was and what is but has no concept of what might be. Let us take a look at some common problems that arise between people and dogs.

Aggression

One of the commonest reasons dogs come into Rescue is aggression. Most perceived aggression is based in fear, though there can also be a genetic or a trained component. Some behaviour studies attempt to create a sub-list of different types of aggression, but if we peel away the layers, again almost all are fear-based. Remove the fear, remove the aggression. Straightforward advice but not always easy to follow, although at times the cause is so easy to remove that it is tragic to find that a dog's owner gave up on it so quickly, possibly because there wasn't the right kind of help immediately available. Indeed, some old-fashioned training methods are guaranteed to increase aggression, because they frighten the dog.

110

We ask such a lot of our dogs. Any other domestic animal can defend itself and we are not horrified. Cats can scratch and bite, horses, donkeys and mules kick and bite, cattle cowkick, butt and gore, as do goats and sheep. Pigs will even eat us given half a chance. All this is understood, and if we put ourselves in a position where these animals attack us, we know we only have ourselves to criticise. Yet a dog only has to growl or lift a lip in its own defence, sometimes under severe and sustained provocation, and it is described as "vicious" and probably "got rid of". Let's have a look at some subtypes of aggression, or, more properly, situations that easily give rise to it.

Dog/Dog Aggression

It's perfectly normal for dogs to display aggression to other dogs. There, I've said it. It is more usual for dogs to dislike or fear other dogs than it is for them to play nicely together in a fluffy pink cosy world of harmony. Other dogs compete for resources, and so at instinctual level are a potential risk. Individual dogs may like individual other dogs, but for the most part, once dogs are adult, their perception of other dogs is that they are a risk until proven otherwise. Therefore the most realistic result we can hope for is that they ignore other dogs, tolerate other dogs and maybe – just maybe – enjoy the company of some other dogs. In general terms, the more dogs enjoy being with people, the less need they have for other dogs. After puppyhood, when youngsters want to meet every dog they come across, those dogs that go over to strange dogs as soon as they see them and ignore their owner are often displaying a relationship with their human that needs attention. But by no means always, because there can be other reasons, and the most usual ones are where dogs are genetically predisposed to fighting, where dogs have been badly-socialised or have gone to the wrong type of puppy-classes and get a buzz out of bullying, and where dogs previously have been attacked by other dogs and according to breed disposition are either trying to drive them away or get the first bite in.

Being a normal behaviour does not mean it is a wanted one or that we should allow it free rein. The correct human role is to take charge by controlling interaction between dogs, and pre-empting anything unwanted before it kicks off. Learning to read the body-language of approaching dogs and their owners is a huge part of this. With practice, we can assess an approaching dog a hundred yards away – crucially, so can your dog, but it doesn't need the practice as it is born with the ability to assess body-language, not just of other dogs but of us and other animals too. Most "aggression" cases are actually one dog being frightened of the other and so lunging and barking ferociously in an attempt to drive it away. If the scared dog is on a lead, its reactions are likely to be more violent because it does not have the option of running away – this is sometimes referred to as "lead aggression". The normal response to fear is one of the Four Fs – "Fight, Flight, Freeze or Fiddle about" (displacement behaviour) but a dog on a lead can only fight or freeze. Curing this type of reaction is straightforward: the handler must commit to increasing the distance between the dogs before their dog starts to react. With practice, people can learn to read their dogs' uneasiness from the first stiffening of the body, and move them well out of the "reaction zone" before the dog becomes really fearful and so reactive. The message is: "I will deal with this". Before long, the dog will start to trust the owner to manage any such situations, and instead of mentally (and then physically) locking on to the other dog, will look at the owner for reassurance that they too have noticed the threat – because it is what the dog perceives as a threat, not the owner, that matters – and know that the owner will take them to a safe distance. This distance will differ dog by dog and day to day, but once the dog is able to trust the owner, the reaction distance will decrease until, over time, the reactive dog can pass any other dog, even close by, without reacting. It does not mean that the dog is any less concerned: what it does mean is that the dog has built a bond of trust with the owner.

When moving a dog that is about to fixate on another, it is important to push rather than pull. Human nature is to go to the safe distance and pull on the dog's lead to get it to follow, but this leaves the dog on its own at the mercy of whatever is causing it disquiet. Instead, we should quietly and without fuss push the dog with our leg and sidestep with it, using our bodies to block between our own dog and the other one. Dogs understand pushing: dogs push each other all the time and are at ease with it, but pulling leaves them feeling vulnerable and so does not work anything like as well.

Having achieved a safe distance, the dog should receive a tiny food reward once it is calm. Thus you are rewarding and reinforcing calm behaviour. If the dog does not take the food, then you are still too close to the fear trigger. Old-fashioned behaviourists claimed that this would cause more problems because it was "rewarding fear" and thus the dog would replicate fearful behaviour in order to get a reward. This is not so because fear is a primary emotion designed to protect, and cannot be rewarded. Some training concepts want the dog to sit, look at the handler or both when the fear trigger approaches, but this again destroys trust. A dog should not be expected to wait immobile while something it dislikes or fears approaches it. But a simple change of order by removing the dog to that safe distance first and then asking for the "sit" or "look" once it feels safe and is calm, is the way to address the fear-aggressive response.

When teaching this discipline, I ask people to imagine that they are phobic about wasps. Everybody is afraid of something, so for the purposes of the exercise, it is wasps. If a wasp came through the window and sat on the sill, they would be concerned. If it flew across and sat in front of them I could tell them until I was blue in the face that it was a nice wasp, wasps don't hurt you, of course it won't sting, and so on, and all they would think was that the wasp was much too close. If they had any spare mental capacity for hearing what I was saying, it would be to register that I was a fool who didn't know much about wasps and couldn't be relied upon in a wasp-induced crisis. I would lose their respect. However, if I took them to the other side of the room and a good distance away from the wasp – and then gave them a hundred pounds – that would set up a different mental process. Next time a wasp arrived, they would look at me to see if I had noticed, and then eagerly accompany me to a suitable distance and wait for their hundred pounds. I would be the right person to have around on three counts. By acknowledging the fear, increasing the distance and then rewarding calmness once there, I would have forged the beginnings of a powerful bond between us. Over time, they would build trust in me to keep them safe from wasps.

It is important to know that, during this trust-building exercise, the rewards have to be valuable and varied. A hundred pounds, fifty pounds, two hundred pounds, but don't expect a fiver to cut the mustard. The dog needs a sliver of sausage, liver, cheese, anything delicious and smelly – a piece of kibble will not do. Vary the rewards but do not be "cheap" with them.

Stress

It is important to understand the part played by stress when dealing with aggression of any kind. Think of stress as a glass of water – empty is zero stress, full to the brim is level ten. Stress fills the glass, but only evaporation from stress-free periods empties it. The dog goes out, has two dog encounters, stress levels go up to four. Next day, stress levels are down to three, dog has one dog encounter, levels go up to five. Dog has two days of no dog encounters, levels go down to two. This is how stress works; the dog does not go down to nil stress after each encounter, and if it has a particularly bad run of incidents, it can get to level ten and stay there for weeks. Stress in other areas of its life will still fill the glass, which is why it is unwise to take a fear-reactive dog to training classes in the first instance, because there are too many "wasps". We cannot train fear, and we cannot train while fear is present, so before we try to train anything, the dog needs to feel safe. We cannot frighten fear away: we cannot aggress aggression away. What we can and should do is build a strong bond of trust in our ability to keep the dog safe.

Part One

This first part of teaching dogs with aggression issues that you will deal with everything and they don't need to, can take a long time, but we need to hold in mind that this stage is not for ever. Although avoidance tactics may seem as if they are not going to teach the dog that other dogs are safe, bear in mind that our dog already knows very well that other dogs are not safe. What the dog has to learn is that whatever we encounter, it doesn't have to take charge of its own protection because we will deal with the situation before it becomes risky. And we must deal with it every time, or we will destroy the trust we are working so hard to build. As our dog trusts us more, so we will be able to reduce the reaction distance in accordance with what our dog finds comfortable, remembering that dogs read other dogs far better than most humans ever will. This means that we must always take note of what our dog is telling us, and when we get better with our dog-reading skills, what the approaching dog is telling us also. We should not believe people who say their dog is friendly or only wants to play, if our dog or that dog's body language tells us otherwise. Our goal is to pass other dogs without ours being afraid, not to create the friendship award for the dog that likes the most dogs. With good support, fear-reactive dogs will become much less reactive, but we cannot train it out of them because fear does not respond to training. What we can do is counter-condition when the feared object appears by making the dog feel safe. Dogs are only too ready to absolve themselves of the responsibility for their own safety if they can trust us to take over for them. We work on removing the need to be fearful, and the so-called aggression reduces in tandem with that. We must get this foundation layer secure before we move on to the next phase, or else we are building on an insecure base, which will mean at some time in the future that the whole structure may collapse. Think of building trust as a brick wall – if there is a wobbly layer, it has to be stripped back to the first sound layer before we build up again.

Fear or Something Else?

There are occasions when the primary drive for aggression is not fear. In these cases, the behaviour is either caused by a genetic component, specific training, or is hormonal. Examples of genetic aggression include breeds created to attack people, dogs, other animals or all of these. Sometimes the dog is not of such a breed but has an inborn anomaly that makes it aggressive. Hormone-driven aggression includes maternal aggression, breeding aggression, which is seen when male dogs spar over a bitch on heat, and most of all in those cases where the dog has learned to bully other dogs or threaten humans, and gets a huge rush of feelgood hormones from it. This quickly becomes addictive. Dogs displaying bullying behaviour often learn it at the wrong type of puppy classes, or in the wrong type of home where they are forced to be aggressive in order to keep or gain resources. Any breed can become a bully and get such pleasure from it that it rapidly overtakes the pleasure it gets from anything else, and this is doubly so if the dog does not have much else of interest in its life and is left to find its own fun.

It is straightforward to manage breeding aggression by controlling the circumstances; with genetic aggression we can keep the dog away from triggers, keep it occupied and arrange its life so that it never displays that side of its personality, but bullying needs an actual programme of retraining because the dog gets so much pleasure out of it and eventually becomes addicted to the hormone rush. Mostly the bully develops the behaviour to this point before the owner realises that there is any problem at all; they think the dog is "playing" then "playing a bit roughly" (but still playing) and it is only when it goes out of its way to injure or terrify other dogs, or another dog owner is rude to them, that they see what is really going on.

Defusing the Bully

With the bully, we need to change the hormone addiction from the buzzy ones such as adrenaline and cortisol to the calming ones of dopamine and serotonin. Any one of us who has had to give up a dangerous exciting sport will have some empathy for just how difficult this is, but nevertheless it can be done and it must be done. It is inexcusable to allow one dog to bully another, and can cause significant behaviour problems with hitherto pleasant-natured dogs. Other people may be working with fear-reactive dogs, and don't want all their hard graft and dedication ruined by an uncontrolled lout of a dog pitching into theirs just to get a thrill. So we need total commitment, and this starts in the home by avoiding anything that gets the dog worked up into a state of excitement and thus an unwanted hormone rush. So no rough-and-tumble, no running about and shouting, no ball-throwing or frantic toy-tugging. If there are noisy children who need to let off steam, this must occur well away from the dog and yes I do appreciate the difficulties but this is aggression we are containing. The dog must live in an oasis of calm, and we create this first by removing anything that might lead to agitation and so feed the craving for the hormone rush. But we don't do this in a vacuum. Instead we actively seek to release the velvet-smooth and equally addictive hormones of calm pleasure. We do this by building the dog's confidence – sounds odd I know, but bullies by definition are underconfident. Confident dogs (and people) don't have to bully others in order to feel good. Confident dogs are calm. Does the calm create the confidence or the confidence create the calm? It's some of each. What we are teaching the bully dog is that calm and confident feels great. So how do we do that?

We make the dog work mentally on tasks that will give it a feeling of achievement. Note that this is achievement in dog terms not human. The dog cannot get any of these tasks "wrong". We give it mind games such as those described in Chapter Three . We arrange its meals so that it has to work for its food by getting it out of puzzle toys or finding it as part of a scenting game. When out, we take all the decisions for it, not in a hectoring manner but as part of quiet control of its environment. There will be extinction behaviour, but if we are quiet and consistent, we will win the day. We may always have to watch and anticipate when our bully sees other dogs, because some of those dogs will be sending out either "victim" or "antagonist" signals of their own, which is the equivalent of a whiff of alcohol to an alcoholic. But if we commit to doing so, we can get the bullying down to an easily controllable level. However, the long-term success of this type of behaviour modification depends on substituting another reward – we can't simply ditch a hugely pleasurable behaviour and leave the dog in an emotional vacuum. Think how many people give up smoking and put on weight because they are replacing the mouth-satisfying behaviour of smoking – which is very close to suckling – by eating more. So it is with dogs, too. We need to commit to supplanting the unwanted behaviour by first acknowledging that it gave a great deal of pleasure and encouraged its own self-reinforcing dependence, and then substituting with new behaviour that we like and, more to the point, the dog will enjoy.

To find what the dog is likely to enjoy most, we need to go back to those tasks genetically imprinted on it, and then introduce occupation that satisfies those needs. With crossbred dogs, we have more options to explore – for instance, the collie/spaniel cross might like herding, seeking out by scent, problem-solving and retrieving. If we have a dog bred this way that has been exhibiting bullying behaviour, we would not be putting it into a situation where excited hormones flow, such as Agility or Flyball, but quieter occupations where there is a sense of achievement from an absorbing task, such as finding and collecting together a number of hidden tennis balls. There may be some time in the future when we can re-introduce ball-throwing or tug games, but these are a long way off and should only be considered once the dog's general behaviour has improved to the point that it is no longer bullying. Then we change the nature of those games by keeping excitement levels low: no shouting or whipping up a frenzy. It is perfectly possible to play "tug" and ball-throwing in a quiet and friendly manner.

All the while we work with the bully, we need to remember that the dog is not being a bully because it is a bad, horrible animal. It has simply found a rewarding behaviour and is seeking to replicate the reward. We are not failures for owning a bullying dog, and the dog is not a disaster because it has learned to bully. We need to detach from the emotional side of the behaviour and think of it as an unlevel layer in the brick wall that we need to fix. By changing our own mindset, we make the task much easier on ourselves and also approach it from a far more comfortable angle psychologically. This way we distance ourselves from any temptation to punish, and instead hold in our attitude the essential need of replacing an unwanted behaviour with a wanted one, and then "fixing" the wanted behaviour in place by making it really worthwhile for the dog.

Dog/Man Aggression

There is a chasm between dog/dog and dog/man aggression, which is why we so often see dog-aggressive dogs oozing "attitude" as they bear down on our own animal, while the owner, oblivious to what is really going on, assures us that their dog is "fine" "soft as anything", "all right" and similar epithets. The dog may be all of these things with people, but is displaying dog-aggression to our dog, and sadly so many owners are unaware that dog/dog aggression is another world from dog/man aggression, or even that there is any difference at all. Just because a dog is friendly with people doesn't mean it is automatically pleasant to other dogs. Man-aggression in its true form is far more difficult to handle than dog-on-dog aggression, because the dog evolved to live with us in a co-operative manner, and so man-aggression has been bred out of most breeds to the extent that it takes a pretty bad incident or series of incidents, or else specialist training, to turn dogs against people, unless there is a genetic component. A genuine attack on humans with the objective of maiming or killing is a rarity in the everyday domestic dog. But most of what is reported as "man-aggression" is in fact fear.

If the dog is afraid, it does not matter one jot if we think that the dog is being "stupid". It is afraid, and we need to identify the cause of the fear and then remove it, replacing it not with a vacuum but instead with the equivalent situation modified into safety. Lie on the ground for a moment, and see the world from your dog's perspective. Imagine (or try in reality if you have the nerve) what it is like to be this size on the pavement, outside the shops, in the park, by the school, any of those places we take our dogs. Notice how people appear to have enormous feet moving right by your face, huge staring eyes, and hands that come out of the sky towards you. Big bared teeth clack at you while loud sounds come from behind them. It really is scary, even when you know what is going on and speak the language. At home, kneel into the dog crate and ask family members to stick their fingers through the wire at you, or bend down and stare at you while talking gibberish. Even though you know them and you know what is going on, at an animal level you will experience a frisson of fear before your intellect takes over.

Now you have the perspective, think how our loud voices and hard stares can seem to a dog. Add shouting, lashing out with hands or feet, rolled-up newspapers or any of the other aversives we humans might visit on our dogs, the inconsistencies of our rules and tempers, and it becomes plain that our world can be a scary place for the average pet dog. Even if humans shout or aim blows at each other rather than the dog, it is frightening for the dog caught in the crossfire. It might hide away and build up stress levels to the point of becoming physically ill, such as with skin eruptions, develop inappropriate coping mechanisms such as self-mutilation or forgetting its house-training, or it might try to fight its way out and – behold – we have an aggressive display.

Adults

There is a big division between aggression towards adults and that aimed at children. Adult humans can trigger aggression in dogs by deliberately training them to be so, or accidentally "training" them by unintentionally creating a set of circumstances to which the dog is likely to respond with aggression, such as by frightening, frustrating or doing something that makes the dog think it has to defend itself.

Many of us have a relative or friend tucked away that scares the dog. This person might be really nice and never have done anything intentionally to upset the dog, but they smell or sound or look frightening to the dog. We have to respect this. No matter how this person would like to prove to the dog that they are kind and loving, the dog is afraid. With rescue dogs, this may be due to some baggage from the past, especially with scents. I knew about an ex-laboratory dog that attacked "out of the blue" when a woman came to the house in her work clothes. The lady was a hairdresser, and smelled of bleach, which was enough to trigger a terrified attack from the dog. Taking such a dog into rescue and then rehoming it without a full understanding of its past had set it up for failure. Similarly, there are dogs that cannot bear the smell of other substances if they have made a connection between those and past abuse. There are dogs that are reactive to the smell of alcohol, certain types of cigarette, pipe or cigar smoke, social or medical drugs, even certain sweets, lotions or perfumes may throw them back into the past and trigger aggression. Some medication-induced behaviour in humans can have the same effect, too, and so can some of our illnesses. When we are so pleased to see dogs in an "assistance" capacity, where they work to help incapacitated people, it is easy not to realise that, to many dogs, some kinds of ill person can be absolutely terrifying. Any illness that alters the human mindset can be seen by dogs as an overpowering threat. We must never underestimate this, nor sweep the idea under the carpet for the sake of political correctness: the dog is not PC, it is afraid, and it is well-armed. But it can only communicate its fears like a dog. It is our responsibility to see that it never has to.

Children

The version of "aggression" most often seen is when a dog snaps at a child. What has actually happened is that the child has done something, right then or in the past, that the dog finds threatening. Dogs normally go through a great many appeasing signals before they are driven to snap, so it is likely that the dog has moved away but been followed and possibly cornered, that it has turned its head and given the "whale eye" showing the whites, raised a forepaw, growled softly, growled louder, moved its whiskers forward, snarled, and still not been listened to, so escalated into an air-snap. Following on from the air-snap is the closed-mouth punch, then the open-mouthed punch, teeth on skin, broken skin and then a harder bite that penetrates flesh. This is still inhibited bite, as a small dog can do a lot more damage than most of us think, and a medium-sized dog is capable of shearing straight through any human bone with little discernable effort. However, we don't see it as such: what we do see is the bite "out of nowhere" because we have to be taught how to read what the dog is telling us. Even sadder are those cases with very submissive dogs that lie in a curl and raise one or two legs, the classic stance of "I am afraid: please leave me alone". This is so often interpreted as inviting a tummy-rub, which further indiscretion takes the dog way over threshold and with a human bending over it too, which to a dog is very threatening indeed. The resulting bite has to be to the face, sometimes with awful consequences.

We humans are programmed to test boundaries, so we cannot blame children too young to understand consequences for pushing the boundaries with a dog. Therefore we must keep dogs and small children apart unless directly supervised, and that does not mean being in the same room but

Fighting or playing?

doing something else – it means watching the dog/child interaction the whole time and actively stopping anything that could lead to an incident. This does not mean either dog or child is "bad", it is simply recognising that each will respond to a given situation according to its genetic legacy, and if you tell a child not to touch a dog and then leave the room, it's a racing certainty that the child will touch the dog – and this happens almost as much with adults that are not dog-aware too. Children by nature are supremely concerned with themselves, and do not develop empathy until later, and also when very young they mostly live in the immediate. A child does not mentally project what might happen if it runs across the room and jumps onto a sleeping dog, nor if it takes the dog's food when it is eating, so we adults need to be vigilant so that the dog/child relationship is as pleasant as possible for both parties. If a child wants to "ride" on the dog's back, few parents realise that this presents a huge threat to the dog at instinctual level, because this situation would only occur otherwise if a predator were about to kill the dog. It can also cause the dog a lot of physical pain, and do permanent damage. That phrase "he's so good: the children pull him around and he never retaliates" should never be heard; no dog should be put through that and no child should learn that it is acceptable. Just as we would not leave a child by an unguarded fire or a pot of boiling water, so we should commit at the same level of keeping dog and child protected. That way they too can enjoy each other's company, but respectfully and safely.

The New Baby

Sadly, few people use pregnancy time to prepare the family dog for the arrival of a baby, and the consequent disruption of the dog's life. Babies scare the bejasus out of dogs: they make loud discordant noises, they smell of body fluids, they move erratically, and they have big stary eyes. So often the arrival of a baby means that the dog gets far less attention and exercise, or even drops off the bottom of the "to-do" list entirely. By the time the baby is crawling, some dogs are in a state of escalating stress, and for every dog that tolerates whatever the tot dishes out and even helps it learn to stand and walk, there are many others that are living in constant fear. The noises get louder, the eyes stare harder, the fingers twist and poke, and the child follows the dog about and tries to provoke a reaction. The reaction it gets is often devastating for the child and family, and terminal for the dog. And it could all be so easily avoided.

Preparation for the Child

Adding children to the family reduces available time and energy to a marked degree, and some tasks have to be delegated or else forgotten entirely. There will be times when the dog simply cannot be given attention, or when it has to be shut away from the child for their mutual safety. Some people are happy for dog and child to interact closely, and others are concerned about hygiene. Some feel that animals in the home challenge the young immune system in a beneficial way, and others feel that their presence is a health risk. Neither is incorrect, and it is a matter of doing whatever we feel comfortable with. However, if that means the dog is shut away from its human family most of the time, then its needs are not being properly addressed, and owners have a responsibility here. But back to the family dog's preparation during the pregnancy: this is the time to introduce changes of routine, such as getting the dog accustomed to the adults carrying "a bundle" and talking to it, shutting the dog out of certain rooms when bundle is being "fed" or "bathed" if this is to be the case when the real baby arrives, playing recordings of baby noises, moving around more at night, placing crib and pram where they will be kept in future, and teaching the dog to walk calmly with the pram or pushchair. If outsiders will be walking the dog while baby takes up most of the parents' time, now is when they should be introduced, to walk first with the owner accompanying, and then with the new person alone. This gives us a chance to demonstrate how we would like our dog to be exercised, and what we prefer to be done when it meets other dogs. Time spent in preparation is never wasted, because then not only is it less of a shock to the dog when the real baby arrives, but also less stress on the parents as the dog will be ensconced in its new way of life and therefore calmer with the changes. Dogs can smell the hormonal differences that occur during pregnancy, so they have some idea that a little one is on the way, but of course they can only behave like dogs and have no way of understanding how different human child-rearing is from their own genetic programming. Some very empathetic dogs will choose to lie beside the "bump", rest their heads on it, or sniff it frequently and gently; some become extra clingy during the owner's pregnancy. Some of course do not show any change in behaviour at all.

We do not know beforehand whether we will get a placid, easy baby or a fretful demanding one, nor will we know until baby comes home whether the dog will like it or want to get as far away as possible, so it makes sound sense to prepare for all eventualities and lay good foundations before they are needed. Ideally, before the baby comes home, parents will have brought some baby-scented clothing or bedding back from the hospital and let the dog have a good smell of it, so that it is prepared for the new scents of this specific baby. When baby actually arrives home, owners should leave him or her in the car for a few moments and greet the dog without the new arrival. Then is the time to bring the baby indoors, once the dog has expressed its joy at having both of its owners home again, absorbed the new scents, and is much better prepared for the baby being brought indoors as a calm, matter-of-fact process than if everything new and exciting happens in one go.

Some dogs adore babies and children, and are never happier than with their human family right in the midst of all the goings-on. Others prefer to stay away, and interact only with the adults of the family. We never know in advance which our dogs are going to be, but we cannot change the way they feel, so we must accept and go along with how they prefer to live with us. Dogs need their own space, and family dogs especially so, because there will be times when the house is full of visiting children and parents, which means a houseful of noise and strangers, not all of whom will be dog-aware. This is a happy time for some dogs and anathema to others, so we should always provide a safe haven for the dog where nobody else goes (a place where people can peer into the crate or over the baby-gates and try to touch or otherwise interact with the dog does not make a safe retreat) and be prepared to be firm with our guests if needed.

Prey Trigger?

Seldom a year goes by without a baby being attacked and badly injured or even killed by a family dog, sometimes one that actually jumps into the pram to get at the baby, shaking and wounding it with frightening ease. These tragedies are often said to be triggered by the prey drive igniting in the dog, where the shrill cries, body fluid smells (no matter how clean the baby, it smells strongly to a dog) and helplessness trigger a predator/prey response. But these attacks do not "come out of the blue". Scratching the surface of any such incident, a background of errors and mismanagement unfolds, where dogs have not been prepared for the baby's arrival, and most of all, have not had their own needs attended to in the way of proper attention, training and exercise, for some considerable time, if ever. A bored, rejected, frustrated, unfulfilled dog that has no trust in its owners and no environmental management to make it feel safe, explodes into action and

Rescued dog.

deals with the new thing in the way its instincts demand, with awful results. These incidents do not mean that there is anything "bad" with that dog or with any dogs, but it does show that we must not underestimate their reactions to severely disruptive changes in their environment. They are dogs, not furry people or soft toys, and when their needs are not met, they can still only behave as dogs. If a dog cannot get away from an environment that is causing it major misery, then we have to expect it to react. It associates the unpleasant changes in its life with the arrival of the newcomer, and deals with it in a dog way. This is why many rescues will not rehome dogs to families with young children, because in so many cases too much is expected of the dog, and although a crisis might be approaching like a runaway train, far too many people simply do not accept that there might be a problem until something far bigger and more dreadful than they could ever imagine has resulted.

Toddlers

If the baby is frightening to a dog, at least it is reasonably static. Toddlers present the most difficult issues of all, because they are so mobile, so astute, so fixated on what they want to do and so unaware of likely consequences that whenever toddlers and dogs are together, they must be very closely supervised indeed. This includes when under other people's care. In fact, so real are the dangers to dog and child alike that this short time in human development is better organised either so that toddler and dog never meet (for instance on visits to relatives, where it is far safer for the dog to be elsewhere, or at least somewhere that cannot be accessed by others for the duration of the visit) or that only the most aware and trustworthy adults are ever in charge of the child. Grandparents, aunts and uncles who have a dog should be every bit as careful to prepare their own dog for baby visits as the parents. The dog can only be a dog and the child can only be a child; neither can take responsibility for any disaster occurring. This is particularly important with dogs that have old injuries that might still give pain, or else the discomforts of old age in the shape of arthritis, deafness or inadequate sight. Anything that hurts or scares a dog may result in a snap, and little children are so very vulnerable. The dog only has a few ways to warn of its discomfiture, and children do not understand these warnings; if ever a dog shows aggression to a child, then it is the child's guardians that are at fault, not the dog or the child, because neither should ever be put in that position.

Older Children

Sometimes we hear about dreadful injuries incurred in older children too, but again, there is always background to this, although maybe not with the unfortunate child that got injured. So often there is a history of a dog being teased; this is human bullying and commonly misrepresented as "a bit of fun" even by adults, who should know better. Combine this with overstressed underexercised dogs and it is an accident waiting to happen. A few years ago, a pre-teen child was killed by a trio of dogs in a neighbour's garden. It transpired that this child was fond of hanging over the fence tormenting the dogs; one day he overbalanced and fell in. This again was so easily avoidable, but one child and three dogs paid with their lives, and two human families were left traumatised. These stories will continue all the while dogs are passively abused by not having their needs met, and humans accidentally or deliberately exacerbate an already explosive situation. Incidentally, any child getting a buzz from tormenting animals isn't having its own needs met either.

But we also have all the good relationships between dogs and children, and all the adults who remember a dog as a wonderful companion when they were growing up. We can be sure that for the most part, there was at least one adult in the background making sure that everything went well. Times change in terms of social responsibility, and few youngsters now can enjoy the "Enid Blyton" kind of freedom to roam with a canine companion, so we adults still need to supervise. Any incident that takes place between dog and dog or dog and person while with a minor has the potential to backfire very easily, and in legal terms, the adult who owns the dog is liable, even if not present. Whereas many of us, myself included, can remember exercising dogs by ourselves from a very early age, those days are now over. There are far too many badly-behaved dogs and unaware owners around to take that risk, and even if our own dogs are well-trained, the majority of dogs that we encounter will not be. Having established that, there is still plenty of opportunity for children and dogs to be together, but under adult supervision. Children and dogs can still be "best friends" and teaching our children to read the dog, anticipate its needs, take responsibility for its care, get involved in its training and learn how best to behave round their own and other dogs, is one of the greatest gifts we can give them.

The Trigger

Aggression is reactive: there is always a trigger, though there are times when that trigger was installed in the distant past and may not be instantly recognisable at the time the dog attacks. Aggression is an "expensive" behaviour in survival terms. Aggressive dogs risk getting hurt, and injured dogs, in a primitive setting, often die. Though our own dogs are never likely to be in that situation, it is the primitive mindset which takes over whenever a dog is in extremis. This means that, for a normal dog to show aggression, it has already been driven to the point where it feels severely threatened, and then a trigger is activated. We humans are not the best judges of what, to a dog, is a severe threat, so we need to watch and listen to our dogs. With rescue dogs, we usually have no idea of the trigger/s or the past, so we need to observe the dog closely and take heed at once if it appears to be stressed, before this spills over into aggression. This is not to say that every rescue dog will have aggression issues, but instead that we need to be aware of the possibility and take care not to push the dog beyond the point where it feels at ease. It may have been pushed too far in its previous home, and so react earlier, harder and faster than the current situation seems to demand. Remember that everything a dog does is the best option so far as that dog is concerned at that time, and it is the dog's reading of the situation, not ours, which matters to the dog.

The Motherhood Problem

Hormonal changes associated with pregnancy, lactation and motherhood happen with every mammal including us humans, and this has the potential to create two problems. One is that the months of waiting before a human baby arrives prompt the mother-to-be to get a puppy to satisfy those maternal longings. If addressed consciously, the idea may also have roots in a remembered dog-friend from childhood, and the romantic idea that baby and puppy can grow up together and be best friends. Stark common sense is that puppies and babies are each incredibly demanding, and don't go well together at all. Good breeders know this phenomenon all too well, and will not sell a puppy to a pregnant woman, but bad breeders have no such regard and will happily pocket the money and forget all about their responsibilities. Here is a pup that is highly likely to end up in Rescue round about the time baby starts toddling, which coincides with puppy adolescence, when they are at their most needy as well as most difficult to rehome, having lost all their puppy charm and probably having had no training either.

The other frequently encountered issue often involves an existing family dog rather than a newly acquired puppy. Maternal protectiveness perceives the dog as a threat, and the mother will not be satisfied until the dog has been "got rid of" because she sees it as a danger to the baby. There is no gainsaying this because it is hormones talking at a very strong primitive level, which means the idea cannot be deflected by logic or common sense. Sometimes compromise may be reached by keeping the dog kennelled in the garden, and if this is the solution, that dog is owed plenty of extra attention, exercise and occupation, rather than just being shut away from its family. Nor must it have to put up with being tormented and used as entertainment for visiting children while confined in its kennel. I come across this attitude constantly; whatever it does for the human relationship is none of my business, but it is immensely sad for the dog.

Maternal Aggression

It is natural and correct for bitches to protect their puppies. The hormone prolactin is mainly responsible for maternal aggression, and as a litter of puppies develops and the bitch's milk dries up, so her protectiveness lessens.

However, if you keep one or more puppies, individual bitches can display protectiveness for some considerable time, even in a few cases when the "puppy" is fully grown. Prolactin isn't the whole story, though, because most creatures, mammals or not, display maternal aggression and great protectiveness of their young. But for the most part, maternal aggression is self-solving. It is simply a matter of being reasonable about restricting strangers' access to bitch and pups while she is suckling. Of course, people will want to come and see the puppies, and how you handle this depends on the individual bitch. Some don't mind at all, and others get very angry and stressed. If yours is one of the latter, then separate her from the pups when people come to choose, and don't allow any visitors until the pups are at least five weeks old, by which time most bitches only visit a couple of times a day anyway. Even if your bitch does not make overtly aggressive gestures, watch her for signs of stress such as lip-licking, puffing, and head-turning when people arrive to see the puppies, and if she is at all unhappy, keep strangers away from her. A few bitches become so distressed that they eat their own puppies in an overdose of maternal protectiveness, and even if yours isn't as extreme, stress hormones in her milk will be bad for the puppies. It is old kennelman's wisdom that stressy bitches breed stressy puppies, and while some of this is genetic, frequent exposure to stress hormones may quite possibly have a long-term effect on puppies' characters and general development.

Protective mother dog.

When we go to view a litter, much is made by contemporary behaviourists of seeing the bitch with the puppies. Occasionally this is not ideal because of an individual bitch's protectiveness. This does not necessarily mean that the bitch has a bad character. You need to make sure that she is indeed the mother of the litter by seeing her with them, but if the breeder shuts her away while you interact with the pups, do not take this amiss.

I remember going to see a two-day-old litter sired by my stud dog. Obviously the bitch was very protective at that time, and I sat across the room from her so that I could see the puppies while not being too close to them. Appealing as new puppies are, it is advisable that strangers do not touch them because it really stresses most bitches, and some are even wary of their own human family touching the whelps as well. It is so important to listen to a mother dog. This bitch wanted to go for a walk when the other dogs in the family made ready to leave, but she was also very concerned about me being there. I duly told her to go ahead and I wouldn't touch her puppies; she gathered the meaning if not the words and glowered at me all the way out as she left, to let me know how serious she was. I didn't touch the pups, and would not in any case have done so while she was out – if we want dogs to respect us, we do well to respect them also. When she came back she did not go to her pups but straight to me, and sniffed my hands. She then made strong eye contact, wagged her tail and went to suckle her litter. I came to know that dog very well, and she was always very pleased to see me, as a contrast to being aloof with most people. I like to think it was because I left her puppies alone that day.

Redirected Aggression

This is a posh name for "frustration". It is often seen when a dog is prevented from running up to another because it is on the lead, so it turns and bites at the lead or its owner's hands, legs or clothing. Some people redirect aggression all the time – think of someone who gets a dressing-down at work and then takes out their feelings on an underling, or the family when they get home. Or the mother struggling with recalcitrant children, a buggy and the dog, who jerks the lead impatiently and gives the dog a painful moment. The trick with redirected aggression is for the handler to anticipate it, and redirect in turn. So for the dog that gets "mouthy" when excited, you push a toy into its mouth and then tell it to "sit" or "down", thus occupying the jaws and then the mind. It is mighty difficult for a dog to get hold of you when its mouth is already full and you have also changed its body posture to one that reduces its ability to get at you. We also see redirected aggression at such times when one dog has made another submit, and that dog spends the rest of the walk looking for a weaker dog that it can make submit in turn. The way to handle this is to "change the subject" by interacting with the dog in a way that makes it happy and secure again, which means giving it a ball to chase or a few seconds of quiet "tug" with its tuggy-toy, rather than fussing and sympathising with it, because physical movement dispels stress hormones. It is common for dogs being taught to walk nicely on the lead to redirect aggression to the lead, biting at it or even getting hold of it and pulling. Using a chain lead makes the lead unpleasant in the dog's mouth and takes all the fun out of it for the dog – but remember not to leave a void in mouth or mind, and get the dog to carry a toy instead.

Genetic Aggression

Some breeds, notably fighting breeds, have been deliberately created by selective breeding for a behavioural glitch that drives them to kill other dogs. Such animals ignore the usual canine submissive postures which make other types back off once the weaker dog has rolled over, and instead drive in and kill. It does not mean that dogs of this breeding will inevitably become fighters, and responsible people can keep generations of them without a whiff of mishap. What it does mean is that if this type of dog does get into a fight it will derive enormous pleasure from it. Even if prevented from killing that particular opponent at that time, the dog will have experienced an endorphin rush that nothing else can equal, and will seek to repeat the experience.

Many fighting breeds have been created to be exceptionally friendly with people, as even in the heat of a fight, they have to be handled, and because they all bite above their weight, some types considerably so, there must be no risk of redirected aggression to the handlers. Coupled with this, they have a very high pain threshold in tandem with a huge endorphin release as a pain response. These attributes make them very forgiving of accidental hurt, which encourages their promotion as "family dogs" because it takes an abnormal level of being poked, prodded, twisted or sat upon before they react uncomfortably. This tolerance emphatically does not extend to other dogs: fighting breeds are very quick to take offence, and if they are to be kept, should never be allowed antagonistic opportunities. It would be as well for the companion dog world if these attributes were to be honestly accepted, rather than as at present, where some fighting breeds are actively promoted because of their wonderful tolerance of humans without adding the corollary that they are highly intolerant of other dogs.

Dogs that are genetically dog-aggressive are seldom man-aggressive, but those bred to be man-aggressive are almost always dog-aggressive too. Mastiff and flock-guarding types that have a breed history of fighting can be very awkward to handle once they have been allowed to explore the man-aggressive side of their nature. In their countries of origin, this type of dog was fought not only as a spectacle for entertainment, but also to ensure that the very fiercest were the ones that were bred from.

also to ensure that the very fiercest were the ones that were bred from. Guarding flocks against large predators needed that kind of attitude, and even though those breeds that have come down to us many generations away from such origins are much less combative than their ancestors, the trait can still be brought to the surface all too easily. These dogs are not traditionally handled when fighting, and because their task was to protect flocks against human as well as animal raiders, they retain an easy capability to be aggressive with humans too. Many behaviourists will not take on man-aggressive dogs in this group, and those who do have to be very careful indeed. The final group of man-aggressive types encompasses those which historically guarded people from robbers, and this type bonds with its owner and usually its immediate circle of family and friends, while being readily antagonistic to others. There are some obvious dogs in this category and a few surprising ones as well, until their history is delved into a little deeper and we realise that they have a guarding ancestry. If diligently socialised, this last group can show no signs of man-aggression unless something goes wrong, but they are not keen on other dogs any more than the rest in this group.

Predatory Aggression

This is actually a misnomer, but one that won't go away. Like "pack" and "dominance", the real meaning has been lost in popular parlance, and instead the phrase is applied to that group of domesticated canines that hunt with us for a living. Dogs that predate by trade are mostly very genial types; often they are kept in large groups, living, feeding and working together, under the direction of a small group of humans and working to one specific prey. Centuries of keeping packs of scent-hunting hounds together in lodges mean that the surly ones get weeded out; it would not be the best of results if they turned on the horses and people who follow the hunt. Where hounds hunted for food for people, it would be counter-productive if they ate their quarry before the huntsmen caught up. Dogs that kill other animals for human consumption, or indeed their own (hunting beagles in UK were allowed to eat the hares they caught, but packs of staghounds were never allowed to touch deer, which were shot after being brought to bay) are not displaying aggression when they hunt or when they kill. Due to the hunting ban in UK in 2004 we do not now have the opportunity to show this as readily as we once could, and there is a real danger of a made-up theory going unchallenged in the future from lack of study and first-hand experience.

As ever, there are exceptions, most notably with those dogs used for pest control that are bred and trained to tackle quarry that fights back. Some quarry species deliver a nasty bite (e.g. rats, squirrels, mink) some if taken wrongly can do a lot of damage (e.g. fox, otter) and a few are capable of killing a dog, and most dogs would avoid them unless specially bred for the task (e.g. wolf, coyote, boar). Multi-purpose hunting dogs know which prey is likely to hurt them, and which not, and as predators don't waste energy, tend to treat their catch according to its potential to damage them. Even dogs used regularly on savage quarry are bred to be benign with people, though terrier types when fired up after a tough task can be very prone to redirection, and need to be handled with care. So genuine predators are highly unlikely to be aggressive dogs per se, but we do encounter a widespread misconception that, because these dogs are used to kill other animals, they are vicious, unpredictable or dangerous as a blanket attitude to other dogs and people. It is worth remembering that, while some dogs are bred to be killers of other animals, all dogs would kill prey species given half a chance and the right physique. It is important that we see this as normal behaviour. A few people try to perpetuate an idea that once a dog has killed another animal, it will become incurably vicious to both animals and people. Certainly a dog that has caught a prey species will have experienced a buzz that it could not get from any other experience, and will seek to repeat that thrill, but its attitude to people will not change because it has caught an animal or bird. Professional hunting dogs remain steady to species not designated as prey, and most pet dogs can be trained to do this as well, though there will always be some that cannot, not because they are in any way nasty but because dogs are predators by nature. If we do not want our dogs to catch prey species, we should manage their lives so that they never get the chance, and instead apply ourselves to satisfying their instincts in a way we as individuals find acceptable.

Territorial Aggression

This is a fundamental drive in most creatures, because without territory there is little hope of survival for any length of time. Animals need territory to breed, to feed, to sleep safely, and without it they are deeply stressed. When I lecture, I tell people that if they want to see naked territorial aggression, they should park in someone else's space. This deep need exists in all of us too: "good fences make good neighbours" and better not cross the boundary line when you build it!

It is logical to assume therefore that all dogs will have the potential for territory issues, and after all, that is one of the reasons we started keeping them – to guard our territory. Territory to a dog is flexible: it can be wherever the dog is at the time, only the home area, the area outside the home too, the whole street, wherever the owner is (we are territory too) or where its bed and bowl are. It is reasonable to assume that those breeds which have been created to guard will show territorial aggression a lot quicker and more decisively than those that were not, but all dogs will guard if they feel under threat. The difference is that guarding breeds will guard whether under threat or not, and they usually display patrolling behaviour when given free range over what they perceive to be their territory. We cannot train out a genetic behaviour and therefore we have to manage it: giving non-guarding breeds no reason to guard will usually be sufficient until their confidence is threatened, but guarding breeds actually need structure to their guarding. Therefore we should establish a life where we accompany them on their "rounds" say by a walk around the perimeter of the garden or property, and then they are "off duty" as their patrolling need has been satisfied. They will of course need sufficient other exercise and occupation to hold boredom at bay, because otherwise they will create guarding situations for themselves. If they find the result suitably satisfying, then we run the risk of inadvertently creating a self-rewarding behaviour that will be difficult to eradicate.

Protectiveness

Dogs can get very protective of their owners, and tales abound of how canine heroes defend us. Actually, they are not protecting us – they are protecting themselves. Where we have a good relationship with our dogs, and are the source of all good things including being that "safe place", we assume huge value to them. They will sometimes put themselves at considerable risk to defend their interest in us, and countless humans have been grateful for that. Whether you want your dogs to protect you or not is an individual matter: I find it useful. But if you go this route, you must be certain that you can control that protectiveness, because the dog has no concept of human laws, and may otherwise protect you to the point of its own death sentence. Overt protectiveness in a non-guarding breed is often a sign of insecurity, and if such a dog has its confidence boosted by sympathetic management, then it is usually happy to withdraw from direct conflict and let the human make the decisions and manage the outcome. Nervy people tend to have nervous dogs; the more confident and calm the person is, the calmer the dog. If you have issues with confidence, be careful what type of dog you choose. It might seem that one of the guarding breeds would be ideal for the under-confident person but in fact these dogs would not guard if confidence was an inborn asset: it is the under-confident dog that guards. Many big powerful breeds used as guards are nothing like as confident as their appearance and willingness to give the alarm seems to tell us. The socially inadequate person with the big savage-looking dog is a stereotype; however the bite from an under-confident dog hurts just as much. People who lack confidence are better to choose their dogs from genial types that ooze bonhomie to dogs and humans alike; it is the calm, confident person who does best with the overtly guarding breeds.

Relationships

Couples may find that when they want to sit together, cuddle and smooch, the dog can become unsettled. Some slink away, some try and push between them, some stand and bark at them, some stand and tremble. The reason is that to a dog, face to face contact and limbs around each other is a threat. Dogs only do that if they are fighting with intent to kill. So they find it very unsettling when two prime resources appear to be about to injure each other. Given time and tact, most dogs will come to realise that such human interaction is benign.

Rows however are not, and couples that shout and throw things, hit each other and go overboard at a touch of dispute, are immensely frightening to dogs. Even families that are simply loud and given to physical pulling and hitting in a non-aggressive context can freak dogs out to the point that the dog develops behavioural problems due to being severely and unpredictably stressed. Thus if we take a dog on that has come into Rescue following a relationship break-up, that dog is highly likely to have behavioural problems as a direct result of having felt insecure over a long time, and quite possibly as a result of redirected aggression onto itself.

Food Aggression

It is natural, normal and should be unremarkable to defend one's food. Food is another primary life resource: no food and we die. Some dogs are extreme food-guarders, but this should be seen as a variant on a normal behaviour and not a dreadful fault. Old-style dog training included quite a fetish about being able to remove a dog's food "to show who is boss". It doesn't show who is boss at all, but it really upsets even the nicest dogs and can quickly cause major guarding issues with insecure ones. Removing a dog's food and then giving it back "to show you control the resources" is pretty dumb. Supposing I took your wallet and then gave it back – would you think I was a nice person because I gave it back, or would you focus on making sure I never had the chance to take your wallet again? That's how dogs think too. A very astute behaviourist I know once snatched a slice of pizza off a friend's plate, ducked the punch that immediately followed and said, "THAT is what you are doing to your dog". She says that if you decide to use that method, make sure it is with finger food not anything eaten with knife and fork, or else you risk cutlery in the back of your hand.

Food aggression can start in puppyhood, if puppies are all fed out of one bowl and so have to fight for their share. It can also start at any age afterwards, if a dog feels vulnerable when it eats. Dogs should be able to eat in peace even if it means feeding in separate areas. Personally I like to watch my dogs eating because it is a good way of seeing any health problems starting, not only with something obvious such as one dog not wanting its food, but also the subtler message of one dog that is normally polite trying to snark another one away from its meal, which tells me that there is a health problem beginning with the dog that is being challenged. I do not allow dogs to eyeball each other or in any way attempt to take another's food; periodically we have had dogs that are obsessed with food as well as shy eaters which are easily put off, and in each case these are fed separately. Some dogs like company when they eat and others prefer to be alone; this should be respected.

The meal or meals are the most important part of the day apart from exercise (moot point!) and a dog should be able to enjoy its meal, not feel tense and unhappy about it. Some dogs can have a difficult attitude to food when they come out of Rescue, maybe because of the barking and clattering that accompanies feeding times in kennels, maybe because they were kennelled with a dog that threatened them out of their food, maybe because they didn't actually like the food. Some Rescues can use confrontational methods to test for food guarding, such as putting an artificial "hand" in the dog's bowl when it is eating and labelling the dog "aggressive" if it growls. This is often justified by the observation that a child might put its hand in the dog's food when the dog is rehomed, but any home that allows a child anywhere near a dog that is eating is not suitable for either. Some people like to make a dog sit and wait for its food; again this can be taken to unreasonable extremes. While a dog should have the manners to wait until its food bowl is on the ground rather than knocking it out of our hand, making a dog sit and wait beyond this time smacks of power-play and is a rather unsavoury glimpse of human attitude. Similarly, some dogs like to take time over their food (owners of certain breeds might express disbelief at this concept) so the bossy "take up the bowl after ten minutes whether the dog has finished or not" instruction is not appropriate with this type of dog, and again might trigger food-guarding where there was none before. The time to take up the bowl is when the dog walks away from it having finished what it wanted, and if this action worries the dog into coming back to guard an empty bowl, then we can use our superior human intellect by luring the dog out of the room in a friendly manner, giving it something nice such as a tasty titbit or a toy it likes, and then picking its bowl up when it is not there to see.

Where the dog arrives with a well-developed food-guarding habit, it takes remarkably little to change its ideas. To begin with, we make sure that our attitude is one of understanding that the dog is being reasonable, and its fears are very likely justified because of what has happened in its past. We change its "now" by making sure that it can eat undisturbed, and we do this by getting its food ready and then summoning the dog, rather than raising tension by allowing the dog to watch the preparation of its food. The dog needs to "wait" only until the bowl is put on the floor, and if it is so stressed that it dives straight in, defuse this by scattering a small number of very tiny treats behind it, and then placing the bowl on the floor while it is mopping up these. However, I have found that dogs quickly adjust to good manners as long as they know that the food really is coming their way and is theirs to enjoy. Once the bowl is down and the dog is released to eat, we should withdraw to a place in the same room where we are able to observe but not posing a threat. If there is other family, the room in which the dog is fed is out of bounds to them while it eats, no matter how much they want something they think they need right now. Most dogs that are left to eat in peace with a human observer quietly present will reduce in food aggressiveness over time with no other treatment whatsoever.

With a dog that is profoundly aggressive around food, we change its thought processes by starting with three empty bowls at a reasonable distance from each other, so the dog has to walk to each rather than just stretch across. The handler walks past one bowl and drops a small amount of food in it, and walks away. The dog is allowed to eat the food, and as it finishes, the handler walks past another bowl and does the same. The dog quickly learns that the handler's presence is a positive thing because food arrives with the handler, and no dog can guard three bowls. Only one bowl should have food in it at a time. Once the dog is completely calm with the three-bowl process, which normally does not take all that many meals but has to depend on each individual dog's level of fear – because food aggression is all about fear – reduce the bowls at each meal to two, then one, but continue to feed by walking past and dropping small amounts of food in at a time. When this is established with one bowl, give almost all the meal in the bowl, and add a few morsels by walking past and dropping them as the dog eats. It is important not to bend over or linger by the bowls, as these acts are seen as threatening by the dog that fears to lose its food.

Some people treat food-aggression by hand-feeding. This is a good way with slight food-aggression, especially from very young puppies, but not recommended with an adult dog, especially if that dog has other fear issues. Sometimes dogs come in close because they want the food, but then panic because they are too close to a human they don't yet trust. Some of these dogs will then bite. So, while hand-feeding is a good way to build trust, and a way I use myself with some dogs, it has to be suited to the individual dog at a particular stage of its rehabilitation, and if in doubt, don't.

Free Feeding

Leaving a bowl of food down for dogs to pick at as they please is not a good idea on several counts. To begin with, we do not have a clear idea of how much the dog is eating, so if any health problems are brewing, we do not see them as early as we would if sticking to set mealtimes. House-training is more difficult, because a dog fed to a schedule will empty out to a schedule as well, and this is particularly useful if we have one of those dogs that needs to move its bowels in the middle of the night. By altering the timing of the last meal or feeding a larger meal early on and a smaller one later, we can manipulate the dog's digestion to be more convenient to us. No matter how much we love our dog, standing out in the cold night waiting for it to find just the right spot can be very irritating. If we have multiple dogs then we do not have a clear idea of which one is eating what, and if one needs to watch its weight, we have no control over that. Some dogs self-regulate and only eat what they need, while others will eat as long as there is food on the planet. When training using food rewards, we "set ourselves up for success" if the dog is hungry; if it has chosen to ingest a bellyful just before we start, we are not going to get anywhere. There are physical dangers in exercising a dog with a full stomach too, as that can create "bloat" where the gut can start to twist under the load of food. Bloat can kill; some breeds, notably deep-chested ones, are more at risk than others, but any dog can get bloat, and it is a risk not worth taking. However, the biggest danger with free-feeding is that it can really stress some dogs because they feel they have to guard the food. With overt guarding behaviour, we at least see straight away what is going on, but some dogs instead develop stress patterns of behaviour which can manifest as anything from self-mutilation to attacks on visitors. By committing to a suitable feeding schedule for the particular dog you have and with no food available otherwise, the stress is wiped out. Incidentally, any food left lying around can be a terrific stressor for some dogs, so if there are cats that are used to having food left available, arrange the home so that the dog has no access to the room the food is in. Cat food (and indeed cat excrement) smells strong and appealing to dogs because of the high meat content plus specially manufactured odours added to make the food more enticing, so the food and the litter tray should be well away from areas to which the dog has access. Similarly with people and food: if we put food away when we have finished with it, and do not allow people to wander about with food in their hands, if we train our dogs to relax on their beds rather than hang around when humans are eating, we not only create dogs that are pleasant to live with, we also avoid unwanted behaviours developing.

Resource Aggression

Anything that a dog values becomes a "resource", including its owner, and the more insecure a dog is, the more it will resource-guard. Unsurprisingly, dogs from guarding breeds guard resources more readily than any other types in that they do not have to be unduly insecure within their breed type for guarding behaviour to present. While dogs are not as concerned with "property" in the way humans are, anything that is in a dog's mouth belongs to it, anything a dog is lying on top of, and anything it has hidden in its bed and placed itself close by, belongs to it also. We need to see this attitude from the dog's point of view because it cannot see it from ours. It has no concept of items that have been bought by us with money we have earned; all that is a closed book to the canine mind. But what it has right now is of value to it, and it is a remarkably insensitive human who then tries to take such objects away by force. A proportion of these humans will be warned by the dog, and some will take no notice and get bitten. So if we have been careless and the dog has acquired something precious or even dangerous, we secure a co-operative handover at the time and for the future by teaching the dog to "trade" one item for another long before we are actually ever in a confrontational position. Teaching dogs to retrieve is also extremely useful, because then when they get hold of something we don't want them to have, they already know that bringing it to us is very rewarding.

Some dogs resource-guard doorways and similar narrow spaces. Space is terribly important to animals, more so than it is to us, and it is easy for us to miss a dog on guard like this until it rushes the unwary human in one of those attacks that we think come without warning. With rescue dogs especially, space becomes extremely valuable, both as a protective bubble around them, and as a means to control who goes where for defensive reasons. Narrow spaces are where animals attack or get attacked: ask any soldier who has seen active service. If a dog has taken up position across a restricted space, we should not confront it but instead lure it into a wider space and if necessary keep it there with a lead or a simple barrier while whatever triggered the behaviour is moved somewhere safer. Those dogs that accept people into their homes and attack as they leave will often do so in a doorway or by the outside door. Very narrow spaces within the home, such as cluttered corridors or blocked corners may also precipitate the space-guarder's reactivity. We often understand it better if we see it as a kind of canine feng shui, but what it is all about is having enough safe open space around the dog, and it is equally as applicable outside as indoors. Look at your home and garden with "space eyes" and see how many tight places there may be. Often narrowing your eyes gives a better picture of the way your dog sees its home environment in terms of open and restricted space.

Pain Aggression

Dogs are very good at concealing pain and illness. Social animals are programmed to attack and either kill or drive away the weak, sick, stupid and old, and so it is in the dog's survival instincts to hide infirmity until it is really bad. This means that many pet dogs are in pain, but we don't realise. The pain can be intermittent, constant, low-level, fluctuating or severe, and unless we are aware, we can miss it completely. This can partly be denial, because we do not like to think of our dogs getting old or ill. I often see ageing dogs or those for whom arthritis or even hip dysplasia are escalating conditions, being made to run behind a bicycle or with a jogger, and I have never yet had a positive response from mentioning it. Old injuries can mean pain, particularly fractures plated or pinned with metal, and if human amputees can suffer phantom pains in the limbs they no longer have, it is logical to suppose that the same happens with dogs. We do not know whether dogs get headaches, but there is no reason to suppose they do not; I have seen dogs press their heads against walls and it does seem as if they are trying to relieve pain. Their teeth can trouble them, broken toes or nails can go undetected, as can joint or spinal injuries, pain or infection in the ears, and a host of other miseries that, unless we are very observant, we plain do not realise are there. I once took a dog to my very good vet with no more information than "he isn't himself". A nose-to-tail examination revealed a swollen prostate, which must have been agony, but he had barely given any indication of being not quite right.

Therefore, with any change in behaviour, but most particularly one that involves aggression, the dog should have a full veterinary check as soon as possible.

Infirmity troubles dogs too: going blind or deaf may not hurt, but they do not understand the mechanics of it, only knowing that the world sounds strange and the light isn't as good as it was. How many dogs are punished for "disobedience" when they cannot hear their people properly, or described as "stupid" when they walk into things they can no longer see? Deterioration of sight or hearing is usually a gradual process, and easy for owners to miss at first. A dog does not have to be old for its faculties to fail, but most dogs lose sight and/or hearing as part of the ageing process. Such dogs feel vulnerable because ancient instinct tells them that other dogs are now a danger to them. Often the first alert we have to a dog becoming ill is a change in behaviour from the dogs around it at home or those it meets on walks. If a dog suddenly starts attacking others, it could mean that either one is becoming weak or ill, because the vulnerability of being so can drive some of the feistier types of dog such as terriers to the pre-emptive strike. We need to be particularly vigilant at home for changing dynamics between dogs. It is sadly quite common for unsuspecting owners to come home to find one dog killed, sometimes even partially eaten, and in one particularly unhappy case I was involved in, a large dog was dismembered and bits of it stashed around the house. This is dogs being dogs, and following their genetic programming, no matter how horrific it is to us. In fact, even in human society, some choose to prey upon the old and weak, and we have to be specifically educated from childhood into a moral stance that finds this unacceptable.

As far as the dog is concerned, if it is ill it is vulnerable and in danger, and so it will display behavioural changes which are sometimes overtly aggressive and sometimes reactive, i.e. has to be triggered by an outside incident.

Therefore if a dog has suddenly become aggressive to other dogs, or else is being targeted as a victim by other dogs, it needs a full veterinary check before any behavioural work is undertaken, and most behaviour consultants will insist on this before they work with the dog. We cannot train away pain or a feeling of being defenceless, and if aggression is based upon pain, removing the pain normally restores confidence to the dog unless it has been attacked in the meantime, in which case we have some behaviour work to do as well. Pain is also high on the list as a cause of dog/human aggression, and yet is seldom given the consideration it needs. Recently I read an article by a well-known dog trainer who commented on a terrier that growled and snapped when picked up. He said that such behaviour was something he "would not stand for", but it is a typical response from a dog that is frightened or in pain, and which only has so many ways of telling us this.

Drug-induced Aggression

Some types of medication can cause aggression as a side-effect in some dogs, so if our dog is prescribed anything, it is important to ask our vet whether there is a likelihood of aggression as a result. It is also useful to do our own research, as we cannot expect our vets to know everything. Steroids, some incontinence treatments and a variety of mind-altering drugs all have this potential, and various other medications as well, so if a dog changes its personality or becomes tetchy after a medication change, it may be the illness or it may be the treatment. There are alternative medications available for most conditions, so it is worth exploring these at the earliest opportunity, as vets cannot always foresee how an individual may react. This can also arise when the vet is experimenting with dosage in order to find the right amount needed by the dog, or when a condition has altered and the medication we have been using is changed or withdrawn. Drug-induced aggression is out of the dog's control; it might become morose, nervous, irritable or ferocious, but the bite causes just as much damage whatever its cause. Therefore we need to be aware of this as a potential issue with any medication, and if it is encountered, we should go back to our vet and work together to find a better treatment. Sometimes this will mean using medication that does not work quite so well, or that is more expensive. If there is no alternative and the condition is long-term, then we have a quality of life issue, ours as well as the dog's, and may need to do some hard thinking.

Love the Growl

So often a dog is described as aggressive because it has growled at somebody. Growling is not aggression: it is communication, and the growl is one of the most valuable communications that there is from a dog, because it tells us that the dog is very uncomfortable with a situation. Dogs have limited vocal communication: they bark, growl, howl, whine, moan, yelp, and some more vocal breeds have additional sounds to use as well. Before a dog is driven to vocalise, it will have used many physical signals, but we humans are rubbish at reading body-language, or even detecting it, until we have been taught. So the growling dog has been trying to get its point across by subtler means for some time, but nobody is listening.

It is all too usual for us to feel offended by the growl. How dare the dog growl at us? We pay the bills, buy its food, own the house it lives in, inconvenience ourselves mightily exercising it and taking it to the vet and it just growled at us! Old-style dominance/pack theory tells us that the dog is being dominant and is about to stage a hierarchal takeover in the household, and so advise punishment in order to remind the dog how lowly it is. If we punish the growl, we do not take away the stress that drove the dog to growling in the first place. We do, however, take away the dog's option of communicating at a reasonable level. Dogs punished for growling escalate pretty fast through the higher stages to a bite. This is typical of the bite that we in our ignorance say "came from nowhere" was "for no reason" or "without warning". There will have been plenty of prior warning at some stage but not necessarily with this situation or even in this household. Sometimes people take on a dog that has been punished for growling in its previous home, and so learned that growling is no use and it has to progress straight to the bite. In cases like these, if we are prepared to work with the dog, and sometimes at some physical risk to ourselves, we can reinstate the growl. If we cannot, then we ought to commit to watching the dog carefully for any signs of discomfiture with any given situation, and to remove it from that type of situation before it feels it has no option but to bite.

When dealing with aggression especially, we need to know that the dog is not aggressive: the dog is displaying aggressive behaviour. It is doing so for one of a variety of very good reasons plus the trigger: no trigger, no aggression. Therefore we need to analyse the reasons and the trigger, then take steps to organise the environment better so that the dog does not need to "shout" in order to express its discomfiture. Aggression is not a personal insult: it is escalated communication because nobody listened before. Once we understand that, aggression ceases to be a behavioural bogeyman and instead presents a journey of discovery where we can work with the dog to help it. This does not mean that we should be complacent, because a bite is a bite whatever its motivation, but we do need to understand that when dogs show aggression, we are opening communication, not closing it.

Separation Anxiety

This is one of the most difficult behaviours to treat, and in many cases it can only be managed, because it is incurable in some dogs. It is particularly prevalent in rescued dogs because those dogs have already experienced a great deal of mental stress for which the canine mind is not equipped. Anecdotally it seems to be far more prevalent in neutered dogs, though that may be because most rescue dogs are neutered before they are rehomed, and early neuters seem to be more prone to it too, but quite possibly for the same reason in many cases, though we always have to consider the effect of neutering on mental development (see Chapter Four).

There are degrees of the condition, and the subtler examples are often not recognised as such. Some affected dogs may simply refuse to eat food left for them, even in a kong or similar, or engage in any activity with toys that they normally like. I had a dog that would not even drink while I was away, but she was never noisy or destructive; it would have been easy to have missed this indication of distress. Such dogs are usually straightforward to rehabilitate, and of course much easier to live with as they are not wrecking the house or driving the neighbours crazy with noise while we are working to change their behaviour. High-end dogs vocalise, often for as many hours as the owner is away, destroy household items, even chewing walls and doors, urinate and defecate more than would be normal, self-mutilate, salivate to the point of soaking their fronts in drool, pace constantly, and/or try to crawl into small dark places. CCTV will show that anxious behaviour such as pacing and panting can start as soon as the owner begins getting ready to go out, and that the destructive behaviour may commence as soon as the owner has left. It is important to hold in our own minds that the dog is not

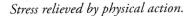

Stress relieved by physical action.

doing this to be spiteful, vengeful, controlling, dominant, change its status within the family or to be plain irritating – the dog is terrified, the dog is unbearably stressed, and dogs do not have the emotional mechanism to deal with being shut away on their own in situations where they are afraid. But stress is relieved by physical action, especially repetitive movements, so they pace, chew, pant, bark and tear things up. Stress hormones stimulate bladder and bowels, so the dog has to empty itself, and if it has been shut in the house, it will have to do this indoors. Howling, constant barking and that piercing whine that often accompanies it is the dog's equivalent of calling the owner on its mobile. It is significant in behaviour terms that other dogs in the vicinity rarely respond to howling, whining or barking that has its source in SA. This is because they can tell that the vocalising dog is vulnerable and weak, and have no desire to put themselves at risk by being associated with it. By contrast, dogs will readily respond to a dog that is barking because it is challenging movement or presence outside that may be a threat. This is a "strong" dog, and therefore worth associating with.

Separation anxiety is most often about a dog's attachment to humans, usually one specific human, and this attachment is normally made very quickly at a time of acute need in the dog. Therefore it is rarely helpful to get another dog when symptoms manifest to a significant degree, because either that dog is okay with being left, in which case it will ignore the other one in its stress (CCTV can be so useful) because dogs do not like neediness in others, or else the second dog will become anxious as well. Behold: we now have two dogs with SA. The attachment to the new owner occurs most usually when a dog has been in Rescue and has either displayed anxiety to an extreme degree, so that the staff have been forced to bring it into the office rather than leave it kennelled, or has completely shut down and so appears calm. With the latter kind, there can be a delayed reaction period lasting a few days to a couple of weeks, and then the demon is unleashed, while the more overtly anxious dogs weld themselves to their new owner at once, and follow them everywhere. Puppies can develop SA too, but the cause is different: too many people bring a puppy home, play with it all day and then leave it to cry the night through on its own. The puppy has never been on its own in its life, has had a journey and maybe been travel-sick, is in a strange place and possibly shut in a crate as well, and panics. Who could blame it? I am always amazed at the many puppies that get over this and become averagely well-adjusted pets in time, but others do not, and the terror of that first night stays with them every time they are left. However, the end result is the same – a dog or pup, but most usually an adolescent, that is petrified of being alone.

We should not underrate the fixation on one particular person. Extreme SA dogs cannot even be left with a dogsitter, or another member of the family, because they only trust one person to keep them safe. They are not displaying SA out of "faithfulness": the dog only feels safe when this

141

one person is present. Others are calm as long as a known person is with them, and some make the transference to a pet-sitter or daycare kennelling without much of a hiccup. The hardline SA dogs are truly a nightmare to their owners, and to everyone within earshot too.

As an issue of underconfidence, we treat SA by building confidence in the dog. Unfortunately many people expect a dog to settle into a new home without any preparation; some of us take a few days off work, but do not always use the time wisely to accustom the dog to being left and then the owner returning. Some of us use the crate but do not realise that a dog has to be habituated to the crate as a good experience, and instead shut it in right away and expect the dog to be fine with that. So to prevent SA developing in the first place, we assume that it is hovering on the horizon, and accustom the dog to its new life with reward-based training, consistent boundaries, and plenty of mental and physical exercise. But very often dogs come into Rescue with SA already established – maybe that is the reason they have come in – and the new owners have to deal with it. We create a multiple approach.

Strategies

Building the dog's confidence in itself means working with it at those mind games, and giving it plenty to do on its own at those times when we want to get on with other things. This is the foundation layer for occupying the dog while we are out. At the same time, we reduce the reward of the dog following us about. We break each household task into small parts, so that the dog following us gives up and settles, because we are boring. For example: we want to make a cup of tea. We get up (dog gets up) go into the kitchen (dog follows) fill kettle, go back, (dog follows) sit down (dog settles) then get up (dog gets up) go into kitchen (dog follows) get cup out of cupboard, go back (dog follows) sit down (dog settles) and so on until the tea is made and ready to carry into the other room to drink. If we do this for every single task, it will be a lot of effort over a short time but it teaches the dog that it might as well stay on its bed when we leave the room, and it is the dog that makes the decision. Of course, a really soft, cosy bed should be provided where we want the dog to stay, and nothing at all where we don't want the dog. There will be times when we do want the dog to come to us, so treat the exercise as a game of "Simon Says" where if we don't want the dog about, such as for the "cup of tea" example, we ignore it totally, but if we do want to include the dog, we make eye contact and talk pleasantly to it, then ask it to come with us. When it does, something nice happens e.g. a titbit or a mind game. If it trails after us without being called, nothing happens and it is ignored. This isn't about ostracising the dog, but teaching it that constantly following us about is pointless and unrewarding, while coming with us when we say it can is very rewarding.

While we bring these matters into the dog's life, we also have to work at de-stressing the departure procedure. Again, it is a matter of "baby steps". It is useful to use a marker signal that indicates we are going out, for instance a towel hung over a chair. We need to use the same towel, because small differences to us can be big ones to dogs. We start with the dog in the same room, our marker is put in place, and we then ignore the dog. If it comes to us, we quietly and without fuss return it to its bed. When we wish to interact with the dog, we remove the marker and then call the dog over and fuss it. The marker is the signal that the dog is going to be ignored. Removing the marker means the dog and owner can interact. Do not over-use the marker: start for very short periods of time – a minute, two minutes – and build up.

Once the dog has accustomed itself to the marker, we integrate it with our departure signals. Again, at first it is a matter of put up the marker, put on shoes, sit down, ignore dog. Take off shoes, remove marker, interact with dog. When putting on shoes makes no difference to the dog any more, add another action in the departure sequence, such as picking up keys. If the dog gets up, resettle it and ignore. Bit by bit we link all our departure signals with the marker, and then we can add the departure, but that to start with is no more than go out, close door, come straight back in, ignore dog, remove marker once dog has settled, then reward dog with interaction. Build up very slowly to going out of the front door and straight back in, then out for half a minute, a minute and so on. If you get the start of SA, for instance the dog starts to pace and whine, you are going too fast: knock back in the sequence and stay at that level for a few days, then move on. It's a huge commitment, it takes as long as it takes because the dog sets the timing, and it must not be rushed. Nor can we cure SA by just doing the last set of procedures because it is vital to build up confidence in the dog at the same time as teaching it that we are going out but always coming back. During this time, our life will be very restricted, but then life with a dog that has SA is pretty restricted anyway. We still need to exercise the dog normally, and while tackling SA we may feel that our whole world revolves round the dog to the detriment of everything else, but improvement does come, and soon we can leave the dog for longer. It is worth trying a dog-sitter in tandem with your going-out training; this works for some dogs but not all. Gradually, the majority of dogs will mellow to the extent that they can be left for a certain amount of time. Where and for how long they can be left depends on the type and extent of the behaviour; many dogs cannot handle the idea of being shut in a crate if they have learned to associate it with being left for hours, but will be calm if confined to, for instance, the kitchen, behind baby-gates. If the dog can jump one gate, put one on top of the other, and always observe the twin precautions of leaving nothing available that the dog can damage, and leaving plenty available that the dog can safely chew.

The most difficult part of re-programming the SA dog is that most of us have to go out from time to time, and the dog that vocalises incessantly until we come back is likely to link its making a noise with our return, which reinforces the behaviour. Few of us have the freedom of routine that it takes to build the SA dog up gradually to the point where we can successfully leave it.

I once saw a different approach to SA which worked very well for that particular dog, though few of us could recreate the circumstances. Coming into Rescue as the result of a Noise Abatement Order (he had been left in the garden to scream his days away) he was taken on by a farmer at the end of one summer. That autumn was very wet, with storms and daily downpours, and the dog was a thin-coated breed with a fastidious dislike of discomfort. The farmer had to work outdoors all day, and the dog followed her about, getting soaked and miserable. Eventually the dog decided it could lie in the back doorway and watch from there, and from this progressed to the kitchen, where there was a cosy bed and the warm range as an alternative to being cold and wet. Because the dog chose to separate itself from its owner, the changeover was made in the dog's time and within its comfort zone.

Calmers

Dogs can become so distressed with SA that there is justification in the use of safe calming agents when you get to the stage of leaving the dog. Beware, however, of certain drugs that leave the dog every bit as distressed but unable to express itself. Your vet will be able to give suitable advice, especially if he or she is knowledgeable about Bach Flower Remedies, calming herbs, homeopathy and other preparations. Herbs are strong remedies and can do harm if wrongly used, but Bach and homeopathic remedies simply don't work if the wrong treatment is given. Additionally, you may consider using diffusers such as Adaptil, which are pheromone-based and supposed to mimic the scents given out by a suckling bitch, or the herbal equivalents of which there are several. Some of these work better than others, and I recommend spraying one dog bed with the calming scent and leaving the others au naturel. Dogs may choose the calming scent-sprayed bed or refuse to go near it, and so we find out if that particular scent is going to help or not. Dogs should always have the means of getting away from scent "comforters" because not all like them. I was given one to review and report back to the manufacturers, and results were dramatic. I used it very sparingly on two dog beds, each in a different room, and none of the dogs would go near either.

Be especially careful with aromatherapy oils because a dog's strong sense of smell means that some scents will be distressing to it: only ever use aromatherapy prescribed in conjunction with a vet who is properly qualified

Safe at last.

in its use. As a qualified aromatherapist myself, there are many remedies I would use before these.

Limitations

Sometimes SA is so severe that, while we can achieve a degree of improvement, we cannot remove it entirely. Depending on how much we are prepared to commit to the dog, we can experiment with kennels that offer daycare, or employ a pet-sitter. Dogs that may not settle in their own home with another person may well settle in a different environment, and I do know of one that went out all day with the dog-walker five days a week, until her owner came home for the evening. Because she was active, she was dispelling stress hormones rather than accumulating them, and she did become much calmer after several months of this.

Poisoned Cues

Where a dog has learned that obeying a verbal instruction leads to pain or fear, we say that the cue, i.e. the word, has been poisoned. Typically with rescued animals there are one or more poisoned cues, and we need to address them by changing the cue words because the cause and effect has become so entrenched in the dog's mind that we cannot "unpoison" the cue. Often this means changing the dog's name, because that is the sound that has been paired with unpleasantness in the past. The dog's name from its previous home may not in any case be the one that the new home has been supplied with, as many animals come into Rescue without names; the kennel staff have to call them something, and favourite names are frequently recycled. It is easy to change a dog's name: simply decide on the new name, pair it with the old one for a few days and use it for calling the dog into any pleasant situation. For instance, suppose the dog is called Suki and you want to call it Rolo, call SukiRolo Dinner, SukiRolo Walkies, SukiRolo Biscuit at appropriate times. Then just drop the Suki part of the name and the dog will respond to Rolo. If a dog has been made to "sit" and then been hurt, change the "sit" cue for another word – any word will do as long as you are consistent. Words are only sounds with consequences as far as dogs are concerned, and if a sound has been paired with a nasty consequence, the dog will fear the word; change the word and pair the desired action with reward and pleasure, and the dog is well on the way to becoming obedient to the new word.

Recall

This is the instruction that is the hardest to establish, and the most important. With dogs that are in their second (or more) homes, recall is likely to be very shaky if it exists at all. A dog cannot be expected to return to a person it does not trust, and trust has to be built gradually: it does not come as soon as the dog changes homes. A dog may have had little or no reason to trust any previous humans in its life: this is not necessarily the result of abuse but often is a matter of misunderstanding. Nor does "love" automatically create trust: love is the last thing these dogs need but very often the first thing they get, which overwhelms and confuses them. Rescue dogs need space and time to adapt to their new environment and to assess their new person or family, which includes any animals in the home. Trust will come slowly while they are adjusting to their new lives; meanwhile what we can offer them is consistency. So many people call a dog and then rant at it or even hit it after it has come back. The dog associates the human behaviour with the last action it has done, so in future will be put off returning. But it also

Recall needs some work.

146

wants to return because it is a domestic dog and wants human company, unless it has been so badly abused that it fears all people, in which case it should not be off the lead just yet. So here is where we see the dog that comes back so far and no further, that circles and backs off but does not come in close enough to be touched. This shows a major flaw in the relationship, just as when a frightened dog runs for the car, or home, or just plain runs away. Trust is there when the dog runs to the owner, and from this you may realise you know several people whose dogs are never abused and have lived with them all their lives, but do not trust them.

Nor will dogs recall if their return is for something less pleasant than whatever it is they were doing or just about to do. People who call a dog and then put it on the lead, signalling the end of its fun, will cause their dogs to become unreliable in recall, because who wants to stop having a good time? Recall should be trained into a dog as offering something better than whatever it was just doing, so we need kidology here. If the dog is running about with a group of other dogs, it isn't going to want to recall any more than we would be happy about leaving a party we were enjoying, and if we call the dog right then, we simply establish in its mind that recall is optional. So in this situation, we can wait until the group has paused in its running about, and that is the time our dog will look back at us. The instant our dog has checked in with us, we need to be interesting. Throw and catch a toy or a ball, run away, hide behind a tree – the stage is ours. Yes we will get some pretty odd looks from time to time, but as with all remedial training, this is a foundation layer: it is not for ever. In the early stages, having rewarded the dog for coming to us, we then release it to return to its fun. Thus the dog realises that coming away from something good when called means a reward and then being allowed to continue its fun, rather than the recall always signalling the end of something pleasant. The time will come when we can call our dog away from any group at any time – but we should still only do this if we need to. If we have allowed our dog to go off and interact with another or a group of other dogs, then it is reasonable to let it enjoy that interaction for a short time, and not take it away just to prove we can. If interaction with a group of dogs is about to turn nasty, we should not call our dog but instead must go and get it. The reason is that if our dog turns its head in response to our call, it leaves itself vulnerable to attack. Thus – again – recall is poisoned.

If we aim to be reasonable, fair, and above all, safe dog owners, as we build trust, so our dogs will return to us because being with us is far better than any amount of dog company. Remember the "domestic" part of being domestic dogs means that they have evolved to live with us, interact with us, and enjoy our company over that of other dogs. And that above all is the root of sound recall.

Recall in the Home

Recall can be practiced in the home, but again has to be reasonable. We should never call our dog for anything unpleasant, such as having eye drops, or being shut away because we are going out. Coming back to us must always be for something better than the dog was just doing. It surprises people that unpleasantness can include what we see as showing the dog affection, but dogs don't always want to be fussed any more than we do, and some dogs actively dislike being touched. This is especially so with rescue dogs, which may have good reason to fear human hands. But many dogs in any case do not want to have their fur ruffled, or their heads patted, and some find cuddles really frightening. We simian types like to clutch, pick up and hug, and many dogs are terrified of this (Jean Donaldson writes eloquently in this in her book *The Culture Clash*). Of those that don't seem to object, some may be actively enjoying the attention but others will be enduring it, and we need to be aware of what the dog is feeling. Some dogs enjoy any form of attention and are very tactile, but others prefer to be left untouched unless they specifically "request" contact. There are plenty of good things to recall dogs for, and practicing recall from room to room in the house, and in and out of the garden, is very useful. Make sure that the rewards are super-rewarding, though, as we need recall to be as high quality as we can get. Similarly, make sure that the dog is awake before planning a recall exercise, and is not immersed in something desirable such as a kong or a chew item. "Set yourself up for success".

100% Recall

There are books, trainers and training courses which claim to achieve 100% recall. While worth investigating up to a point, because they do provide some useful techniques, there comes a time when we don't need to spend any more money to find out what we already know, which is that with a sentient being we can never guarantee 100% anything. With this in mind, we can secure recall as much as possible by making it extremely rewarding, and save our nerves by using management (put the dog on the lead, don't go that way, close the gate etc.) where recall is essential but its likelihood may be in doubt. Whatever our dogs' individual motivators are, we need to be aware of them, anticipate, pre-empt, and, where multiple dogs are concerned, divide and rule. One dog may obey under temptation: two or more dogs are far less likely to, as many a complacent owner has learned, so in the group situation in risky areas, only have one dog off the lead at a time. Recall is very much about the relationship between dog and owner: we have to be worth it. This is nothing to do with love, fear or any other emotion: it is to do with it being more worthwhile for the dog to return to us, and there are a few situations where we owners cannot guarantee that whatever we offer has the edge on what the dog wants to do. This does not mean we have "bad" dogs or that we are ineffectual owners, but is a normal part of intelligent beings making the best use of circumstances. Dogs are opportunists, and they are far quicker than we will ever be at sizing up a situation and acting upon it. Wise dog owners limit those opportunities kindly, and in such a manner that the dog has no idea that there was ever another decision available.

Coprophagia

This means faeces-eating, and is very common in dogs for a variety of reasons. Coprophagia is within the normal spectrum of behaviour for dogs, but is abhorrent to us, and so where it does present, we are anxious to stop it, and the dog would like to continue. Broadly divisible into eating carnivore or herbivore muck, we need to find the reasons (commonly more than one) in order to effect a cure. Sometimes this behaviour is so entrenched that we have to manage it rather than cure it, so first we need to understand it from the dog's point of view.

Herbivore Sources

Herbivore muck is good nourishing food for dogs. It contains vegetable matter partly broken down by the original animal's digestive processes, and so its nutrients are more available to the dog's digestion. Cellulose plant matter is very difficult to digest even for herbivores, which either digest it twice through chewing cud (e.g. cattle) faecal reingestion (e.g. rabbits) or waste a lot of food value (e.g. horses). We humans cook vegetables for the same effect. Dogs eat herbivore muck. It won't harm them unless the herbivores have been given veterinary drugs such as wormers. I find that if my dogs have plenty of vegetables as part of their food rations, they show little inclination to eat herbivore muck, but if we have been low on vegetable supplies, they are more interested in it. Because this method of taking in vegetation is so natural for dogs, we really don't need to stress over it beyond making sure the dog does not lick our faces immediately afterwards. However, for those who find it truly abhorrent, it is a matter of addressing the need by feeding sufficient vegetable matter, while keeping the dog away from places where herbivores graze.

Carnivore/Omnivore Sources

While still within the natural spectrum, the idea of our pets eating carnivore (e.g. dog, cat, fox) or omnivore (e.g. pig, badger, human) faecal matter is extremely unpleasant to us, and we might reflect with a shudder on those more primitive human societies where dogs scavenging on the midden are a part of life, which is why dogs are considered "unclean" to many ethnic groups. Carnivore and omnivore digestions are quite wasteful, so in dog terms they are making use of a good source of available food. Unless a habit has already formed – and coprophagia becomes a habit very quickly because it is so rewarding – feeding dogs in a way that supplies them their necessary nutrients in the form of fresh food that gives occupation in the eating, will most probably prevent this desire developing. Dogs fed processed food are at a disadvantage here because the taste and smell of such food is often artificially enhanced by the use of "digest", a slurry that is sprayed onto it just before it is packed. This mix of ingredients maintains much of its smell through the dog's digestion process and remains in the eliminated faeces, thus still smelling like the original food. Quite often, incipient coprophagia can be halted by changing to a fresh-food diet. However, many dogs find cat faeces irresistible no matter how well they are fed, so if cats and dogs are kept together, it is wise to have the litter-tray somewhere the dog cannot reach.

Some dogs will eat their own faeces, or those of other dogs, which is behavioural as much as dietary. For dogs that have been starved, it may have been their only source of nutrition, and for dogs that have been kept confined in their own filth, their only source of entertainment. For a few dogs it can be a territorial matter, either to remove their own signs from a group of stronger characters, or to dismiss the presence of a weaker character. Where house-training has been carried out in a confrontational or even abusive manner, the dog may think the owner's anger at seeing a mess is about any mess rather than where the mess is, and so as it has no choice but to mess when it needs to, it eats that mess to hide it. This behaviour may also surface where a previously house-trained dog has been housed in kennels where the schedule leaves it no alternative but to soil its living area. While not the exclusive preserve of the rescued dog, it is clear that many forms of thoughtless treatment can push the dog into this behaviour.

Management
So often coprophagia has to be managed, because once established it touches base with the primitive dog mindset, and after all, so far as the dog is concerned, there is no reason not to do it. In managing, we keep the dog's access to faecal matter to a minimum, which means keeping kennel, yard or garden scrupulously clear of droppings. When exercising the dog, we need to be aware of the places where this behaviour might be indulged, and keep the dog on a lead. With some, sufficient distraction in terms of toys and games will occupy the dog, but many others have an almost magnetic attraction to muck, and can find and devour it far faster than most owners can prevent. Muzzling the dog is not a help either, as the dog simply smears filth around its muzzle and leaves us with an equally revolting task later – that is, if we manage to avoid having the soiled muzzle wiped across our legs and hands on the way back. Let's not even talk about the car.

The best we can do is to provide a diet that supplies proper nutrients without added chemicals or flavourings, teach a "leave" command with appropriate rewards the instant a dubious comestible has been resisted, and keep opportunities to indulge the behaviour to a minimum. Established coprophagics will almost always revert to the behaviour if a sufficiently tempting opportunity presents itself, but occasional indulgers can be redirected using vigilance and cunning. Various sources claim that adding this or that to the dog's food, for example pineapple chunks or curry powder, will cure the habit, but experience finds that as many dogs treat this as a condiment as respond to it in the way we would prefer.

Future Harmony

If we expect the rescued dog to manifest some issues as a result of its past, we will not be caught unawares as it begins to unravel whatever is inside it. Remember the dog can only use the coping mechanisms inborn to it, and sometimes we too may be overfaced with a particular behaviour as it presents. Experience, as the saying goes, is something we get after we needed it, and so there is no shame in finding a suitable professional to help us understand the roots of a behavioural glitsch. But you must choose your professional carefully, because they are not all cut from the same cloth. If any suggestion or training method disturbs you, remember you do not have to follow it. In order to work well with a professional, you need to have confidence in them, and there are plenty of us to choose from.

Some rescue dogs appear to slip seamlessly from one home into another, and this is largely due to the good management that came before and which continues in the new home. Another person may have encountered problems, or may have encountered the same settling-in issues and interpreted them as problems. We need to be ready for anything, but that does not necessarily mean that difficulties are inevitable. As long as we go into rescuing a dog with our eyes wide open, there is every chance we can end up with a fine canine companion.

Chapter Seven

Puppy Days

Puppy Development Stages, Training and Socialising

THE PUPPY is not a blank parchment. By the time it slips into the world as a separate entity, it is genetically fifty per cent of each parent and will have traits in turn from most of their forebears. It has inherited temperament and behaviours, looks and health. The dog that develops from this puppy is the sum of all these inborn traits, plus the life experiences that mould its own attitudes. No two puppies in a litter will turn out to be identical, for each will have inherited a different set of genes from the fifty per cent available out of each parent, and each will have had different opportunities to learn. Good training will make the best out of any dog, however unpromising, and bad training can ruin even the pup with the most potential. Puppies are as much work as human toddlers, and even when a dog is adult, we are talking about having to find another four hours in our day in order to keep it properly. If that level of responsibility has not put you off – read on!

As a buyer, you have no control over the choice of parents or the way the bitch is kept during pregnancy. Nor do you have any input into those crucial few weeks that the pups are with the bitch. Therefore the research you do before you choose your puppy is very important. Yes, there are people who do no research at all, pick a puppy from the free-ads paper, off the internet or out of a car boot at a dodgy dog show, and get a good dog. There are equally as many who do the same, and the dog is paying the vet's mortgage or staring through the bars at a Rescue a few months later. It makes sense to put as much research into getting a puppy as you do when choosing a life partner, and human relationships being what they are, you may even have the dog for longer! Let's look at dog breeders.

Breeders

Good breeders plan their litters well in advance, so you may have to go on a waiting list. This gives you time to research and possibly visit the prospective parents. Bear in mind that the breeder will want to check you out as well. It is in the interests of the good breeder that the puppy is well placed and that the owners are happy with it. If a breeder refuses to consider you as a potential puppy owner, do not be offended but instead consider whether your life at the moment is honestly suitable for a dog, or a dog of that breed. So many people choose a breed on the basis of how it looks rather than how it behaves, and then they end up with a dog that is too intelligent, too active, too driven, too hairy, too slobbery, too big – any number of "toos" that mean it does not fit in with their expectations. "Set yourself up for success" and choose a puppy that will suit the way you are – or else commit to making huge changes to your life.

Where do you find a good breeder? Here is sometimes where the best breeders can be unhelpful without intending to be, because the best do not need to advertise. They will probably be on breed lists and websites though, so with a certain amount of research you will come up with a recurring list of names. It can be useful to chat with veterinary practices, and check their noticeboards, and also local dog-training groups, but be careful about being suckered into getting a puppy from an unknown background because someone knows of a litter that needs "rescuing". If of course your objective is to get a rescue puppy, then this is as good a way as any to find one. Once you are in contact with one or two breeders, these will be able to put you in touch with a wider group, because not every breeder breeds every year, but they should be able to put you in touch with another breeder who is planning a litter. The breeder you want to buy from is one who is breeding with the intention of keeping a pup for their own use, and selling the rest of the litter, rather than one hoping to make some money – because properly-reared litters don't make money.

Choosing the Litter

There is nothing wrong with going on several breeders' lists. Matings sometimes don't happen, bitches don't always conceive, litters can be lost during the pregnancy, there may only be one or two puppies born instead of a number of them, or there might not be one of the sex you wanted, but once you have chosen your puppy, do the decent thing and let the other breeders know that you do not need to be on their list any more.

Choosing the litter.

Expect to pay a deposit once you have chosen your puppy. Most breeders will not allow prospective purchasers to visit the litter until the puppies are five or six weeks old, which is largely to reduce the risk of infection being brought into the litter, and also because it takes experience and observation to see puppies' characters any earlier. There is also the bitch to consider. While many bitches are perfectly happy to let strangers touch their puppies, equally many are not. This "maternal aggression" is so common in mothers of any species that it is considered the norm – yet we are led to believe by some dog "experts" that a bitch acting protectively towards her litter is of bad temperament, and therefore we should not buy a puppy from there. This is nonsense: maternal aggression, or as I prefer to call it "maternal protectiveness" is hormonally driven and nothing to do with the day-to-day temperament of the bitch. While some lactating bitches are incredibly mellow and seemingly without any maternal protectiveness at all, others can be very protective indeed, and we should be sympathetic to their needs.

The Outdoor Litter

It is modern "received wisdom" that we should avoid the litter raised outdoors, and I can only think that the proponents of this idea either have very large houses or else own those breeds of dog that have very small litters. Or perhaps they have never raised a litter at all. It is a good idea to keep new whelps in the house for the first three or four weeks, as if something goes wrong with either bitch or pups, it goes wrong very quickly indeed, and the wise breeder is never far away. From then onwards, however, most litters need more space and stimulation than the average house can supply. A good big brood kennel and run keeps puppies safe out of doors, and they can be let out into a paddock or garden (which latter may never be the same again, but puppies' needs come first) whenever the breeder has time to supervise them. At four weeks old, most puppies are well on the way to being weaned, and the bitch will only want to visit a few times a day, to top them up with milk once they have tried out their solid food. So the outdoor-reared litter is not necessarily a neglected one: instead it can have enjoyed far more stimuli and learning experiences than the litter kept shut in one room of the house, plus it teaches puppies the basics of house-training. They should have plenty of opportunities to tell outdoors from sleeping area by means of the different surfaces they encounter – grass, soil, concrete and so on. Individual puppies can be brought indoors to learn about matters such as noise and vibration from domestic appliances, and different indoor surfaces too, though if they started out inside the house, they should already be familiar with these things. By six weeks old, puppies need a lot of space to run around in, especially large litters or large breed puppies. If the breeder has the puppies in a safe outdoor environment, and they run eagerly to investigate you, wanting to touch you and explore your hands and feet, then this tells you they have had plenty of time spent with them. The outdoor litter to avoid is the one that has been raised in a shed, kennel or barn and had little human contact apart from food, water and basic cleaning. If pups are reluctant to approach and interact with you, smell strong, have runny eyes, noses or bums, staring coats, pot bellies or other signs of poor husbandry, then no matter how good the bloodlines are on paper, or how sorry you might feel for them, this is not a litter to buy from. Especially not the "feeling sorry" part, because it is you who will feel sorry, maybe for the lifetime of that pup, as you try to deal with health or temperament issues that are directly related to lack of care in the beginning. If only people would shop with their heads and leave their hearts at home, then good breeders would get the support they need, and bad breeders would give up dogs and find another way of making money. The result would be better dogs in our environs, which in turn would create a wider acceptance of dogs in public places, and greater appreciation of the dog's place in our society.

Rescue Puppies

You might well have decided to get a puppy from Breed Rescue, a general Dog Rescue, or from an unwanted litter you have heard about. If you are willing and able to tackle owning a puppy which has had an iffy start in life, then this is another way to get a puppy. You will know little or nothing about its breeding, parentage, early rearing or background, but if you are willing to take a chance, you will find plenty of puppies available.

Two Puppies Together

If ever a breeder tries to get you to take two puppies together, walk away. This is the sign of a poor breeder, one who knows little and cares less about their dogs. Even if they offer you the other puppy at a reduced rate, or because it is the last one, or free because they can see how nice you are, leave it right there. Two puppies together are significantly more than twice the work and hassle of one, and although a few people can make a good fist of rearing two puppies of the same age, these are people with great experience and exceptional circumstances. For the average dog owner, it creates a nightmare situation.

The subtext is often a misguided idea that two puppies will be company for each other, will play with and entertain each other, and so be less work for the owner. Dream on. With two puppies, you never know which has done what; for their part, they don't need you because they have each other, and so you would need to make time to train and exercise each one quite separately every single day. Otherwise they bond with each other and you can whistle Dixie for their attention: they don't have any reason to oblige you in any way. Two puppies will run off on walks where one would stay with you; two puppies will chase cats and poultry where one could be taught to leave them, two puppies make house-training very trying indeed. And if this is not difficult enough, they then grow up into two hooligan dogs. With maturity comes rivalry: in a more natural world, the young leave home and find their own territory, but two dogs in one household cannot do that, so they start to fight. This can start with "play" that turns ugly, rivalry for your attention, resource-guarding, redirected tension such as somebody coming to the door, two dogs running to the door and then setting about each other, and any number of other triggers.

Two puppies from the same litter are too alike to tolerate each other the

Two puppies together.

157

way two dogs dissimilar in age, size and needs might. Male dogs fight, but bitches fight to the death. The saying is "dogs fight to breed, but bitches fight to breathe". Once the two puppies start to mature and a grudge match kicks off, there is no stopping it until one dies or moves to a new home, unless you, the unsuspecting owner who had two cute puppies and is now living a nightmare, section off your home so that the twain never meet. This means being able to trust every other person in the household to close doors and fasten bolts, every visitor to do as you ask, and every holiday becomes an exercise in logistics. One moment of carelessness can result in a bloodbath, and I do not exaggerate. It takes skilled management to avoid their rivalry building up to the point of fighting, and once that bridge is crossed, there is no going back. I know quite a lot of people who have coped with this once, but not anybody who would tackle it a second time. The best way to have two dogs is to get one, train it to the standard that you want, and when it is about two years old or even older, get the second dog. Ideally this should be of a different type and gender, but we all like the breeds we like and we might want only that type. We might also prefer one gender rather than a mixed household. This is manageable as long as we are prepared for the extra work and attentiveness to detail that avoids giving dogs the opportunity to become rivals. The reason for getting different types is that they will not find the same resources of equal value, so for instance while two gundogs will have a very similar outlook, a gundog and a terrier are very dissimilar mentally. Different genders tend to accept each other more readily because canine programming is to avoid fighting the opposite sex. However, the latter still leads to problems at season times, unless the male can be sent away for the duration. Lots of us have groups of same-sex same-type dogs very successfully, but we have to be aware of what can go wrong and do our level best to see it never does. Age differences and personalities are very important here, and it is wise to have big gaps in age and to choose personalities as different as we can manage especially if we keep similar breed types.

Developmental Fear Periods

Puppies go through a series of developmental fear periods where uncomfortable new experiences have a profound effect on them, and we need to know about these so that we can manage socialising our puppies to best effect. Very young puppies are fearless, and everything in their world is welcomed with glee. Puppies undergoing a fear period find even mildly negative experiences worrying, and this reaction exists to prevent the more mobile but still defenceless puppy from wandering off and getting eaten by something. Negative experiences encountered during a fear period are very hard to eradicate. For instance, if a puppy going through a fear period is hurt or frightened by a man wearing a hat, then it will probably remain fearful of all men wearing hats. Though this attitude can usually be improved by later behaviour modification, the fear will not go away by itself. Fear periods vary slightly within the accepted norm, because each puppy is an individual, and differing breed types have different levels of reactivity. The boldest puppy from some breeds can naturally be more reserved than the least confident puppy from a more ebullient type. So the following is only a guide, and if your puppy tells you that its timings are different, listen to the puppy. Normal print is the accepted scientific conclusion*, and italics are mine, based on personal experience.

Prenatal Period
Conception to Birth
Neonatal Period 0-13 days
Puppies are not able to regulate temperature or waste elimination without their mother's stimulation

I handle pups from birth (as long as the bitch is happy with it) to accustom them to human scent and hands. This is a very useful learning stage, and pups are extremely responsive to touch at this time. Despite not being able to hear to begin with, they are very vocal. Ears and eyes begin to function at around ten days. My own experience is that puppies can control waste elimination within a very few days of birth, and it is not unusual for them to shuffle off the bedding area to eliminate outside it.

Transition Period 13-21 days
Ears and eyes gradually open. Best time to introduce other species and novel items.

I hold fire on other species for health (infection risks) and safety reasons, but I raise the ante with handling, and with introducing safe "novel items" for investigation. Pups are already interacting with each other. It is safest for developing eyesight to keep the puppy-room dimly-lit and to avoid flash photography. Sound can be introduced via a radio on low, plus human voices, and household noises such as vacuum cleaners and washing machines can be introduced. However, puppies must also be accustomed to silence because in their new homes, night-time may be a quiet period.

Awareness Period 21-23 days
Rapid time of sensory development. Best time to introduce new floor surfaces and auditory stimuli.

Not a big window for introduction! Therefore I start this earlier, as above. Pups have different surfaces in their living quarters already, and at three weeks can be taken out to explore under supervision. Eyesight still needs to be guarded: daylight and dim artificial light are okay, but no bright lights or full sunlight.

Canine Socialisation Period 21-49 days

Puppies learn how to stop *respond to* mother's discipline and how to be a dog.

Other safe family dogs may be introduced at this time, but not dogs from outside the home or dogs that dislike puppies. Good mothers are gentle with their discipline.

During 4th and 5th weeks

Short car rides may be introduced and stimuli such as radio, dishwasher, TV, hair dryer, vacuum cleaner etc. increased.

Also garden surfaces under supervision. Pups should have auditory stimuli from as soon as ears open at about 10 days, as described above. Periods of quiet should be maintained as too much stimulus does not give puppies time to absorb information and may instead cause an unacceptable level of stress.

By this time, most bitches only attend pups briefly, suckling them then leaving them for long periods. This teaches pups to be without their parent figure and sets good practice for later life when dogs have to be left "home alone". Bitches should be able to choose when to attend their pups and when to leave them. Bitches forced to stay with their pups may become stressed, and so vigorous with their discipline.

During the 5th and 6th week

Individual attention with humans should be given daily.

They should in my opinion have this from day 1, especially separation from siblings for human attention, returning the pup to the nest as soon as it indicates it wants to go back there. By doing this, pups will accustom to being away from the others. Pups should not be separated and then left alone.

Human Socialisation Period 7-12 weeks

Best time for rehoming. It was believed* that from 7 to 16 weeks of the puppy's life his basic character was set by what he had been taught.

I disagree. Temperament/character is genetic. However, inborn responses to certain stimuli may bring out more or less desirable traits. 7 weeks is a good time for a pup to change homes IF the new home is geared to an infant puppy's needs, and the new owner is committed to fulfilling these. The pup should be exposed to as many pleasant life experiences as possible during this time.

Fear Impact Sub-period 8-10 weeks

Experiences that a pup perceives as traumatic during this time tend to be generalised and may affect them for the rest of their lives.

I'd extend this period to 12 weeks. A lot of separation anxiety is rooted in pups changing homes at this time and then being left alone or shut in with no preparation.

This is also the time when travel-sickness strikes. Most pups will grow out of it at a year or so old, but stressful car journeys, such as to the vet, can lengthen the period of time in which a pup is car-sick from fear as opposed to from movement.

Seniority Classification Period 12-16 weeks

The age of cutting teeth and apron strings. By 16 weeks, the puppy's emotional makeup is fully developed.

I disagree profoundly. Emotional development is critically related to hormonal changes, and until these are complete, that pup cannot be said to be emotionally fully developed. The above concept relates to old science, which does not see the dog as an emotional being but rather a piece of mobile and mildly sentient furniture.

However, during the above-quoted period, pups have established their basic characters, so you can see which are nervous, confident, quiet, boisterous etc., which may be what the scientist meant. At 16 weeks most pups are still very dependent on their owners, and like to follow them about when outside. Recall is generally "perfect" with no warning of the storms to come.

Flight Instinct Period 4-8 months

There is a time during this period lasting 2-4 weeks when the pup will test his wings. He won't come when called and will run away when the owner tries to put on the lead.

In my experience this lasts a lot longer, and tends to start at about 6-8 months. During this time we cannot train reliably, and should relax about it because the pup cannot develop faster than its body and mind allow. This is about management rather than training, avoiding high-risk areas and situations as much as possible. The owner needs to concentrate on developing trust with the pup by protecting it in situations where it shows fear (regardless of whether the human thinks the pup should find the situation fearful) and by being interesting and stimulating company for the pup.

This is also the time when pups lose "puppy amnesty" with adult dogs. Puppy behaviour which has been tolerated up to now will start to be corrected by adult dogs. This is necessary in developmental terms, but if those adult dogs have not acquired correct canine manners and so discipline the pup too roughly, or by contrast allow the pup to bully them, the adolescent pup will not be learning proper manners. Therefore it is essential that the owner controls canine interaction and quietly stops potentially damaging behaviour before it gets to that point.

Second Fear Impact Period 6-14 months
In large breeds, this stage may last longer. This period shows a fear of new situations and novel objects.

This is when humans can really foul up. Bad experiences, neutering now before the hormonal development has completed, getting impatient/ aggressive with the adolescent pup, not dealing with boredom properly, not giving sufficient protection from strange dogs and people, can all have lasting consequences. A single attack from another dog during this period can trigger a lifetime of reactiveness. Many young dogs come into Rescue at this time, just when they are least able to cope with major life changes. Separation Anxiety may become installed for life as a result of this.

Young Adulthood 18-24 months
Many dogs may show a rise in aggression levels during this time. They may become protective and territorial and take advantage of any relaxation of the guidelines set by the owner.

It isn't actually aggression or advantage-taking at all – it is an escalated fear response to change and uncertainty. Owners need to be quietly consistent with "rules", i.e. making it clear to the dog what behaviour is unacceptable while training and rewarding all desired behaviour. Once the pup is past this stage and fully adult, it may be neutered if this is wanted.

Choosing the Right Puppy
This has to be the right puppy for us and our situation now, not the puppy for anyone else and any time in the past or future. Therefore it is best to visit the litter alone, unless we are strong characters who can withstand the "Oh but I like that one" from those we have brought with us. Also we should be

strong if we feel drawn towards a puppy marked the same way as a dog we have had in the past, because a dog is more personality than looks, and we will never get our old dog back in any case. Sometimes it is very hard to see a completely different personality dressed like our old favourite. Sometimes breeders will guide us towards a particular pup, and good breeders know their puppies very well. Bad breeders, however, may try to steer us towards a poor specimen because the good ones will be bought by someone less gullible. We should check the puppy over for obvious physical flaws such as deformed mouth, club foot, umbilical hernia and so on, before we release our heart to it.

Character is important, and we have to match the puppy to our own lifestyle and temperament. If a bold puppy is going to irritate us, a clever puppy outmanoeuvre us or a shy puppy exasperate us, we should avoid that type. If we have other dogs already, we need to factor in their acceptance as well. Nobody needs two strong or two sensitive characters together and it can often end in misery that we would never encounter if we took care to match personalities better. It used to be said that we should take the first puppy that runs up to us. That is good if we want a bold puppy. I tend to choose the last puppy to leave me instead. So often a litter will come bundling up, investigate and play around a visitor, then wander off and resume puppy activities. But one will be left that will continue to interact with or else fall peacefully asleep on me. And that is "my" puppy. Sometimes a puppy stands out from the litter so obviously that we barely see the others, and that too would be a suitable choice. Once I had a prospective puppy owner film the litter playing with his children, and from studying the film, one puppy stood out where it had not seemed so obvious at the time. They had him for sixteen happy years.

Temperament Testing

There was a real fad some years previously for "temperament testing" puppies, which involved subjecting each one to various exercises such as rolling it over and holding it down, making a sudden loud noise behind it, and so on. These actions were supposed to enable the puppy buyer to tell a good-natured pup from a difficult one. Such tests were extremely stressful for puppies, and we can imagine the effect on such youngsters if a series of potential buyers put them through this. With sensitive breeds especially, this would be a great way to cause permanent psychological harm. Good breeders would not countenance anyone doing this to their precious puppies, and are in any case more than able to tell you the character of each puppy.

Changing Homes

The age at which a puppy changes home is very important if this transition is to go well. At the moment, English law states that puppies cannot change homes until eight weeks old, except for going from the breeder to an intermediary home such as a pet shop or dealer, which is legal at five weeks. The law is not necessarily wise, and this is one instance that could do with amendment, because it is preposterous to forbid a puppy to go from one good home to another before a certain age, but still to allow very young puppies to transfer to commercial premises and be held there until they are sold. Good breeders in any case would not sell from such outlets. We can only do our best; good breeders know when their puppies are at the right age for changing homes, and some are certainly ready before eight weeks, while others benefit from staying with the breeder for a little longer. Changing homes is a huge upheaval to a young puppy and the biggest event in its life so far; we owe it not just to the puppy but ourselves as well, to pick the right time for that puppy and so minimise the risk of major behavioural issues caused by a traumatic experience at a vulnerable time.

Running On

Breeders are not generally behaviourists, so while many are brilliant instinctive puppy-rearers, we cannot expect them invariably to be au fait with such matters as fear periods. Often a breeder will "run on" several pups from one litter, to see which is the best one for them to keep – which is not automatically the best puppy or the pick of the litter, but the best one for their purposes, be it show or work. The others then come onto the pet market at about four to six months old. This is, however, not the best time developmentally for puppies to change homes, and such puppies can be trickier to manage than if they had changed homes at a few weeks old. It is by no means impossible to make good dogs out of them, and usually they will have had the best of rearing, but if we decide to take on an older pup, we need to be aware that we are going to have to work harder to get the kind of behaviour we want. For instance, very young puppies want to follow us closely, so we can exploit that by teaching heel and recall at the age the puppy wants to be close to us anyway. The older puppy, like most adolescents, thinks it knows it all, and is far less ready to take direction, far less inclined to want to be with us, and far harder to train in close work. If several puppies have been run on in a way that means they live in a "gang" they may well be much less inclined to prefer human company over that of other dogs, or else they might have started to scrap between themselves and have not learned good dog manners. All of this can be overcome with consistent training, but it is as well to know what we are letting ourselves in for. It is also worth keeping in mind that older puppies have bigger mouths for causing damage, bigger feet for digging holes, and make bigger puddles and piles if they have not been house-trained. On the plus side, we have a much better idea of how the adult dog is going to look.

Preparation and Proofing

Assuming we have chosen our puppy, paid our deposit and will collect when it is ready to leave home, we need to prepare our own home and also make the transition as easy as we can for the puppy. Top of this list is consistency, so the whole family should be agreed on what is and what is not to be allowed, and what words are to be used to communicate training needs (it is no use trying to train a dog that "Sit" means "sit" and "Down" means "lie down" if one family member keeps saying "Sit Down"). We need to ensure either that the garden is securely fenced or that we have a secure area within the garden which the puppy can access as soon as it goes out of any door, that we have fenced off any areas that are precious to us, and any poisonous plants or trees, and also any areas where garden or vehicle chemicals are stored. Anti-freeze, slug pellets, insecticides, herbicides and cocoa mulch are all very dangerous to dogs, and it is better if the puppy cannot get at paint, preservatives, sharp implements or anything else that might hurt it. Inside the house, enclose electricity cables and furniture legs in plastic pipes, and start training the family into a philosophy of "put it away if you don't want it chewed". Decide where the puppy's day bed is going to be, and if you intend to crate-train, where you will put the crate.

Puppy Preparation

Many breeders will assist by allowing us to impregnate a cloth with our own scent which we then take to the breeder, who puts it in the puppy-pen. Thus the puppies get used to the scent of their new family (several different scents from different prospective owners does not present a problem) and then we can take the piece of material back with us when we bring the puppy home, and leave it in its bed. Thus the familiar scents of the litter and dam will be there to help the puppy's transition to its new home. It is best if the puppy is collected in the morning, so that it has all day to accustom itself to its new surroundings rather than undergoing a car journey and then being expected to sleep all night in a strange place.

Names

Choosing a name for our puppy can be fun, but also surprisingly difficult if different members of the family fix on different names. Sometimes we have to wait until the puppy comes home and suggests its own name by its personality, but it is best for the puppy if the name is ready and waiting and can be used from the moment it changes homes. Breeders will often help out by using the name as soon as the buyer has chosen it, and puppies familiarise very quickly to their names. The chosen name should be short and easy to say, ideally no more than two syllables, and should not sound like or shorten to anything you would be embarrassed to say in polite company. One day you may be calling your dog loudly in a public place, so keep that in mind. Nor should the name sound similar to a command (e.g. "Clown" and "Down"), or invite an unfortunate Spoonerism (try saying "Shane, Sit!"). Sometimes people like their dogs to have similar names, such as already owning Poppy and calling the new dog Moppy, but this is very confusing to the dogs and invites needless training problems. Ideally, in a multi-dog household, all dog names should sound completely different from each other.

House-Training

This is one of the most obvious ways that dogs have to learn to live with us, and a lot of misunderstanding between puppy and owner can arise. Dogs are programmed to keep their sleeping and eating areas clean, and that is all. They have no inborn understanding of "indoors" and "outdoors", nor of the revulsion we humans feel about bodily waste. If we have a puppy from a good breeder, it will be well on the way to being clean in its immediate environs, because even tiny whelps that do not yet have their eyes open properly will squirm off their bedding area to eliminate away from it. I have many times read that such young puppies cannot eliminate independently, and need their dam to stimulate bladder and bowels for them, and this is indeed the case for the first few days, but my own observations show that many of them can and do empty themselves without help very soon afterwards (see *Developmental Periods* above). So if the breeder has allowed a clear demarcation between sleeping and playing areas, most puppies will have learned to keep their bedding area clean by the time they come home with their new owners. This is not without the potential for problems though, if the puppies have only had access to one type of surface for elimination, because they may then find it difficult to change from their familiar surface. Substrate is very important to puppies, and those which have not been exposed to a variety of surfaces underfoot may always prefer one in particular. Therefore, if the puppy has been paper-trained, do not leave newspapers on the floor, or homework lying around, because as far as that puppy is concerned, paper is the most appealing substance to empty itself on. Although puppies favour soft absorbent surfaces from choice, those that have been kept in concrete-floored pens will often seek out concrete as a preferred surface. So the puppy that always wees on the kitchen tiles, the post lying on the doormat or the rug, is not being any kind of bad, but instead choosing the surface most like that which it has been accustomed to empty itself. Puppies that have learned to use a variety of substrate will always be easier to housetrain than those that have only one imprinted on them.

Puppies that have had no chance to get away from their own mess, for instance if they have been kept closely confined in a crate, can be difficult to housetrain, because the taboo about fouling their sleeping space has been breached. These are the puppies that will happily foul their beds and lie in the result, and it can take a long time to reprogramme them into using other areas. Here, owner vigilance is especially important, because very young puppies have little control over bladder or bowels, and little desire to "hold on" once they reach a level of fullness that causes them discomfort. Therefore successful house-training means that the owner should have the time and desire to observe the puppy closely when it is awake, and as soon as it shows signs of needing to void itself, it should be taken outside to its preferred surface. This might mean laying out a small area of newspaper, shavings, turf or soil and taking the puppy there each time, using the word we have chosen to associate with elimination. It might seem obvious, but we do need to be careful that the chosen words are not those that come up in ordinary conversation, or that are embarrassing in sensitive company (I confess I have failed with the latter). We need two words, one for bowel and one for bladder emptying, because while it is all undesirable to have in the house, to the puppy there is a vast difference between the two, and it is common for puppies to empty one way and not realise they need to see to the other as well. After it has performed, it should be praised, rewarded with a tiny but desirable food treat, and then allowed to play and explore for five to ten minutes before being taken indoors again. If this is not done, then puppies will start to hold onto their waste until they go back in the house, because being outside is a bit scary or exciting, depending on the puppy. The fearful pup may well be too nervous, and the bolder one too keen to explore, to achieve what we want, which is usually to get the elimination over with and go back indoors to whatever we were doing. Therefore we manipulate that by putting a lead on a puppy when we are outside so that it can't go too far away, and rewarding the desired result three times: praise, treat and play. The feeling of bodily relief is also a reward to the puppy so we need to be extra careful that it only gets this reward in the right place.

Beware the double-barrel effect, where a puppy will eliminate outside, come back in and immediately empty itself again indoors. Always give the puppy plenty of time to see to its second effort. If we know the puppy needs to empty itself but it is distracted at the wrong moment and then forgets and starts to play, take it indoors on the lead, count to five and go straight out again. This usually works well.

Industriousness and application is always rewarded when house-training. If we try to cut corners, we set the whole concept back. Therefore we never put the puppy out: we take it out. We then wait with it kindly and calmly, and are ready with the reward after it has done what we want. If we are lazy and just put the puppy out, we never know what has and has not been accomplished, and the puppy has not had the superb series of rewards that it gets with us, which again is counter-productive to getting reliable house-training.

Elimination is neither here nor there to us, but to dogs it is a very big deal indeed. It is communication: it says I Am Here to any other animals that may be about, it is the equivalent of a graffiti artist's "tag". And to a puppy newly removed from its mother and siblings, it is a dangerous thing to advertise its presence. I wouldn't like to add up the time I have spent, sometimes very uncomfortably, waiting outside for a puppy to perform, but this is vital time if we want a reliably house-trained dog in the future. We should not tut and tick and get annoyed, but try and project zen-like calm before the deed and share great joy afterwards. Puppies are very sensitive to our moods, and if we appear stroppy when we take it out, the puppy will become anxious, and may well associate elimination in front of us with us being out of temper. This often leads to elimination where we cannot see, and is the source of many an unwanted discovery behind the sofa. So we need to keep our mind on the ultimate objective, and our cunning and determination screwed to the sticking-post, which means always being a pleasant companion in front of whom it is absolutely fine to perform bodily functions. This by degrees will lead to that wonderful situation where you can take a dog to an appropriate place, say the words, get the desired result, and then, knowing your dog has emptied out, you can take it anywhere. It is endlessly useful being able to get elimination on command, and often more comfortable for the dog, too, which does not realise that it may be some time before it gets another opportunity.

Not only should we supply the preferred substrate to begin with, it is wise to have this in a sheltered area, for instance behind a beach windbreak or even under a garden table, for those occasions when the weather is inclement. Small wet cold miserable puppies just want to go back indoors, and while many will get the idea of emptying out quickly, others will refuse to, and we have the seeds of a future problem. Many adult dogs can be difficult about going outside in bad weather, but outside they must go; this is non-negotiable if we are to have a civilised dog that we can take anywhere. Therefore our part of the deal is to provide somewhere sufficiently comfortable. Comfort includes not being overlooked, even through a fence by passing people or dogs, because it takes very little to put a puppy off in the beginning. This is not being awkward; the puppy is genuinely anxious. Elimination makes it vulnerable both in the act and in the scent left behind, and this is a primitive programming geared to keeping puppies safe. Later, if we install what we want right from the beginning, we will have a reliably house-trained dog.

Timing

Expect to take a puppy out whenever it wakes up, and at any time it changes from one activity to another. After a play session, a bit of training, a meal, going from one room to another, if it has been with us in the kitchen and we now want to relax in the living-room – take the puppy outside first.

If the puppy has not been out for an hour, it needs to go out. If an hour is too long, cut back to half an hour. If a visitor is due, let them meet the puppy outside, because excitement can have a stimulating effect on bladder and bowels. If the puppy has had a fright, the same applies, because it involves the same hormones which are designed to empty out body waste in preparation for fight or flight. Happy excitement or scared excitement produces the same effect, and there is nothing the puppy can do about it. So take puppy outside before getting it excited, and try not to frighten it at all.

Accidents

A puppy that eliminates in the house is not being bad, awkward or anything else negative – it simply has not yet been fully trained. Most puppies will have "accidents" unless the owners are super-vigilant. If this happens, first put the puppy outside, then clean up with either white vinegar if the surface will stand it, or an enzymatic cleaner. Never use a cleaning agent with ammonia in it, because to a dog, the ammonia smells like urine and therefore encourages it to eliminate there again. Then chalk the incident up to experience and resolve to be more vigilant.

Training Pads

These are a bad idea. Training pads are made of soft material that is impregnated with scent that encourages your puppy to eliminate on the pad. Their use teaches your puppy that voiding itself indoors is acceptable. Once puppies get older, they find the pad makes an irresistible toy, so it tends to get carted around and shredded rather than used as the manufacturer intended. We need to be aware that, while it is all house-training to us, to a dog there is a huge difference between liquid and solid waste, and they don't like to do both in the same area. Therefore anyone using the training pads will need to leave several about, which again is teaching the pup that it can use the whole house as a latrine. For those of us who want a pup to go outside to empty itself, the puppy-pads are a non-starter. There are people who keep indoor dogs and who do intend for their pet to use a specific area inside the home rather than go outside, and in this case, two very large trays filled with turf, soil or cat litter, fixed so that they cannot be moved and not placed too close together for the reasons stated above, will probably be more successful than the puppy pads. This is because puppy pads feel similar in texture to carpet and soft furnishings, so the unwitting user is "training" the puppy to eliminate in exactly those places that we like to keep clean.

Doors

It is tempting to leave the back door open, or even have a dog-flap installed, so that we do not have to put ourselves to the trouble of taking the puppy outside at frequent intervals. However, this is not house-training the puppy, and very often it will be made plain to us as the colder weather draws in and doors need to be kept shut, that the puppy is not as house-trained as we thought it was. Then we have to go back to basics, but this time with a bigger dog that produces more waste, and usually one that has gone from the obliging pup to the unco-operative adolescent. The problem with dog-flaps is that our household insurance will not cover us if someone forces entry that way, and so they should be secured if we go out, and also at night. Again, the dog will not understand that it is supposed to wait until the flap works again before it can empty itself.

At Night

Successful house-training needs to be continued into the night, and the best way to do this is to have the puppy in the bedroom with us, or else we sleep in the puppy's quarters. If we do not want the puppy in the bedroom long-term, it is still all right to have it in the bedroom to begin with, because once it is well enough developed to last all night without needing to empty itself, its sleeping area can gradually be moved to the bedroom door, the landing and thence to wherever its permanent night quarters are to be. A puppy loose in the bedroom, however, is going to be counter-productive, because the puppy's mental programming is merely to eliminate away from its feeding and sleeping areas, and so this is likely to lead to an unpleasant encounter with a bare foot and a puppy "accident" later. So the puppy needs to be confined in some way, such as in a crate or a large cardboard box. Light sleepers will hear a puppy start to fidget because it needs to void itself, and then they can take it outside; heavier sleepers are recommended to set their alarm to wake them every three hours at first. Luckily, puppies acquire bladder and bowel control fairly quickly, and before long the alarm only needs to be set once. Until this time, we need to remember always that the puppy is not being dirty, awkward or stubborn if it has an "accident". It is a young animal and needs to be given the same consideration and tolerance as a human infant. Puppies cannot develop any faster than their bodies allow; some are clean almost from the start and others take longer. Like human young, they have little bowel and bladder control to begin with, are easily distracted from their eliminatory needs, and initially have a very short timespan between realising they need to empty out, and doing so. On the plus side, they mature much faster than human young, so the house-training stage, while wearisome, does not usually last all that long.

Leaky Valves

Some breeds are particularly known for lack of bladder control, and some individuals of any breed may be slow in developing sphincter control. Many puppies "leak" when excited, often filling the unwary shoe as they greet us, and there is also the issue of submissive urination, where anything from a few drops to a fountain is expelled to signal in dog terms that the puppy is young and not a threat. While not threatening to us, it can be an exasperating stage, but we should quell our irritation because the puppy is obeying its genes, not setting out to annoy us. Leaks from excitement and submissive urination are usually grown out of, though some dogs retain the tendency all their lives. A veterinary check is useful, as individual puppies can have incorrect urethral or sphincter development which may benefit from surgery, and some may have a simple urinary infection that is easily cured. Puppies that wet while they are sleeping are more likely to have physical issues as a cause.

Crate Training

Blessed is the breeder whose puppies are used to spending some time in a crate individually before they change homes, but such breeders are few. Proper crate-training is not essential to puppy-keeping, but it certainly makes some aspects much easier. The puppy in the crate is safe: it cannot chew our possessions, it gives us all a break from constant vigilance, gives other household pets some peace, and is the start to teaching the puppy a degree of self-reliance, so that we can leave it for periods of time without it becoming distressed. But we can't just bung a puppy in a crate, shut the door and walk away – we need to train the puppy not just to accept but to enjoy being in the crate. We need to make the crate the best place in the whole house for a puppy to be. Luckily, human cunning is up to this task.

The crate needs to be in a quiet place, where other animals can't get at it, and away from heavy human traffic passing to and fro. There should be the potential for keeping visitors away from the crate, because the puppy will not feel safe if staring, grinning faces and poking fingers can access it while it is crated and can't get away. At the same time, the puppy needs to see that someone is about, rather than being left in the crate in isolation. A blanket

Safely confined.

over the top of the crate creates a den-like feel and also partly obscures vision, so the puppy should only be able to see out of the door side. And, to begin with, this door should be left open.

Nice things should appear in the crate, such as snippets of food, and chew items, to make it always worth the puppy's while to go in there and check. An exceptionally warm and comfortable bed should fill it, so that it is the best place in the house for lying down. When the puppy falls asleep in other places, it should gently be placed in the crate, with the door left open, so that it wakes up there. These persuasions will soon have the puppy very happy to go into its crate, and then we can gradually introduce the concept of closing the door. We do this for very short periods of time to start with, and stay with the puppy doing something nice, such as feeding it bit by bit through the closed door. We can then sit with it for a minute or two, then open the door. Puppies usually accept the restriction of the closed door very well if it is introduced gradually. A very few puppies become claustrophobic and upset even with a gradual introduction to the closed door, and in these cases, a pen leading out from the crate is a better option. These can easily be created with wood and wire, or else from ready-made panels available from manufacturers of dog accessories. If we do go for the pen option, it is wise to place a turf tray at the furthest end of the pen in case of house-training mishaps, but this is not an alternative to house-training and we should still be committed to taking the puppy out as often as it needs to empty out.

Leaving the Puppy

Leading on from crate-training or pen-training, we introduce the concept of being left. This again needs to be gradual, and the puppy should be tired and comfortable before we start. Leaving a puppy chewing on something nice or settling down on a warm soft bed is psychologically a great deal easier for it than leaving a puppy that has become increasingly anxious about the going-out ritual of shoes and coat on, picking up keys, saying goodbye-be-a-good-dog and so on. Leaving is just something we do: out of the room and back in again before the puppy has a chance to fret. A radio left on softly in the background can be a great help, but it needs to be on frequently during the day so that its sound does not specifically herald our departure – dogs are so quick to pick up on this kind of link. We gradually accustom the puppy to our being out of the room it is in, but so that it can hear us moving around the rest of our home. From minutes, we build up to longer, going out of one door and back in at another a few minutes later, down the garden, into the car, starting the car, driving round the block, until the puppy is relaxed about being left alone. He must always have plenty of occupation at those times when we leave him, because he is still very young with a short attention span, and needs readily-available comfort from having a choice of things to do. It is worth consulting a vet who is familiar with safe calming treatments such as Adaptil diffusers or Bach Flower Remedies, because ideally our pup should never have the opportunity to become stressed at being left, rather than our trying to fight a rearguard action with burgeoning separation anxiety.

All too often people see the new puppy as a weekend exercise, and expect it to be sorted out in time for leaving it all day when they go to work. I do not apologise for emphasising once more the amount of work and attention a puppy needs, just as the equivalent small human would, and if we are not in a position to be home, have someone home, or arrange for someone reliable and dedicated to look after the puppy during those times when we have to be out for extended periods, then we are not at the right time in our lives to have a puppy. Yes a dog has to fit in with our lives, but a puppy means we have to address its needs before our own if we are not to raise a flawed and unhappy dog. Careful introduction to being alone will pay dividends all the dog's life, and it is well worth spending a lot of time in the initial stages.

Teething

Puppies teethe, and when they do, they need to chew. If we do not give them plenty of safe items to chew, while at the same time protecting those of our possessions that we do not want chewed, then the puppy will damage our property. Puppies have no concept of what they should or should not chew, only what will feel nice in the mouth and what does not feel so good. Some items sold as chews by pet shops often appeal to human eyes but not to puppy mouths. If a puppy can chew something it will; it is not being bad or spiteful: it is fulfilling a compelling need.

There are two main teething periods in a puppy's development. The first starts with the shedding of milk teeth from about four months old, and the next deals with setting the permanent teeth in the jaw at about a year. These times vary according to the individual puppy. Many breeds have a further chewing period at eighteen months or so, which is short but very intense, and a few breeds, notably Labradors, remain inclined to chew for their whole lifetime. To preserve both our homes and our sanity during these spells, we need to arrange the puppy's accommodation so that it cannot get at anything valuable or dangerous, while supplying a variety of safe chew items. Chewing is not just about teeth: it releases endorphins and so is a comforting behaviour. Chewing relaxes and is pleasantly tiring, so it is a useful behaviour to direct in an appropriate way: we should not attempt to stop it. Safe chew items include deer antler, cardboard boxes without staples, big raw vegetables, the bigger the better, and raw meaty bones (See Chapter Five). Unsafe ones include maize cobs, rawhide chews and cooked bones – never give these. Protect your own home by hiding electrical wires and furniture legs inside strong plastic tubing, and training the family to close doors and keep possessions out of puppy reach. It may seem for a while as if you are living with a furry chainsaw, but the extreme intensity does pass with most dogs, though providing safe chew items should be a lifetime task, as most adult dogs feel better for chewing from time to time.

Socialising Classes

Nowadays we are more aware of the importance of socialising our puppies during the fairly brief time that they are receptive to new experiences. It is extremely important to give the right kind of socialising, though, and this path is strewn with hazards. Many "Puppy Socialising" classes, while held with the best of intentions, are exactly what we do not want our puppies to experience, and it is easy to set our puppies up for failure and all sorts of behavioural problems by exposing them to the wrong classes.

Because the socialising period is so short, one class a week does not give many opportunities for our puppies to be exposed to learning; it would be much better to have a class every day for two weeks than once a week for twelve weeks. This allows time for latent learning, because puppies learn at different rates. Ideally, each class should be at a different venue, so that the puppies can feel, smell, hear and see different surfaces and backgrounds while they learn, but this is hard to achieve and we will probably have to compromise with this one. I have heard it suggested that each class should be held in a different home, which from a puppy point of view would be a great learning experience, but from a householder point of view would be a potential disaster, because not everyone is vigilant and on the ball to prevent "accidents", and excited puppies need to pee and poo even more than is normal. Stress and tension in humans resulting from this does not make a good atmosphere for puppy learning.

Size Matters

Puppies in class should be carefully grouped for size and age to avoid injury. In a litter, puppies are the same size, have the same motivations and characteristics, and have interacted with each other right from the first independent breath. But a random group of puppies making up a class may be very different in size, and a Labrador pup bouncing on a Chihuahua of the same age the way it would with its own siblings would be likely to cause injury. Some breeds are naturally feistier and some naturally shyer than others; confident puppies should not be allowed to bully less confident ones. Aloof breeds should not be forced into interaction with either people or other puppies; indeed no interaction should be forced at all, and if a puppy wants to spend its classes under its owner's chair, it should be allowed to do that. We often have well-meaning jolly-hockey-sticks types of trainers who think shy puppies are better to be pushed into being with the others, but this is dangerously counterproductive. Shy puppies "shut down" if out of their depth in a situation, which "jolly" people can mistake for them being "fine with the others now". They are very much not fine: they have gone into a defensive behaviour out of which they may explode if pushed too far. Some dogs develop into shut-down as default mode, and it is impossible to train them when they are in this condition. Long-term, the dog may well become susceptible to certain types of illness, and vets are beginning to recognise the link between psychological upset and physical disturbance. So the puppy class should make allowances for shy puppies, and let them come out of their shells in their own time. This may take weeks, or even a second run of classes, but the puppy should always drive the schedule if damage is to be avoided.

The Bully

Bullying is rife in the wrong sort of puppy classes, and very seldom seen for what it is, instead being thought of as boisterous play. Some breeds are more prone to bullying behaviour than others, and within their peer group, little comes of it, but within a mixed-breed class, some puppies will seek out others and bully them. The astute trainer stops this at once, and should be prepared to move puppies with a tendency to bullying behaviour into a different class if necessary. Bullying is as bad for the bully as for the bullied, and very difficult for the bully's owner. Bullying releases a potent cocktail of hormones, and bullying dogs quickly become addicted to the buzz they get from intimidating weaker, smaller or gentler puppies. They then take this behaviour out into the real world, with predictable results. I have many times deflected potential bullying behaviour towards my own dogs and been told, "He needs someone to teach him a lesson". Indeed he does, but that someone should be his owner, and with professional help if necessary. People do not get their pet dogs in order to train other people's, and it is irresponsible to risk turning an amiable dog into a fighter. Bullies pick on the weak, and adults can be very astute at judging which dogs they can tackle without fear of retribution, but they can also get it wrong, and this is visiting one person's problem on another. Bullies cannot be retrained but they can be managed; so many people inadvertently end up with a bullying dog whose behaviour started in puppy-classes, but that does not mean we have to put up with it. What's done is done; better never started, but so many behaviour issues begin by happenstance (see also Chapter Six). Back to the puppy class, for which the most important members are just about to be discussed, and it is a rare puppy class that has them.

The Grown-Up World

Puppies know how to be puppies. What they have to learn is how to behave in our world, and with adult dogs. Most puppies never meet an adult dog apart from their mother, and badly-reared puppies may not get proper mothering at all, which includes being taught manners. After the first few weeks, most bitches from choice do not spend a great deal of time with their litters, but they do drop by, feed and clean, snuggle and interact with them several times a day. Some bitches are indulgent mothers, others are stricter, but the puppies learn to mind their manners in response to soft growls and air-snaps. Obstreperous puppies may be held down with a nose or paw, or receive a soft but firm mouth-hold across their muzzles. The ideal puppy class contains a few adult dogs which are used to puppies, maybe from having raised a litter of their own or else having lived in a household where they have met puppies. Many adult dogs, especially males, do not know what on earth to do with a puppy, while others are naturals. Older puppies, those dogs that might look adult but are still maturing, are not good for training younger puppies either, for they often see the very young puppy as a squeaky toy. The puppies being trained need exposure to calm adult dogs which do not fear or dislike them, not those which will allow all sorts of liberties of the ear-chewing or tail-pulling kind. Instead they should meet well-adjusted dogs of either sex who will tolerate polite interaction but warn off any puppy that forgets its manners. This is the ideal way for puppies to begin to be socialised with other dogs. Outside in the real world, our puppy will unfortunately have to meet badly-socialised and unruly dogs, so the importance of its first experiences around adult dogs being positive ones cannot be overstated. With the assistance of trainers who keep an eye on everything that is going on and explain what they are doing and why, and the input of well-adjusted adult dogs, owners can help their puppies bloom into confident, likeable, well-rounded animals. Along with dog manners, these are the classes that should be teaching mannerly greetings to people, settling down when told, controlling excitement, polite lead-walking and recall. Those classes that just allow puppies to jump all over other puppies are a waste of time and money.

World Manners

In the first weeks of a puppy's life, they have so much to encounter, but they are too vulnerable to be left to deal with things themselves. Assuming that the breeder has started them off on a socialising programme, new owners have a sound base to build upon, but there is still an awesome amount of work to do, and early on, our day and night has to revolve around the puppy. Ideally, the pup needs to encounter as much in the way of pleasant new experiences as we can give it. Inevitably some of these experiences may go wrong, and it is our responsibility to protect the puppy from anything very nasty, while allowing it to experience small unpleasantnesses. For instance, it is just as well if we don't let it eat a wasp, but letting it play and take the odd tumble on rough ground, getting wet and mucky, is a necessity. If it goes up to an adult dog and gets growled at, that is fine, but avoid the kind of dog that is going to pick it up and shake it. Puppies are programmed to scream blue murder if another dog threatens them or gets hold of them, and this is designed to make that other dog let go and back off, whereupon if our relationship is sound, our sobbing puppy will run to us for comfort, which should be given unstintingly. However, not all adult dogs pull their punches, and a lamentable few may be so excited by the puppy's cries that they push on into injuring it, so we must control all interactions with adult dogs, and never believe other owners who say their dog loves puppies and only wants to play, because they mostly don't and it isn't play.

Approach and Meeting

Surprising as it may seem, socialising is not about teaching puppies that the world is their friend. Our aim instead should be to have a puppy, and thus a dog, that politely ignores other dogs and people unless those dogs and people want to interact. Whether such interaction is to be allowed should be the owner's choice not the puppy's. We must always bear in mind that some people are frightened of or antagonistic towards dogs, that other dogs may have a raft of reasons for not wanting to be charged at and bounced all over, and that an amazing amount of damage can be done by uncontrolled interaction, both physical and psychological, in a very short time. Mannerly dogs exchange a lot of body-language before they ever get to touching distance: they never charge at each other and try to knock each other over. Most dogs go through a stage in adolescence where their manners disappear, and this is the time for owners to take strong control over any kind of meeting and greeting behaviour until the young dog has grown out of teenage pushiness. The message is "you can only meet and greet other dogs and people if you display good manners". For many dogs, a calm reminder is enough, but for others this developmental stage means temporarily keeping them away from any meetings because they become too dizzy to take direction. This is not for ever: it takes as long as it takes for the impolite young dog to grow out of its challenging behaviour, which is weeks for some and months for others. Reinforcement by practice of an unwanted behaviour is the last thing we want, so we have to take a step back and prevent it. Remember that even unwanted attention is better in the dog's mind than no attention, so even though the youngster is the only party enjoying itself when it charges up to another dog and threatens it, the accelerated reactions of the people involved and that other dog give the miscreant great pleasure. This is a "zero tolerance" matter: the dog must never be allowed to do this, because the more it does, the more it will, and it is totally unacceptable. The culmination of such behaviour may be injury to any of the dogs and people involved (there is a leg fracture in humans commonly known as a "dog walker's fracture") and almost always an exchange of owner opinions that may be loud and judgemental. So until the dog has learned the right way to approach others, the human side of the arrangement needs to keep a good lookout for potential targets and get the dog back on the lead before it reacts. Then – so important and so often forgotten – the dog needs to be rewarded lavishly for being calm. The dogs may meet under strict control, and the nanosecond that behaviour looks like deteriorating into loutishness, they should be parted, gently, quietly, firmly and non-confrontationally. We do not improve the situation with raised voices.

Similarly, the dog needs to be taught that there is only one way to greet people, and that is with "four on the floor". Jumping up at people, grabbing their hands, tearing at their clothing, is absolutely not on. Which is why the last kind of puppy class we should go to is one where the puppy learns that every human hand holds titbits, and every pocket has treats in it. We do not want our puppies to run up to every person they meet and expect a welcome, food and caressing. We do want our puppies to walk past people confidently and quietly. If we stop to chat, we would like our dog to stay with us calmly and patiently. Thus the good puppy class includes "stooge" adult dogs and people that the puppy learns to ignore. Only the owner should be the source of pleasant experiences, and this is the root of the best recall as well as desirable manners.

Learning by Age

It is all too tempting to "hothouse" puppies because we want the best possible adult dog, but development can only be directed by the puppy, and while we can accept this with physical development, it often requires a pause-and-think to understand that mental development comes in stages too. In effect, we need to remember that when a puppy is in kindergarten, we should not be expecting it to produce responses at PhD level. However, we can make a good fist of teaching it kindergarten things, which will later prove good preparation for more complex skills.

Very young puppies have short attention spans, and live mostly in the present. They want to be with us, and this is the time that we build exercises that align with this, such as recall, heel work, lead-training and retrieving. Behaviourally, the puppy is heavily reliant on us for protection, entertainment and guidance, but it is still a puppy and can only communicate as a puppy. This means that behaviour such as mouthing, which in many breeds can escalate to quite painful biting, barking, jumping up or pulling at our clothes for attention is normal for the puppy because we haven't yet shown it better ways. And we must keep our side of the arrangement too, and give the puppy the right kind of attention when it asks in a way we find more acceptable, for instance by sitting in front of us and making eye contact. The puppy is father of the dog, and if we teach puppies the behaviour we want, or by accident, behaviour we don't want, that will be carried through into the adult dog. Whatever we teach the puppy, we need to be aware of the dog it will become, and if the thought of a slavering beast standing at the table looming over your dinner is off-putting, don't feed the puppy from your plate during your own meal.

Pre-empting is our starting point. By taking on a puppy, we effectively commit ourselves to a huge investment in time, because we start with an infant that we are bringing through life stages to adulthood. Once we have this idea in place, the amount of time we have to devote to teaching manners becomes more agreeable. We can't just take the batteries out of them when we are tired, out of sorts or have other tasks in mind – the puppy's needs always come first. So when the puppy asks for attention in a way we don't like, our first understanding is that we have not been giving it enough attention at that time. If it has had its food, had a nap, been outside, it has used up all its own resources and needs something to do. This is why we provide it with items it can rip up or work with on its own, preferably before it asks, to teach it the beginnings of self-reliance. To a puppy, the world is its toy, so if you aren't pleased that it has turned out the laundry basket, recollect that this is a human failing in not keeping the laundry basket out of bounds and not providing the puppy with something acceptable for its amusement.

Then we need to show the puppy how we would like it to ask for attention, and this is the equivalent of teaching a child the difference between "Please may I" and "Gimme". Very young puppies "sit" almost as default mode; they often run up to us and tumble over into a "sit" because their centre of gravity encourages it. Even breeds that find "sit" rather difficult as adults can manage easily when they are small puppies. So when a puppy charges up and stops abruptly into anything resembling "sit", reward it with food, a caress or a kind voice, but most of all by giving it attention of the right kind – which is quiet, interactive, and offers it something to do. A minute or so of interaction, then a suitable toy that it can play with by itself, rewards the polite approach, and they very soon learn it.

By asking for attention, the puppy is not being rude, manipulative, dominant or any other negative epithet we might consider. It has a need and it is looking to us to meet it. If it is hungry or has to go outside to be clean, then we are fortunate to have such a communicative puppy. Seeking attention is not a bad behaviour either, because attention is something it needs as well. It might be less obvious than physical needs, but it is every bit as important. After we have reared a few puppies, attention-getting happens less and less because we learn to identify the next need and pre-empt it by providing it before we are asked. But at first we have to establish lines of communication, so that the puppy learns to "whisper" instead of "shout". Here's how to manage the impolite approaches.

Mouthing

Dogs are a very mouth-oriented species, and those breeds created to retrieve can be extra strong in this respect. Their genes create the feeling of great satisfaction when they have something in their mouths, and it feels right to them. But we do not like being grabbed by those needle teeth. From the puppy's point of view, mouthing gives great results, because we make a noise, pull away, flap around and even bleed sometimes. So a bored puppy that is mouthing at us for attention is getting exactly that, with a side-dish of excitement if we really carry on at them. Very mouthy breeds often use their jaws as a first option for anything, simply because the feeling is so satisfying to them. So we have to understand that mouthing does not come from a desire to hurt us, and if the puppy starts with a nudge and escalates to a bite, then a harder bite, to gain our attention, it is because we have not yet taught it a more acceptable way of interacting with us.

Many such puppies go through a stage where they have very little self-control, so we use management until they grow up more and develop it. We reduce the temptation of flapping sleeves and trouser legs by dressing in a more puppy-proof manner, even if it does mean tucking trouser bottoms into socks for the while, and when the little monster gets that look in its eyes, we pre-empt by putting a toy in its mouth instead. This means being prepared by having suitable toys around the home at a level the pup can neither see nor get at, so there is always something to hand. Each pup has trigger areas, such as by the front door where people appear and disappear accompanied by noise and excitement, and we can learn these and make sure we always have a toy within our reach. It does not mean spending a fortune on pet-shop toys unless we want to, as strips cut from an old fleece can be plaited and knotted to give something that fits nicely as a mouth toy even for large breeds. At first it is as if we are always behind the action, but soon we are able to get the puppy to "sit" or at least be calm in order to be given this toy. "Calm" is the watchword, and if we want a well-mannered dog, we do not do anything that involves getting it excited, particularly not rough-and-tumble games with other humans. This is the surest way I know to teach a pup that people can be mouthed and jumped all over; it gives all the wrong messages and creates a lot of potential for trouble later. Sometimes other people can be a dog's worst enemy in this respect, and as soon as the owner is out of sight, they are playing power games with the puppy, getting it over-excited and effectively teaching it all the things we don't want it to do. If you have people in your life that cannot be trusted to behave properly around a puppy (and I certainly have some in mine) make sure you never give them the chance to ruin your puppy's manners, even if that means seeing to it that they don't meet. The equivalent of "tears before bedtime" people just love to razz a puppy up and then walk away leaving the hapless owner with the equivalent of nuclear fallout in excitement terms, because all that adrenaline has to go somewhere and it is only dispelled by physical activity. With older dogs that have learned self-control, we can if we choose utilise higher levels of excitement to give performance in whatever discipline we need it, but it is not something to bring out in puppies. Puppies need to learn that we are delicate creatures, untouchable by tooth, and that all good things cease if this happens. But we must not forget the other half of the training equation, which is to ensure that a polite approach always results in the right kind of attention. Even if the puppy has just nipped us, and then recollected itself, let go and offered a "sit" or similar, we should reward the wanted behaviour as soon as it occurs, and not loiter in the past being annoyed about the nip. It can be a rocky road with some mouthy puppies, but if we are utterly consistent, the behaviour is straightforward to re-programme.

Parading

Once the dog has proceeded past the mouthing stage, it often redirects to toys to such good effect that it comes to greet you with a toy already in its mouth. This is called "parading" and should be seen as the lovely greeting it is. The dog does not want you to take the toy, but would like you to acknowledge it. Some dogs parade even though they have never mouthed. Predictably, trainers locked into dominance theory would have it that parading is "alpha" and is a kind of canine jeering that the dog has a toy and you do not, but anyone seeing the dog's soft benign body-language realises that it is a kindly interaction not a challenge.

Chewing

All puppies chew, and many adult dogs too. We manage this because the dog needs to do it – chewing is very much a part of normal development and indeed is essential at teething times. Chewing releases endorphins and so is a major comforter. There are many objects in our homes that we don't want chewed, but the puppy has no knowledge of anything being valuable to us or dangerous to it. So we need to protect the puppy and our possessions by ensuring that each is safe from the other. We also need to provide adequate safe items for the puppy to chew (see above). Some breeds are destructive by nature, and their version of play is to shred every toy they get. This is not wrong: this is how they like to use their toys. It is therefore far better to find them an array of inexpensive items that they can destroy without harming themselves, because they are never going to "learn" to treat their toys another way. Other dogs are gentle with their toys, and a number will keep the same soft toys all their lives, with only minor nibbles to edges or labels.

We should not expect the puppy to differentiate between our possessions and its own toys. If something looks as if it would be pleasant to chew, it

Loving the hand that feeds you.

will be. It is pointless our stressing about a shredded doormat when it was obviously a great deal more fun to chew at that moment than anything else the puppy could reach. Puppies teach the family to be tidy or rue the day! Everything we don't want chewed should be put where the puppy can't get at it, and in the case of furniture, either the puppy is never left unsupervised near the Chippendale chairs, or it is kept out of certain places until it grows out of its phases. Some dogs take to gnawing walls and doorsteps if not given more appropriate release for their need; while the house damage can be mended, the adult teeth cannot. Plenty of safe chewing and mental exercise will reduce this need in most dogs unless it is a stress response in which case all bets are off, and prevention by management is key. Indoors, baby gates and crates are very helpful, and there is no reason why a kennel and proper run out of doors cannot be used as an alternative for those times when we cannot concentrate on the puppy (put the weldmesh on the inside of the run so that wood cannot be chewed). Bad-tasting sprays added to furniture etc. may distract some pups from chewing as long as they are given other items they can gnaw, but others will regard it as a condiment. It is no good shouting, flapping, punishing or bearing a grudge if a pup chews something of ours: they have no idea what the matter is and we simply frighten them. The way to address chewing is to understand that it is normal, provide a variety of safe items to chew alongside plenty of other occupation, and keep our own possessions out of reach of the pup.

Tugging

Behaviour trainers are divided over the value of playing tug games, and the decider should be what jobs you want the dog to do. With those that have to retrieve game for a living, such as gundogs or working sighthounds, it is better that they learn to release whatever they have in their mouths as soon as a human hand touches it. With police and military dogs, a soft mouth is not needed and the training reward is often a game of tug. With pet dogs too, tugging is often very rewarding, because it combines the pleasure of the bite with pulling and shaking. If you do decide to use tug games as the potent reward that they are, make sure the dog knows that teeth are never to touch hands, and if they do, the game stops right then and the human walks away. Dominance trainers say that the dog should never be allowed to "win" a game of tug, but this again is reading something human into something dog. It is perfectly fine and very rewarding to the dog if it is allowed to keep the tug toy once the human has decided the game is over. Tug games should never last for long, and care must be taken not to damage the dog's teeth particularly at the stage when they are shedding deciduous teeth and getting their adult mouths. With small pups, be very careful not to use too much strength, and with any dog at any age, be aware of the pressure being experienced by the neck vertebrae.

Stealing

Puppies will help themselves to anything interesting, and this is not stealing because dogs have no concept of property except that whatever is in their mouths is theirs, so the astute puppy owner learns to put everything away. Some dogs are extraordinarily athletic, and can reach items we might have thought were safely put away. Others can use their paws to great effect, opening doors we might have thought were safely closed. Certain items, such as the rubbish bin and the laundry basket, contain a plethora of deliciously smelling and therefore rewarding treasures that just beg a dog to investigate. In each case, we waste our time if we think we can train the dog not to touch, and have total effectiveness if we learn to shut doors and put temptation out of the dog's reach. Stealing is also a great attention-getter, even if the attention is somewhat negative. If we teach our puppies to retrieve, then they will bring items to us and get a reward, rather than tearing off down the garden with them or even being frightened into swallowing what they have in their mouths if we turn hostile. If we teach puppies to "swap" what they have in their mouths for a higher-value item, then they will happily bring whatever they have to us for a better swap. Thus human cunning and manipulation once again wins the day.

Time-Out

Correctly done, the time-out is very effective when the dog produces unwanted behaviour. We can time-out the puppy by removing it from the room, or time-out ourselves by leaving the room so that the puppy loses our company. Time-outs should instantly follow the unwanted action, and be no longer than ten seconds. Any longer means the dog will adapt to the new situation and look for occupation, rather than linking the time-out with the last behaviour it displayed. Depriving a dog of our company should not be underrated as an aversive, and very sensitive dogs might only need a five-second separation. When we time-out, we should say nothing and avoid eye contact, as the message we give is that no interaction will result from the unwanted behaviour. To begin with, we might feel as if we are constantly up and down, but if we are consistent, the dog rapidly learns to avoid the undesired behaviour. Again, it is essential for us to show the dog what alternative behaviour we want and then reward it; simply giving a time-out is only half the task and will produce only half the result.

Star Charts

Involving children in puppy-training is useful learning for them, but again needs to be geared to the age of the child as well as the age of the puppy. Children have little decision-making power in their own lives and so being in charge of a puppy tempts some into bossiness. The puppy should not be seen as a soft toy, or a machine that obeys when buttons are pressed, and it is better that all training is conducted by the adults involved, as it is all too easy to bore a puppy into resentment or misery by repeating commands, or even its name, endlessly. Instead, children have a valuable potential as "best friends" which does not mean being all over the puppy physically, or ordering it about, but being on-side with helping it succeed. Children are our best helpers in making occupational toys for puppies and older dogs, (see Chapter Three) and can also have great fun compiling star charts for progress, measuring growth, and being in charge of such matters as clean water dishes.

Older Puppies and Adolescence

Puppyhood does not end with the eruption of second teeth. Most breeds can be considered puppies until two years old, giant breeds being immature until three or even four. Adolescence starts at around six months, and is a

Older puppies.

rocky ride with most puppies, so we need to hold on to our mental picture of the finished article, the grown dog, which will appear at the end of this process. Adolescence is better looked back at than gone through, and each puppy presents us with different challenges as its brain rewires from self-centred puppy through boundary-testing youth and comes out (I promise!) at the other end as a co-operative animal. The more work done with the puppy before adolescence, the less is needed once it comes out of it. We need enormous patience, and it is helpful if we hold onto the thought that the youngster is not deliberately trying to annoy us. Testing boundaries is what adolescents do, and it is not a time for us to try and fine-tune various exercises and disciplines, or introduce complex new ones. Adolescence tails off gradually: the challenging behaviours reduce in frequency and potency until one day the clouds will clear and the dog we always wanted will be there.

At the same time that Scott and Fuller were conducting groundbreaking research into puppy developmental phases, Clarence Pfaffenberger was formulating a series of tests to be conducted on very young puppies in order to determine their characters and suitability for training. Their work is well worth reading, but with a critical eye, as our understanding of dog behaviour has come on a long way since these mid-20th century experiments.

Chapter Eight

Aberrant Behaviour Analysis

Reasons and Remedies

WHEN WE SEEK to change a dog's behaviour for whatever reason, we need to be objective, analytical, and free from emotions and pride. This last part can be really hard, because it is natural for us to see matters from our own point of view, and we have to turn situations around in order to see them from the dog's side instead. We need to accept that the dog is not being dominant, stupid, stubborn, nasty, vengeful or anything else – it is taking the action that seems most likely to bring it what it wants. If we change our mindset so that we are not looking at "good" or "bad" behaviour, instead seeing it purely as "behaviour", we can then alter our understanding so that we have "wanted" and "unwanted" behaviour. This gives us a chance to breathe out and relax; instead of taking everything personally and so getting annoyed at the dog, we can see the behaviour clearly, and behind it, the reasons for it, which is the base for creating change successfully. Because, like an alcoholic starting rehabilitation – the dog has to really want to change. For the dog to want to change, when after all the behaviour it offered was perfectly reasonable to it and brought the results it wanted, we have to provide a better reward for it than the unwanted behaviour does, and we need a good answer to the dog's unspoken question, "What's in it for me?".

Analysis

We have to look at behaviour holistically, i.e. the whole dog, its lifestyle, genetic predispositions, health, motivation, history and environment. We may not know all of these things, especially if we have a second-hand dog, but we can take an educated guess. Sometimes, like a good detective, we take the "crime" and work backwards to the dog, and sometimes we look at the dog and move forwards into predictable behaviour. But first we need to see the bigger picture before we start to trim behaviour down into stages that we can tackle. Again, it is human nature to look for a single cause, but in practice, a single unwanted behaviour often has several causes. We need to find all the causes if we are to succeed.

Health

We cannot embark on a successful programme of behaviour modification if the root cause is ill health: we have to restore health as much as possible before we start to train, and where we cannot do this, we need to trim our sails and settle for what can be trained and what must be managed. Physical and mental health are entwined with each other, and often when a behaviour has a physical cause, dealing with that will improve the behaviour without very much else being done. A dog that is ill, in pain, or taking medication that affects its mind, cannot be expected to change the behaviour that it has chosen as a coping mechanism without help. First we need to improve its circumstances, and the behavioural changes can then follow. We cannot work outside the dog's own abilities. Therefore our first port of call is the vet.

Check-Up

The behavioural check-up is a little different from the standard clinical one, and unless we specifically ask, certain aspects may not be included. The whole dog needs to be checked: sight, hearing (for which the BAER* test currently gives the most detailed results) teeth, bloods for organ function to include a full thyroid profile, because the normal test is not comprehensive enough, faeces, urine, skeleton, joints, skin, feet, nails, and for male dogs, castrated or entire, a prostate check. If the dog is taking medication, then with the help of the vet, side-effects of that medication should be fully investigated, especially if more than one medication is being prescribed and there is a chance those drugs might be interacting to produce a behavioural result (see Chapter Six). There is often a spit-the-tea-out moment when assessing a dog at the start of a behavioural consultation to hear a throwaway remark on the lines of the dog is taking medication for epilepsy, or is on steroids, or has a plated fracture, or any one of so many similar pieces of information that are neither here nor there to the owner but provide a vital key to aberrant behaviour. Similarly, a dog with house-training issues may have a urinary tract infection or be suffering from surgically-induced incontinence, for instance as the result of spaying, or have a physical deformity that affects its sphincter control. This is why veterinary input is vital, and why many behaviour trainers will not see a dog until the vet has provided a clean bill of health. Vets themselves do not always make the link about what is to them a "cured" condition, such as a healed fracture, which is actually still causing behavioural issues because it is giving the dog pain, impeding its ability to run, or making it feel vulnerable, or else that popularly-prescribed drugs may be creating behavioural side-effects of which the vet is unaware. Manufacturers do list a complete range of side-effects and caveats in their "small print", so it is always worth researching these, and then discussing options with the vet. though we need to remember that behavioural responses to drugs are still the "poor relation" so far as medicine is concerned, and has been studied far less. This is as much due to the greater difficulty of studying behaviour in comparison to physical side-effects as it is to underestimating the importance of a behavioural presentation at all. Most drug-related studies continue to be conducted on laboratory animals, and we know that dogs do not always display normal behaviour under these conditions in any case. Only vets can prescribe or change medication, conduct tests or recommend treatment; no matter how experienced the behaviour trainer, they are not allowed by law to get involved in veterinary matters, so it is very important to have the vet involved with and supportive of their fellow professional in order to get the best results.

Vulnerability
Ailing dogs feel vulnerable, and according to inborn disposition, they may react defensively, offensively, or shut down and try to become invisible. It is commonly assumed that broken bones heal "as good as new" and it is not until one has a bad fracture oneself that the truth comes out – some healed fractures always hurt, and some of those hurt a lot, especially those with metal in them. The level of pain may change according to the weather, temperatures, air pressure and humidity, so the dog may be "grumpy" some days and "fine" on others. Blind, partially-sighted, deaf and reduced-hearing dogs all feel vulnerable, and are regarded as lesser beings by dogs that have all their faculties. Dogs on mind-altering drugs may appear to be quiet and so "better" – but are they better or are they confused? Steroids can cause marked behavioural changes, some rather alarming, but they are very commonly prescribed, and sometimes are the only treatment available for a particular condition. Dogs that are taking medication smell different and often act differently from dogs that are not, and other dogs don't like it. Amputees move strangely and are unable to run and turn like healthy dogs. Social animals respond to weakness, sickness or "difference" by ignoring, threatening or attacking, and this can happen under our noses in our

own homes, and go unnoticed until it escalates into a full-on attack that causes damage. After that, the matter is not over, because one dog will feel vulnerable and the other may be considering a repeat performance. Dogs can and do become "depressed" as a result of some medication, when the dog feels poorly or disoriented and therefore shuts down so as not to attract attention. This can easily be written off as "getting older" or even "getting better" by us (if the challenging behaviour has disappeared), if we are not looking at the wider picture. This is why it is vitally important for vet, owner and behaviour trainer to work together.

Diet

Though this is covered in detail in Chapter Five, it is worth reiterating here that an important part of any behavioural consultation is to identify what, how, when and where the dog is being fed, and whether it feels safe when it eats.

Genetics

Assuming a clean bill of health, we need to look at the original task of the dog breed/breed mix in front of us, because that gives us specific information about its drives and responses. We cannot alter these any more than we can change the dog's coat or the shape of its head, so we have to work within their restrictions, and find ways of supplying those things that the dog finds rewarding. We cannot make a dog food, toy or action-oriented if by genetics it has no interest in those things. We cannot make a dog bold if it is shy, effusive if it is reserved or co-operative if it is aloof. We need to work with that particular dog's needs, drives and abilities, because that is all the dog has to work with. It can only improve itself within its inborn parameters: it cannot become a different dog.

Previous Dogs

So often when assessing a dog for behaviour work, we are told that the owner has had many dogs before, and none has displayed this particular behaviour. This is partly an understandable human response in that owners are anxious to confirm that they have experience with dogs, are not ignorant or at fault, and that the dog is unusual because it has not conformed to the expected pattern. Nobody wants to be thought of as an inadequate owner – but no proper behaviour consultant would think that way in any case. Most behaviour issues are due to misunderstanding and miscommunication, and the role of the behaviour trainer is to rectify those discrepancies. However, what needs to be understood from the start is that we must train the dog in front of us, not any previous dogs or any future dogs. This dog here and now is the one that needs the help. None of us will ever know it all, and each dog brings new challenges no matter how experienced we are. As a starting point, we need to leave those previous dogs – especially those childhood dogs – behind us, and look at the one which needs our help now.

Environment
Dogs are extremely sensitive to their environment. Small changes to us can be huge changes to the dog, and big upheavals in our lives can be colossal to our dogs. If a behaviour has started suddenly, and there are no health issues behind it, we next need to look at what may have happened in the environment to trigger that change. When we do so, we must include all the dog's senses, for changes in sound, touch or scent are every bit as important to the dog as the more visual ones that catch human attention. Let's start with changes in the home.

Layout and Surfaces
While we may not have the dog at the forefront of our thoughts when we decorate our homes, we need to understand that certain aspects of house layout and surfaces can be problematical to the dog. Tight enclosed spaces are stressful at an instinctive level, especially when entry and exit are not clear. For instance, a small crowded utility room, through which the dog has to pass in order to go to and from the garden, can cause fear because the dog feels trapped. Dogs like clear paths through, and are very much concerned where there is the possibility of being cornered. This applies whether or not anything unpleasant has actually happened, because the need for a safe space "bubble" is important to all dogs. Space isn't just about visual matters either, and I have treated a number of dogs for fear issues where the deciding factor was the noise and vibration made by the washing machine that the dog had to go round in order to get outside. Sometimes dogs have even been shut in kitchens or utility rooms with domestic machinery working, and while some take no notice, others are extremely frightened. Similarly, cluttered rooms where the dog cannot pass through with ease can cause tension, which might never increase to anything serious, or might be enough to tip a reactive dog over the edge, particularly if there are other stressors in its everyday life. When you aren't even safe at home, life is pretty grim. Mirrors, and figurines with big staring eyes can also freak out sensitive dogs, while others seem to take no notice. One of the reasons dogs persistently get onto furniture is so that they are not as enclosed as they are at ground level. Given that, it may seem puzzling that frightened dogs will seek out small dark spaces to hide in, but there is a crucial difference in that, in the places they choose, they can control what else enters that space because they are backed up against a dead-end and facing the only way in and out. A lot of people when in strange places instinctively choose to sit with their back to the wall and facing the door too, and this preference has the same primitive basis. But having to traverse narrow places is another subject entirely in the

dog's mind, and many fearful dogs feel much better once they have had these spaces opened out.

We don't always give enough thought to floor surfaces either. Static shock is common with certain surfaces and absolutely terrifying to dogs because they cannot rationalise what has happened and so cannot take avoiding action. Even some cheap dog beds when on certain kinds of floor are capable of delivering a static shock. Cars can do the same, and this may manifest in the dog as a fear of getting into the car or else car-sickness. Floor surfaces where they slip and slide and cannot grip properly can be traumatic to dogs as well, and it amazes me how humans can so lack empathy over this that they laugh when the dog slips, tumbles or does the splits. How unsafe such dogs must feel. Dogs can sustain injuries from losing their footing like this, and it is an extra misery if they already have pain from old injuries to manage, or are arthritic. The stress has to come out some way, and a variety of unwanted behaviours can appear as a result, from loss of house-training to self-mutilation or generalised reactiveness. So we do need to consider the dog's needs when deciding on our décor, and it is a matter for compromise. For instance, a non-slip runner on top of slippery surfaces can make all the difference to the dog's security.

Noise and Light

Many dogs are sensitive to noise, many don't care, and some like to join in with volleys of barking. To a large extent, living the way we do, a lot of noise is unavoidable. We can even use acceptable noise to muffle unacceptable, for instance having a radio or television on low to render external noise less intrusive. Dogs that wake up very early or bark during the night are probably being disturbed by noise, especially if these incidents are predictable by time, such as when a neighbour is leaving early for work. Most dogs have a different bark to indicate humans or animals, and some, most of my own included, do not bark at passing animals in the night but will always warn of any human presence close to the house.

Light wakes dogs up just as it wakes many of us, so keeping the dog room dark helps with dogs that want to start the day too early. Some dogs, notably border collies and GSDs, are extremely sensitive to flickering light, and lights that strobe or flash can be so disturbing to them that they can develop a variety of stress-related behaviours, or even epilepsy from the continual bombardment of stress hormones. Laser lights sold as cat toys, where the cat is encouraged to chase the light spot, must never ever be used with any dog. They can trigger irreparable damage very quickly, though cats seem unaffected.

Temperature

At the risk of stating the obvious, long spells of severe discomfort from being too hot or too cold will affect a dog's stress levels. This is more likely to apply in the "too hot" range, where most of us live in centrally-heated houses which might be comfortable to a person wearing summer clothes but very hot to certain types of dog. A dense coat can act as insulation, but some breeds suffer very much from the heat. Equally, a hot summer can be very uncomfortable for a dog that has insufficient access to shade or a cool surface to lie on. Where dogs are left while the owner is at work, care should be taken to provide adequate shelter from temperature extremes. We should think very hard before getting a heavy-coated breed if we live in a warm climate, and similarly a thin-coated type if we cannot cater for its needs in the cold. It is easier to put a coat on a cold dog than cool down a hot one; groomers will show us how to care for a heavy coat and thin it out for summer. It is not a good idea to clip a double coat, as then the guard hairs and the undercoat end up the same length for ever after, and cannot do their job of insulating the dog. Where does behaviour come into this? Hot dogs get grouchy and cold dogs are miserable; add other stressors and we have the roots of a behaviour issue.

Scents

It is hard for human imagination to empathise with how much more powerful a dog's sense of smell is compared to our own. It is like a Ferrari next to a pushbike. If we like to fill our homes with scents that are delightful to us, we need to pause and consider a) whether they are nice for the dog, and b) if the dog can get away from them. Just as most of us have never had the desire to roll in fox muck, dogs do not find pot-pourri, scented candles or carpet powder appealing. Highly-scented cosmetics and bath preparations, perfumes, household cleaners and laundry fresheners can be as miserable an experience for the dog as living next to raw sewage might be for us. So, while we have the freedom to scent our homes and clothing how we wish, we should be aware of the effect on our dogs and make sure that the dog can get away from the scents if it wants to. Similarly, we should never apply scent to a collar or bandana that the dog has to wear. If the dog can choose whether to accept a scent or not, then all is well, but if it has no escape from scents that it hates, again we create stress that we should not underestimate. There may be times when we want to use a scented product on a dog for instance as a flea repellent or a medical treatment, and if so we should choose these carefully, follow the advice of a trained practitioner, and keep these experiences to a minimum.

Occupants

New people or new animals in the home can be difficult for dogs. They need to work out the rearranged dynamics, the changes in routine, and how this affects them. As far as possible we should smooth the way for the dog; so often change is sprung upon it when it could have been introduced gradually, and the dog is supposed to "just get used to it". Where extra people are going to live in the home, it is helpful to the dog if it can meet them first on neutral territory that has pleasant associations, for instance joining at the car park and going for a walk together. Much as we want dogs to love us at once, less is more as far as dogs are concerned, and it is far better for new people to ignore the dog and let it approach them in its own time. Many dogs will go straight into a new human relationship and offer themselves for caresses and interaction, but equally many others prefer to assess at a distance and over time. Several walks together with the owner, while the stranger ignores the dog, will build a far better relationship with a new person than if they start offering food and stroking right away. Where circumstances mean that the new person moves into the home with no time to prepare the dog, again, ignoring the dog is the way to build friendships. The dog will approach in its own time, will offer touch when it feels ready, and eventually solicit touch in turn. There are correct and incorrect ways to touch dogs, just as there are appropriate and inappropriate ways of touching in human society, and just as some humans and some societies are very much more tactile than others, so are some dogs. Those contacts that are acceptable between dogs and owners are not the ones that should be given by strangers. For instance, dogs are very protective about their heads, and while owners can stroke and rub a dog's head, with the dog enjoying every moment, a stranger should not expect to do the same. Patting heads is always unwise, being quite unpleasant to the dog. Less offensive touch is on the flanks and chest, with stroking rather than patting in every case. Touch should only be offered when solicited by the dog, and we should always stop before the dog wants us to; in the best stage traditions "leave them wanting more". There is a vast difference between "giving" affection and "taking" it, and many of us, without truly realising what we are doing, help ourselves to the dog because we want to touch it, not because it wants us to touch it. Let the dog "ask" for touch: we never get it wrong by taking our time and letting the dog set the pace.

New Animals

Dogs are predators. Introducing a new animal triggers a predatory response no matter how much we would like them all to be "friends". Interspecies friendships are not natural except between domestic animals and people, and we still have to work at those. Some dogs will learn to tolerate other species and some will actively appear to like them, but it isn't a given, and no matter how well managed, there is always a risk that the dog will continue to see the other creature as a meal. If we are not careful, dogs will learn quickly that any attention paid by the dog to the new animal results in attention for the dog, remembering that even unpleasant attention is better to the dog than none. So when we plan to add a new animal, we should anticipate the worst case by creating a safe area for that creature to occupy. Ideally this should be a room to which the dog has no access. Some dogs can be trained to leave other animals alone, and some cannot; best not to find out the hard way.

Cats

Specifically with regard to cats, many dogs live in harmony with a cat or cats, but will still chase strange cats, while other dogs can be trained to leave all cats alone. In the domestic situation, the best success lies with introducing a puppy to resident cats, but this needs to be closely supervised and they should never be left alone together. Cats can injure a puppy and have an especial liking for clawing eyes; bigger puppies can be too rambunctious for cats. Some cats will deliberately taunt a dog. The success of a cat/dog relationship depends very much on the specific natures of each; if it doesn't work out, we face a lifetime of keeping them apart. If this is the case, do not feed the cat where the dog can see, but instead keep them entirely separate.

Other Dogs

Most of us reach a time when we think about introducing another dog to our homes. We do this for various reasons of our own: one is nice so wouldn't two be even more fun? Maybe one is getting old and we think a younger one will be there to help us through the inevitable bereavement, and meantime go for longer walks than the oldie can now manage. Perhaps we have a dog-related hobby or we work our dogs and we need another to give us greater potential in our chosen sphere. Maybe a child is now old enough and capable enough to merit a dog of their own. Perhaps a friend is in a situation where they can no longer keep the dog, and we have offered to take it. There may be a change in household dynamics and somebody new is coming to live with us, bringing their dog. All of these are perfectly sound reasons for having another dog in the household. We need to be clear, though, that we are getting the dog for ourselves, not as a treat for our dog, because it is highly likely that our existing dog is not going to find the idea at all appealing. It is not going to think it is getting a little brother or sister, a friend or playmate. It is getting a rival, competition for everything it holds dear, and we had better be very clear about that.

The analogy I use – change the gender to suit the situation – is that our life partner is bringing a new woman/man to live with us. And we are sure to be friends, aren't we? We can lunch together, play golf, go shopping, share clothes – how wonderful is that? Yep, that's how your dog feels too.

In time, the dogs may settle together and enjoy each other's company – or they may not, and everyone will be living on tenterhooks. In extreme cases, the dogs may fight to the extent that they have to be kept separate for the remainder of their lives. We then need to be able to trust every household member to maintain security, and visitors have to either do as they are told or be kept well away from the dogs. I know of a number of cases where a visitor "felt sorry" for the dogs being shut away separately and so let them out together, with predictable results. We cannot make dogs like each other: we don't like everyone we meet either. Add the stresses of being in the same territory, and it is easy to see why it can so often go wrong.

There are no guarantees, but there are ways of minimising the potential for conflict. To begin with, the dogs should meet on neutral territory and go for a walk together, the layout being dog-person-person-dog, and dogs on-lead at first. The dogs should not be allowed to eyeball or challenge each other. If all goes well, next time they can start the walk on-lead and towards the end, be let off together. After a few such walks, we gain a much better idea of whether they are likely to get along. These walks should not involve the throwing of balls, use of toys or anything else exciting, and there should be nothing over which the dogs might want to compete. Each owner should handle their own dog. After a number of incident-free walks together, the dogs can then come back to the new household to see how they manage on one dog's home territory. When the permanent move in is made, there should be at least one extra bed and one extra water bowl (i.e. three of each for a two-dog household) and feeding should be arranged so that the dogs are a good distance from each other or even in separate rooms. This "sets us up for success", but even so it will only work for certain dogs.

Where one dog is to be moved into a multi-dog household, or more than one dog into a one-dog household, the same principles apply, but the single dog should meet the others one dog at a time before they meet as a group, and the same with the subsequent introduction to the household, which should be one dog at a time. When the time comes to move in for good, the dogs should all go for a walk together first and then go back into the house together.

Talking Birds

A special case here is with birds that mimic the human voice. If you really want to freak out your dog, even a normal well-adjusted dog, and certainly one that already has issues, get a bird that talks. The bird will learn to call the dog, and also repeat anything else that is regularly said to the dog, bark and whine like the dog, and probably repeat human laughter as well, all of which is traumatic to the dog. I submit that most of us would be freaked out too if we constantly heard disembodied voices in the tones of people we knew calling to us. Most birds that mimic are pretty intelligent, and will love the fracas this creates, so repeating the behaviour. This is not cute: this is torture. If you have a bird that mimics, and you are set on getting a dog, keep it right away from the dog and preferably out of earshot. If you already have a dog, don't get a bird that mimics. It's that serious, and we need to know about this.

Helping People

Due to sentimental tales and films about dogs whose lives are spent helping people, we are easily beguiled into thinking that this is what dogs like to do, and that any dog will transform into a cross between Florence Nightingale and an archangel when presented with a human who is in need of help. This is a wheel on which countless dogs are broken.

Helping people by herding, guarding and hunting is very different from helping people who are in emotional need. Dogs have been bred for the first skills for untold generations, but we should not expect them naturally to have the mindset and the will to achieve the second. Dogs most of all need to feel safe, and the majority of them cannot feel that if their human is in extra need of support. Dogs simply do not have the mental equipment to handle this level of insecurity full-time, and the resulting stresses come out sometimes physically, usually behaviourally, and very often both ways. It is tough on any creature to live under tension for the greater part of its life.

Those dogs that choose to support their person emotionally – and here the key word is "choose" – are ones that are confident, steady in character, and secure in their lives. But so often, people think that a dog taken from Rescue will morph into a good assistance dog simply because it should be so grateful to have a home and regular meals. We fail these dogs if we think this way, because many have been to hell and are not back yet; they do not trust humans and don't have any spare strength to give away. It could be that a year or two down the line, in a good home that makes no demands on them and sees to their every need, such a dog would then become mentally strong enough to offer comfort in return, but this cannot be predicted and should not be anticipated. Even we people, with all the help we can access, never recover fully from trauma, and our deepest insecurities lurk within us all our lives. How can we then expect a dog to cast off its unhappy past and don the mantle of a major supporting role, without a backward glance?

Even with dogs that have been specially bred to offer physical support – so much easier and more within a dog's remit than anything to do with the human mind – there is a huge drop-out rate from early training. These dogs are carefully raised and schooled, but not all can manage their intended future task. Recently I met a golden retriever/poodle cross, specifically bred to assist, and trained by experts, who had failed her placement because she would not recall. The pressures of her intended career were such that she had developed the behaviour of bolting. Any dog that is out of its depth only has so many ways of demonstrating that, so the relatively harmless tactic demonstrated by the bred-for-purpose dog would not necessarily be the chosen option for a dog that has already had a bad start in life and has therefore learned more intimidating responses.

That some dogs can be trained to assist, apparently enjoy that life and bring untold comfort to their human on many levels should be understood as the specific skill-set that it is, not extended to the whole of dogdom, and particularly not to dogs who have been failed by people in their past. Most of us have been honoured by the level of empathy that means a dog offers comfort with a paw on the knee, a lick of the face or its friendly presence pressed closely to us. This is about a dog that chooses the pace, extent and form of its interaction, and equally can choose to back off and recharge its mental batteries at any time it needs to.

Dogs don't do political correctness, and vulnerable people can seem frightening to them. So often a dog is visualised as the perfect easy-option everyday companion for somebody who actually requires more human help and company. Most of us have times when we are lonely and unhappy, and most of our dogs not only cope readily with this but actively seem to go out of their way to offer help and comfort. This is, however, very different from placing a dog with a strange human who is not for whatever reason able to cope emotionally with the world on a permanent basis. If a dog has had a mutually pleasurable and secure long-term relationship with someone, then it may well offer company and apparent empathy to a marked degree to that specific person. Many instances exist of dogs predicting or detecting illness, or offering assistance and comfort over and above that which we might think normal for a dog. Equally, many dogs would rather not get involved with poorly owners on any level. Dogs are much better at coping with human physical illness than emotional and mental, because the inconsistencies of the latter two make them feel insecure. However, we need to be aware that even deteriorating physical health in the owner is enough to create fear in many dogs, which may then display unwanted behaviour in the shape of anything from forgetting house-training to actual aggression. Dogs that have had an adequate but not particularly empathetic relationship with an owner might become really freaked out by escalating illness, and medical help such as mobility aids should have careful introduction rather than just arriving in the home, smelling strange, restricting space and sometimes making odd noises. Even the "clump" of a walking aid approaching can make some dogs uneasy. Others of course take such matters in their stride, but we never know how it will be until it happens, so it is always best to assume an incipient problem and work towards its avoidance. Sympathetic introduction of such appliances coupled with reward – classical conditioning – does not take long and is well worth the trouble.

The great success of assistance dogs pushes boundaries in our expectations of human/dog relationships. Such dogs are normally carefully bred from specific types that are phlegmatic, enjoy human interaction and are task-driven. Introduced to their new owners as part of a detailed programme of integration, with each stage robustly managed, such dogs enrich the lives of their people profoundly. The best organisations take care to ensure that assistance dogs have adequate "downtime" when they can relax and be

Goldendoodle assistance dog.

dogs; problems arise when this aspect is neglected, which is one of many reasons why there is such a high "wastage" rate for dogs failing training. Because while dogs are co-operative with humans, living with a "weakness" in their owner demands a very specific character and background in the dog. It also requires outstanding puppy socialising, and the input of those who rear potential assistance dogs to the point of starting their interactive training is incredibly important.

Fetching, carrying and alerting are extensions of natural dog behaviour, and assistance dogs for the physically disabled, when well-chosen and matched, should manage well. Sadly, the success of this scheme has persuaded people less dog-savvy but with the best of intentions to extend the remit beyond what is safe or pleasant for the dog. There have been attempts to take in rescued dogs from a variety of backgrounds, often unknown, and made up of breeds unsuitable for assistance work, with the idea that this is mutually beneficial. But such dogs have often had a dreadful start in life, no trust in and not much liking for people; they are the last creatures to benefit from being housed with a human that cannot give them security and confidence. No matter how much "love" a dog is given, it is not enough: they need to feel safe, and they can't feel safe when their human is vulnerable or behaves erratically. Currently, some well-meaning agencies are planning to place dogs with dementia sufferers, seemingly being unaware of the welfare implications for the dogs. There are also significant welfare implications for the patients, because insecure dogs can produce behaviour for which the patient is unprepared, or unable to manage. The concept of dogs helping people should never be misted over with sentiment or anthropomorphism: they help us best when carrying out tasks for which they are physically and mentally suited, and no amount of "aaah factor" justifies using dogs for situations and people who really need kind, well-motivated humans. Those of us who pick up the pieces after dogs have been subjected to lifestyles that are beyond their natural coping strategies are very much aware of the drawbacks to using dogs in this way.

Dogs that can choose how much they help, and otherwise lead a normal life, often stretch scientific understanding as they display empathy and communication skills far beyond the expected. I know a dog who will scour the house for a certain toy and bring it to her owner's son, who is so profoundly handicapped that he cannot even talk. This dog visits his day centre too, and is incredibly gentle and communicative with a variety of patients, but she chooses with whom she interacts, and she leads a suitable life otherwise, with plenty of time to be a dog. The difference in welfare terms is crucial. And if we want to avoid aberrant behaviour in any dog that is used to assist people, we need to observe the unfolding situation carefully and continuously rather than take it for granted that everything will be all right, because it has the potential to go terribly wrong, with everyone involved being the loser when it does.

Changes

Given the foregoing, then, it may be easier to understand how a change in home dynamics can create unwanted behaviour in the dog. It is hard enough for us to weather the changes sometimes, whether the natural evolution of child into teenager, the addition of an elderly parent in deteriorating health, or the arrival of a baby – and these are matters that we expect. The dog, however, has no idea that any of this is happening until it does. New partners, grandchildren, people experimenting with drink or drugs, all cause hiccups in the dog's perception of security. While the ebb and flow of changing circumstances is something we all have to manage, we need to be aware of how these changes affect the dog. Some handle change seemingly effortlessly, but others can become stressed out and so produce unwanted behaviour as a direct response. Before we start remedial work on the dog, we need to uncover what has changed in its life at around the time this behaviour first presented.

Strangers in the Home

Workmen in and around the house can present stress to the dog, because it wants to guard its territory but is prevented from doing so. Some dogs enjoy human company so much that they have "the more, the merrier" as an approach, and so do not worry, but others are more insular types and take invasion of their home territory very hard indeed. It is worth taking steps to avoid unsettling the dog; it shouldn't be expected just to accept the experience because again, the true effects may manifest after the event. Time taken to familiarise the dog with the strangers is well spent, but this should not be in the form of getting the strangers to feed the dog titbits or stroke it. This is because some dogs could get out of their depth after coming in to take the food or accept the hand, panic and then snap. It is usually sufficient for the householder to "introduce" the stranger by standing in his or her space, then going over to the dog; the dog then sees that the stranger is not to be feared and neither is required to approach the other. Some very nervous dogs, guarding breeds, or those with previous history of reactivity, are better to be out of the home while strangers are working in it, perhaps instead staying with friends or in daycare at kennels. We need to understand that work done outside the home with the dog inside is frightening – for instance, window-cleaners or roofers appear at a great height and move from place to place around the house exterior, waving their arms and being accompanied by odd noises. Dogs should never be expected to remain in the home without the owner present, if workmen are there. It is very unfair to each, because dynamics change vividly once the owner is out and the dog takes a major drop in security. Many incidents of serious attacks by dogs occur in the home environment but without the owner present.

Outside Behaviour

Creating a safe haven in the home is paramount, but we also need to take our dogs outside the home too, for exercising and because we enjoy their company. Some of the dogs we meet will not be well socialised or trained, and some of the people will not like dogs. Therefore we need to think ahead, taking the responsibility for everything that our dog is permitted to do. We are not helplessly floundering in our dog's wake: we can see further, so we see potential issues before the dog can, and we have the advantage of superior intellect. We can learn to read situations unfolding so that we adjust our reactions in a way that not only keeps our own dog safe but keeps all other beings safe as well. It is good practice to go to places where lots of people walk their dogs and watch closely the interactions between dog and dog, and human and dog. Soon we can get our eye in and so are able to anticipate which dogs are feeling antagonistic or insecure, and which owners notice. This study is best conducted without our own dog, so that we can concentrate fully on the legion mini dramas that unfold every day where people walk dogs. We also need to take in environmental stressors such as unfamiliar or particularly unpleasant noises, smells, or incidents that might cause a dog to react fearfully, such as people shouting in the immediate vicinity, or trucks reversing with accompanying diesel fumes and beeping sounds.

Reading the Walk

Walks are the high spot of most dogs' days, and should be pretty high on our list too. When we walk, we should be on full alert with all senses, not in a fearful way but so we can share whatever sensory messages our dog is getting. Because our senses are not as keen, we apply intellect to fill in the gaps, which means paying attention to what is going on around us. Watching the dog, we find that it frequently makes eye contact, and for a moment we are taken back to our studies in the park, where so many dogs try to make contact with their owners, and after repeated failures, slope off to find their own entertainment. But if we let them catch our eye, and we smile and acknowledge by word or gesture that we are paying attention to them, then dogs are more willing to increase communication with us. This can transmute independence to co-dependence, for instance "shall we go?" instead of "I'm off!" simply because we are worth the communication. The more we "listen" the more they "talk" to us. Dog-walking is no place to catch up on work, telephone calls, electronic distractions or gossip – it is a time to catch up with the dog. It is fun to watch them involved in scenting and try to guess what the smells are telling them, to see them exploring different textures of ground, to anticipate and deflect such temptations as

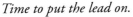

Time to put the lead on.

scavenging, or rolling in stinking patches, guiding them away and rewarding that response before the dog has fully realised that here was an opportunity to eat something rotten or slather itself in foulness. We keep our eyes open for hazards such as barbed wire, broken glass, edible litter or creatures that tempt a dog to chase, using our superior height and usually superior sight to pre-empt so gracefully that the dog is unaware of missed opportunities. Most of all, we learn to assess approaching dogs and owners, avoiding if we need to, passing without incident because we have backtracked to avoid the tight space where even the best-adjusted dog would feel tense, body-blocking the ill-mannered dog out to cause trouble, allowing a pleasant greeting between well-adjusted dogs, or even a supervised run-around together with them where it is safe to do so. Dogs exchange rapid-fire communication well before they meet, so fast that even the aware student of canine body-language is pushed to keep up, and by the time dogs are close enough to touch each other, they already know how the other is going to behave. The lift of an ear, the height of a tail, weight on all feet or some feet, hard eyes or soft, even something as subtle to us as the position of the whiskers, all is conversation between dogs, and we can practice our observation skills so that we know what is likely to happen next. Simple precautions keep everyone safe: we humans are very linear and want our walk to be from here to there and back again, but there is no shame or loss of face by taking sensible detours to avoid trouble on the brew. Humans are outstandingly obtuse sometimes about standing in gateways or blocking narrow tracks, but we don't need to detonate a potentially explosive situation if we only recognise how our dog perceives narrow spaces. Equally, if another dog is going into "guard" mode, we are better to keep ours well away from it than to call its bluff – because it won't be bluff. So many dogs are tipped into reactive behaviour by owner carelessness, which if experienced at a vulnerable time can escalate into an established attitude that needs a lot of subsequent work. Instead, if we commit to reading the walk and avoiding conflict, we have a happy secure dog that does not feel the need to fight its own battles. People will tell us how lucky we are.

Hunting

Hunting is not in fact an aberrant behaviour, but many dog owners see it as such. They cannot understand that their gentle family pet could possibly kill other animals, never mind actually enjoy the process. This is odd of us when we consider that dogs are predators and carnivores. Their programming is to kill animals and eat them. Some breeds are more predatory than others, but any dog, given the chance, will chase such creatures as rabbits and rats with the intent of killing them. This may be natural, but is not wanted by the average pet owner, so we need to do several things to address the dog's needs.

Any dog will be tempted to worry sheep.

First we should assess the degree of predatory nature our own dog has. Predictably, dogs bred for hunting and catching – that is, hounds and terriers – will be more hunting-oriented than other breeds. This is not to say that other breeds have less hunting instinct, but that these specific breeds have more. Next we have to understand that any catchable creature will trigger this instinct. Any dog of any breed at all can become a sheep-worrier or a poultry-killer. Therefore it is our explicit responsibility to keep our dogs from doing this. We achieve that either by specifically training the dog to ignore domestic livestock, which is what owners of working dogs do, or else we avoid having the dog offlead anywhere that livestock is about. We must address this with commitment; it is no good thinking that because it hasn't happened, it won't – the truth is that if it can happen, it will. Because the act of killing prey fulfils a dog's instincts in the way few other experiences can, the dog that has hunted and killed once will always want to do so again, and there is nothing that we can offer as a reward that compares with it. We should never kid ourselves that a dog "only wants to play" with the prey species. It is not playing and it has every intention of killing. This does not mean that the dog is bad or dangerous or will take to attacking people. It is a normal dog behaving in a normal dog way. If it were a cat, nobody would bat an eyelid, because we are used to thinking of cats as predators. Therefore we have to think ahead on every walk, and whenever we are anywhere that wild animals or domestic livestock live, we should keep our dog under close control. This is especially important when on holiday or in unfamiliar areas, where we don't know what livestock is about, and the dog is in a state of heightened awareness because it is somewhere strange. Specifically for sheep-worrying and poultry-killing, if the dog has shown an interest by staring or even chasing but has not actually caught, then it can usually be trained out of the behaviour, albeit only by the use of strong aversives teamed with rewards. The timing of each needs to be so exquisite if it is to succeed that professional help should be sought, and not all professionals are capable of this either. We cannot use pure reward to change this behaviour because we cannot offer any reward that comes near to matching the sheer pleasure and fulfilment

204

Something to chase.

experienced by the dog. If, however, the dog has actually killed sheep or poultry, it cannot be retrained and must be managed robustly by ensuring it never has the opportunity to cut loose and kill again. All livestock should also be treated with respect; while horses and cattle are more capable of defending themselves, and there are cases every year where cattle have killed dogs and sometimes their walkers as well, they can still abort, damage themselves by running on rough ground, or run into fences with tragic results. It is better to avoid fields with horses or cattle in, even if it means turning back or making a short diversion.

We cannot take away the need to hunt, so we are obliged to provide other outlets for this instinct. Some of the tracking and finding games described in Chapter Three are excellent substitutes. If we are in a situation where rabbits or squirrels can be chased (this is illegal in some countries, and in UK a dog may chase a rabbit but not a squirrel, and only if the owner has specific permission from the landowner) squirrels go up trees and rabbits go down holes, so the dog can get a lot of pleasure from hunting without bothering the prey species much (rabbits spend their lives being chased) or a great deal of risk of catching either, though it might connect with the odd weak or very young animal. If we can't cope with that, then we are best to keep away from wildlife-rich areas, as it is torture to the dog to see and scent so many huntable creatures but never be allowed to chase them. If we own a hunting breed as a pet, we have to keep in mind that terriers will go down holes, sighthounds will be away so fast that they can be out of earshot while we are still inhaling to call them, and scenting hounds will follow scent, even old scent, for hours. It is therefore our responsibility to keep terriers right away from holes in the ground, maintain a very good look-out while exercising sighthound types, and lead scenthounds not into temptation. Chasing a ball may be an acceptable substitute for non-hunting breeds, but it won't cut the mustard for those types hardwired to hunt, and

Keep away from holes in the ground.
Photo: F. Sechiari.

bred from generations of hunters. A lot of breeders will not home their working-bred dogs to pet owners because of this, but of course anyone unknowingly getting such a dog from Rescue is in for a baptism of fire and a fair few anxious moments until they become accustomed to what can and can't be expected from such animals. Pet dogs of non-hunting breeds bred from generations of pet stock are a lot easier to manage, and most will be delighted to chase balls, fetch toys, hunt out food treats and snort down the odd rabbit-hole, but they do need some kind of hunting substitute of this nature if they are to be kept in good spirits.

Instinct and Learning

Dogs, any dogs, will hunt instinctively without any teaching, but dogs learn a lot faster from other dogs, and given half a chance will become efficient hunters when experience and opportunity meet. This means that if we want to keep our dogs away from learning about hunting, we should also keep them away from dogs that know how to hunt. Ignorance is bliss, and hunting is a Pandora's Box better kept closed to the pet dog. Studying hunting dogs, however, will teach the behaviour trainer a great deal that is hidden from those who do not have any experience of them. For instance, when breeding and rearing a litter of puppies, these must of necessity be confined safely and not allowed to roam woods and fields with their mother. As the pups become more independent, their dam spends less time with them, and by the age when most go to their new homes, she is seldom with them more than once or twice a day. Yet if we run a puppy on and give it the opportunity to spend time with its mother, she will teach it to hunt. I have seen bitches take a line of puppies along a hedgerow and bolt rabbits for them to chase, or dig mice out for them to catch. My last pup was eighteen weeks old when her mother caught a rabbit, disabled it with a nip, and then dropped it in front of the pup. The humanitarian part of me was very uneasy about the rabbit, but the scientist side recognised this as an amazing opportunity for study. Over the next few weeks, the bitch repeated this behaviour, and at twenty-two weeks the pup had a young but uninjured rabbit dropped in front of her, which she chased and caught. What a tremendous piece of teaching from the mother dog. I know from experience that we can take a hunting-bred dog as a pup and it will learn by itself to be an impressive catcher of game, but there can be relatively few people, and fewer scientists, who ever get the chance to see how a mother dog will train her pups to hunt.

Motivation

Having thoroughly investigated the environment, our next task is to find the motivation for the behaviour. What happens when the dog presents the behaviour, how is the dog likely to be feeling immediately before and immediately afterwards, how do its humans react, what is the reward it receives from the behaviour? How can we change this reward to provide equal or better which we can offer as the result of a more desirable behaviour? What behaviour would we find more acceptable? And not forgetting the most obvious question of all, which is: why don't we want the behaviour the dog is offering? This is not as straightforward as it seems, because while we can easily say why we don't want the dog to eat a bone on our bed, sometimes owner ambitions are out of touch with what is really important, such as wanting the dog to eat in one particular place while the dog finds that place unpleasant to eat in. No matter how much we want the dog to eat there, the dog does not want to eat in that spot. Wise trainers choose their battles: there is no need to try and force the dog to eat somewhere it does not want to eat, and the win/win is achieved by finding a place where we and the dog are happy for it to eat instead, or else finding why our ideal place for it to eat is unpleasant to the dog, and making appropriate changes. If we work on the old-fashioned dominance idea of the dog eats where we want or goes hungry, we are causing conflict at every mealtime for no good reason, and this can start stress-related health problems for dog and owner.

It also strains the bond between the two, which can have a knock-on effect with such matters as recall and general obedience. The dog is entitled to an opinion, but we have the casting vote: we do not have to run our lives around the dog, but nor should we expect the dog to endure situations that make it miserable. The objective is that we enjoy living with each other.

Alternative Behaviour

Then we decide exactly what we want the dog to do instead of whatever it is that it is doing which we don't want. It is easy for humans to slip into a negative mindset of "I want him to stop …" or "I hate it when he …". But the dog does not know what we do want. And if we wait for the dog to substitute a variety of alternative behaviours until it accidentally hits on the right one, we risk ending up with a whole series of behaviours we don't want. Therefore we have to fix in our minds something simple and achievable that we do want. Then we set about substituting the new behaviour for the old. Always we need to check with ourselves whether we are asking something reasonable. Don't ask the dog to "sit" on a nettle patch and yes I have seen it done. Then we have to sell the new behaviour to the dog by making it the easiest or the only option, adding a reward that the dog finds worthwhile immediately we get the result we want. Rewards need to be superior to those provided by the unwanted behaviour. After that, we proof the new behaviour in a variety of situations – this room, that room, the garden, the village green, wherever the dog goes day to day and could exhibit the unwanted behaviour – and then the wanted one is established instead

Analysing aberrant behaviour is a matter of gathering up all the contributing threads, seeing the whole picture instead of just the behaviour, and then taking everything back to the point where the dog last felt safe. By re-establishing its faith in us, dealing with those things that have been upsetting it, and working within the natural canine mindset, we then know how far we can amend the unwanted behaviour and how much of it we need to manage. It is immensely rewarding.

BAER – Brainstem Auditory Evoked Response

Chapter Nine

The Elderly Dog

Managing Behavioural Changes in the Final Years

WE EXPECT physical changes with ageing, but we aren't always prepared for the behavioural ones that go with it, so when our elderly dog, instead of simply gently declining, starts to show character changes that aren't easy to live with, we need information on how best to support our old friend. We may also be unprepared for the way other dogs react to the elderly and infirm among their species, and there is very little guidance available for dog owners to follow. There are quite a few parallels with the human condition here, and as we cannot ask our dogs, sometimes we need to make a likely interpretation based on what we know from people. This is not anthropomorphising, because we are all mammals, and degenerative changes are similar throughout the mammalian world. The main difference is that wild animals heading for old age tend to be killed by other animals, or starve once they cannot find, chew or digest food. They don't as a rule make it as far as extreme old age. With domestic animals, livestock is usually converted to meat while young; only horses, cats and dogs get to retirement age, and even this is fairly recent in terms of their association with people. When I was a child, you rarely saw a dog older than eight or so; if they could not be useful, there was seldom the money to spare to support them into old age. Elderly cats tended to disappear, and few owners could afford to keep a horse as a field ornament, nor was there the medical knowledge necessary to maintain quality of life. Veterinary advances on the one hand and more disposable income on the other means that nowadays more of us keep elderly animals into their dotage. And what a learning curve that can be.

Hearing

We expect blindness and deafness to creep up on our old dogs, and it generally does, sometimes so subtly that it is only when these conditions are well advanced that we notice them. A dog that does not hear us call it for dinner or a walk is obviously going deaf, but we may have thought it was simply being disobedient when it failed to respond to us out on walks. Some humans suffer badly from tinnitus: we have no way of knowing if our dogs do as well, but it is certainly possible. There can be other hearing damage caused by a variety of exposures to loud noise: working gundogs usually become deaf from midlife onwards, but dogs consistently experiencing loud noise, from televisions and music played in the house to the radio turned right up in the car, are also vulnerable. Deafness is not simply hearing less but hearing differently, and dogs can behave as if they are confused because they cannot adjust to the new sounds they hear, while some can become morose because nobody talks to them any more. While some degenerative hearing changes are inevitable, complete deafness is not, and if you suspect your dog is becoming deaf, a check-up from your vet using the BAER test will ascertain if the dog is actually going deaf or has a problem such as an infection or debris in the ear that can be helped with medication, as well as establishing the extent of the deafness in each ear. Preparing your dog for deafness later in life includes training it to follow hand-signals, so you still have communication, and it will still understand what you want. A plus is that dogs with noise phobias will no longer hear the sounds that used to frighten them. We are ever grateful for small mercies.

Sight

Dogs cope well with failing sight, but when the last of their light is extinguished, they cannot tell night from day, and if furniture is moved to different areas in the house, they may have trouble locating "outside" and so appear to lose their house-training. They may bark helplessly at walls, or wake in the night and bark for help, or become so frightened after a few incidents of walking into walls or doors that they cry or bark whenever they want to move, or sit shaking and not daring to go anywhere. Conversely, some dogs manage so well without their sight that owners are unaware that there is any problem at all. Once again, our vet should be consulted in order to establish the extent of the blindness and if possible the cause, so that we have an idea of how the condition will progress. We can make these changes easier for the dog by leaving furniture in the same place and interior doors open, plus arranging different floor surfaces in each room, or a runner

An old friend.

leading between doors, so that the dog can find its way outside by the feel and scent of whatever it is walking on. Out on walks, the dog will still be able to enjoy checking out scents, and can keep track of its owner by listening if it still has some hearing. I know someone whose dog went blind overnight, and he has established a command that tells the dog an obstacle is in its way, so if the dog hears "careful" it knows to stop and check out whatever is in its way by scent and cautious touch. Of course this needs a caring commitment from the owner always to watch where the dog is going, no matter what distractions are about. One of the most important matters to realise is that sighted dogs approaching the blind one are not doing so from any desire to "say hello" or play. Unless they already are familiar with the blind dog, they have recognised its vulnerability and may well be intending to bother it. Part of the responsibility of owning a blind dog is protecting it from its own kind, and this is an area where owners must never let their guard down, because an unseen attack is terribly frightening for the blind dog, and takes away not only its pleasure from its walks, but its trust in its owner. Once that has gone, it doesn't have a lot left.

Scent and Taste

In most dogs, their scenting powers are the strongest sense and the one that appears to outlast the others. Dogs do not have extensive taste detectors in comparison with us: much of their enjoyment of food comes through the nose rather than the tongue. However, elderly dogs quite often change their appetites so that food they have eaten apparently happily up to then becomes unpalatable. This may be due to scent/taste detection changes in the dog, or, in the case of commercial food, a change in ingredients that the manufacturer has made. Also, old age may accelerate tooth problems, or there may be other trouble starting in the mouth, throat or further along the digestive system. Often the first indications we get are loss of appetite, changes in coat, body scent, and sometimes bowel and bladder habits. Elderly dogs should not smell bad in coat, body or breath: if they do, this is an indication that veterinary help is needed. Often the changes necessary are very small, and then we have a contented dog again that eats well and smells healthy. It is all too easy to assume that some new behaviour we don't like is due to general "old age" when in reality it can often be a physical issue that is treatable, and so our dog is not as "old" as we thought.

When other senses start to decline, the ones that remain give proportionately more support, both physical and mental, to the dog, so the elderly dog may well become more fixated on scent, especially when out walking. Where once it would sniff briefly and move on, the older dog may take several seconds to inhale and process the scent before taking a decision whether to scent-mark, and if so from this position or – just a minute while it turns round – that one. With all the calls we humans have on our time, it would be easy to allow this behaviour to become irritating because we want to get on with the walk, but we should instead change our expectations. The dog is enjoying its walk in its own way, and it is not important whether we get from A to B at all, never mind within a certain timescale. As with young puppies, a very old dog will sometimes enjoy an outing more if we drive it somewhere and then let it take its time pottering about checking the weemails and snuffling around the wild animal scents. There is a simple joy in allowing ourselves to share the old dog's pleasure, especially when, having had a good sniff round, it comes back to us, mouth open in a wide grin and mind fully refreshed, ready either to move on and check out another area, or to go home and relax.

Touch

Here is a sense usually underrated because we are all so familiar with it, but it is extremely important, and even more so to elderly dogs. Old dogs sleep more deeply: it is never wise to wake a sleeping dog by touching it, but instead we can tap on the floor beside it so that the vibrations wake it gently. Dogs that can't hear us talking to them any more may become extra needy for a friendly touch, and dogs that can no longer see their environment are helped a great deal by the feel of different surfaces under their paws, and the protection of their whiskers (vibrissae). Most of us are aware that a cat uses its whiskers extensively, but relatively few of us ever give that any thought

212

within a canine context. Dogs' whiskers are not just on the muzzle, but also on the cheeks, under the chin and around the eyes, and their function is protective – the whiskers touch something first and so prevent the dog from hurting a sensitive area. But some breeds of dog need specialist grooming from professionals, and part of this can involve the removal of the vibrissae, sometimes because of fashion and show requirements, and sometimes because it is very difficult to trim a dog's face and leave the whiskers on. A dog with all its senses in place can still manage without its vibrissae, but this becomes a more complex issue when the dog is declining physically and possibly cognitively too. What we will see is a dog that appears to have become clumsy and is clouting its face on what are, to us, perfectly obvious surfaces, or else is underconfident or even frightened in some situations and reluctant to move from one place to another.

Old dogs that crave more contact should be given it whenever possible. Some like to lean against us, lie on our feet so we can't move without them knowing, or weave between our legs so that they have touch on either side. Others like to get on laps, or rest their head on our lap if the whole dog won't fit, and I have one that likes to lie on the back of an armchair, thence to slide down and drape herself around my neck. Being prodded with nose or paw becomes a more frequent occurrence, but although this can get irritating, remember that the dog cannot help being needy, and is not doing this to annoy you. The best way to respond to a dog that seeks attention is to give it attention of the right kind, and this actually diminishes attention-seeking in the long run, because the dog then feels more secure. A few moments of stroking or grooming the old dog will be quite enough to satisfy most of them, and if you do have a little more time, a gentle massage will delight the elderly one. Touch will tell you if there is illness in the body by finding areas of excessive heat or cold, lumps, unaccustomed tenderness or flinching, or a need for more pressure by leaning into your hand.

Pain
Dogs are very good at hiding pain, so by the time we notice that they are troubled, the pain may be quite considerable. Arthritic changes are almost inevitable as a dog gets older, and there is a lot of help available. Nutritional supplements can make a huge difference without the side-effects inherent in painkilling drugs. Later in a dog's life these drugs may become necessary, but it makes sense to avoid them for as long as possible, as all of them are designed, according to the manufacturers, for short-term use only. But arthritis is a long-term condition that changes in severity according to weather conditions, diet, the overall health of the dog, whether it is the ideal weight or could do with losing a few pounds. If a dog flinches from touch, or grumbles when hands come near it, heed the information you are getting about pain. A dog seeking warmth or coolness beyond its normal ways

might be in discomfort. Changes in temperature and humidity can have a profound effect on pain, so see if there is a link between pain response and the weather at the time, which will give you guidance for the future. Above all, if you suspect or know pain is present, protect your dog from the unwanted touch of others who are less aware, because dogs in pain can bite. People don't always remember, even if you told them only a few minutes ago, and it would be so easy for a happy tactile human greeting to cause a rush of pain to the dog, which snaps as a reflex.

Lumps

Most elderly dogs develop lumps of some kind, and most of these are benign. It is the owner's decision whether to do something about these lumps or not, using as help in the process knowledge that the dog has no self-image that is disturbed by not looking as it once did. Some lumps can be very unsightly while others might be well-hidden, only found by the stroking hand (another reason to check out our dogs all over and frequently). Together with our vets, we have to make an informed decision whether to have lumps biopsied or removed. The basis for this is discerning whether the dog's welfare would be improved by this action. If nothing can be done about the lump, it might as well stay in situ, rather than putting the old dog through surgery. If there are lumps on the outside, it's a fair assumption that there are lumps on the inside too, and some of these may be hampering normal internal processes. A dog can live a happy life, lumps and all, for some time, or it can grow a cancerous lump which rapidly affects its quality of life. It is between owner and vet to discuss the best way to manage such a situation. Behaviourally, we need to recognise that quality of life is different for a dog from the way it is with us. The ailing dog cannot phone its friends, surf the Internet, read or write, join its relatives for a party, or indulge any of the pleasures that make an impaired life worthwhile for us. Prolonging a life for a few extra months for the sake of the owner is questionable in terms of kindness to the dog.

Other Dogs

Social animals do not, as a rule, feel protective towards the old, any more than they do towards the sick, weak or disabled. Indeed, even in human society, care for the elderly is a social skill that has to be taught rather than a natural response to infirmity. Most dogs either ignore an old dog – it becomes a non-dog – or try to drive it away or kill it. This does not mean that those dogs are vicious or nasty: they are simply obeying their inborn imperatives. One of the first reminders we may get of our dog ageing is a change in the attitude of other dogs towards it, and we must act upon these signs before our dog is frightened or injured. When exercising our old dog, we need to look out for other dogs just as diligently as we would with a reactive dog, and use body-blocking to protect the old dog from unwanted contact, especially if our dog cannot move all that well and so the options of changing direction or moving off the path are limited. We need to commit totally to the protection of our ageing friend, and should not be embarrassed into going against what we know we should be doing by our own social pressures of not wanting to offend the other dog owner. Bumptious young dogs do not want to "say hello" or "play" when they run up to old weak dogs; they want to knock the oldie off its feet and buzz up their own happy hormones by doing so. A frail old dog can have the last of its quality of life extinguished by being afraid of being hurt every time it goes out, so don't let it happen.

Confusion

Old age does alter perception and memory, but in animals we only see the results rather than the process. The old dog may take to standing in doorways as if wondering what it meant to do, or have problems with doors in general, wanting them open all the time and woofing pathetically when they are closed. Old dogs can have what look like vague moments, when they can't remember what to do with a toy they used to enjoy playing with, or an item they used to love to retrieve. They might take a few moments to recognise people they know well, or even their owners at times. This is not always the effect of old age, and we should be aware that there can be other causes. Top of the list is a urinary tract infection (UTI), which so often does not show any other way except as confusion. There may not even be a temperature. Always have your oldie checked out for this; it is easily treated with antibiotics, and then we discover the old dog is nothing like as senile as we had thought. If your dog is on veterinary drugs, check out whether there are side-effects that affect cognitive ability. The dog that panics when

Kept safe and happy.

in the garden on its own, and can't find its way back to the house, has not necessarily gone irretrievably dotty, but may be suffering from a condition that is easy to remedy.

It is usual for old dogs to get into "loops" of repetitive behaviour with barking, pawing at items, wanting to be fed because it has forgotten it just has been, or walking constantly between one place and another. Tolerate this within the realms of safety: it can get exasperating for us, but they don't intend to annoy. It is often possible to break into the behaviour by something as simple as offering a small highly smelly treat, or giving the dog some fuss. You don't have to concern yourself about creating bad habits for the future, because by the time dogs are at this stage, the future is now, and they might as well do what makes them happy.

Incontinence

Incontinence is sometimes the result of mental degeneration, where the dog loses the ability to tell outside from indoors, or perhaps fails to recognise the meaning of internal pressures until it is too late, and of course it can be due to physical reasons as well, such as weakening sphincter muscles. In a house dog, this is very distressing to manage; less so with kennelled dogs. As covered in Chapter Four there are ways to make this condition easier for the humans in the household, but we also need to understand that incontinence which comes as a result of old age may be indicative of internal problems that are going to get worse. For instance, a sluggish bowel that delivers its contents without warning is not just sluggish at the sphincter end, but all the way along, which means that toxins may be building up inside the dog from poor digestion. Therefore the dog's quality of life may be deteriorating quite considerably by the time this condition presents. We can feel guilty because we think of ending the life of an incontinent dog simply due to the difficulties it gives us, but we also need to be aware that there are many instances where this is exactly the right thing to do for the dog's sake too, and not just because of our domestic situation. It is a very individual decision how much we put up with and how long we put up with it; we need also to see the picture from the point of view of the degenerating health of the dog. Some dogs become very upset at their incontinence while others couldn't give a fig, and some households include very old or very young humans too, which become a big part of the equation. There can be real difficulties trying to keep vulnerable family and elderly dog separate, and the resulting tensions will be apparent to the dog, which may suffer a diminishing quality of life because everyone in its immediate circle seems to be annoyed or resentful.

The End

Call it euthanasia, putting to sleep, putting down, whatever we like, there comes a time with most dogs where we need to end their lives because they are no longer enjoying them. Few dogs pass away in their sleep: for most owners there comes that heartbreaking time where we need to step in and prevent suffering. That is the arrangement we take a dog on with in the first place, but no matter how many times we go through it, it never gets any easier. "Better a week too soon than a day too late" is a useful maxim; some of us tend towards denial, and others can be very astute for judging that time when an erstwhile happy old dog looks at us and says, in effect "I don't want to do this any more". As a vet said to me long ago "It isn't a growing-older competition: it's all about quality of life". How we deal with it is up to us, but this is a book on dog behaviour, and so we need to see this from a canine point of view.

If you have only one dog, the main decision is whether you have a home euthanasia or go to the veterinary surgery, and that can depend on available funds, how the dog feels about the veterinary building, whether there are children in the family, and how ill the dog is. There is no shame in opting for euthanasia at the surgery if money is a big consideration, if there are others in the household who are unlikely to be able to manage their emotions, which in turn would distress the dog, and if the dog is unconcerned about being at the surgery. If, however, the dog has always been nervous at the surgery, then opt for a home euthanasia if you possibly can, not just because you want your old friend to pass away calmly, but for the physical side of the task being a lot harder and so more upsetting if the dog is agitated and full of adrenaline. It is up to the family if children witness the event or are sent away, but – as a digression into human behaviour – it is far more upsetting for children to be lied to, or to come home unsuspectingly from school or a day at Granny's to find the dog has disappeared, than it is to include them in the befores and afters, even if not at the actual event. Even if the vet removes the mortal remains for cremation or other disposal, it can be immensely grounding for children to be involved in some kind of ceremony of remembrance for the dog, and we adults need closure as well.

If there are other dogs in the household, then behaviourally this needs a lot of planning. Some issues can be managed, and others may need riding out as they happen, for better or worse. As dogs become elderly, sometimes their influence on other dogs in the household changes, depending on the number, type, gender and character of the mix of animals. If there is one other dog, then the effect of the death of the other can have one of several results, depending on the relationship. If they were great companions, then the remaining dog may be bereft. It may be reluctant to eat or go for walks, might become more vocal, retreat into itself and appear depressed, become clingy and needy, or conversely, avoid interaction with its human family. It may display behaviour that it never has before, for instance starting to chew items, forget its housetraining, or show repetitive behaviour such as self-mutilation or tail-chasing. In cases such as this, the human reaction is often immediately to get another dog, which sometimes works and sometimes is disastrous. I would recommend returning the existing dog to a more stable frame of mind before commencing the upheaval of adding another dog, both for the dog's sake and that of the other people in the household. It is all too easy for someone to dislike the new dog, even on a subconscious level, because it isn't the old one, or for the remaining dog to have its life made trying at a vulnerable time by having to shake down new dynamics with a different dog. The new dog comes into a strange and vaguely hostile environment, which does not help either.

The remaining dog is best helped by a calm attitude, rather than overt sympathy and extra treats trying to help it feel better, because in fact excessive emotional displays make dogs uneasy. The exercise regime should be kept up, feeding should be reduced to small portions at the usual times until the appetite is back – most pet dogs could easily lose a few pounds – safe chew items should be provided for the chewer, remembering that the act of chewing releases endorphins and so offers comfort, and more occupation, such as interactive games and puzzle toys, used to distract the self-mutilator. Check with your vet for treatments that help a dog through stress, such as the use of calming pheromones, Bach Flower remedies, and veterinary-approved herbal treatments. Keep away from drugs that alter the mind, as this is absolutely the wrong time to use them. Helping a dog adjust to grief should be a gentle process, and it needs normal mental function in order to process it.

Some dogs, by contrast, do not appear any different when their companion dies, and show no sign of missing them at all. Though this might seem shocking to the human mourning the loss of a dear canine friend, it is the most normal reaction among dogs. And some dogs positively blossom after the death of the old dog, and it is only then that we realise just how much one was being affected by the other.

With multiple-dog households, the effects on group dynamics of losing one member can be profound. Depending on how much the departed dog influenced the rest of them, this can result in anarchy as several characters seek to establish new roles, or if carefully managed, a bloodless coup whereby the most suitable dog fills the senior role. Even if the missing dog was not ostensibly a strong character, its contribution may have been as mediator, or a calming influence, which is now missing. This might be sufficient for a more volatile character to push its luck under circumstances that normally pass without incident, so that, for instance, someone ringing the doorbell tempts that dog to redirect aggression onto one of the others. Once again, the root is insecurity, because the gentle dog that never appeared to be doing anything within the group, but in fact was a crucial peacekeeper, is now missing. We handle this best by increasing mental and physical exercise so that the dogs have less energy and are more fulfilled. We need to anticipate and sidestep flashpoints, for instance by a change in where we feed each dog or the behaviour we ask for before leads are put on, by finding time to walk each dog separately several times a week to strengthen the bonds between us and each separate dog rather than letting them try each other's strength, and by watching them. Time spent observing our dogs is never wasted, and those people who have the fewest problems are usually the ones who do the most watching. As ever with animals, we do best when we are proactive rather than reactive. Eventually the group will settle down to its new arrangements, and we can all draw breath again.

In the case of two dogs in the household, it is better if the surviving dog is allowed to see and sniff the deceased dog after the euthanasia. If the vet is removing the euthanased dog, then this process is unavoidably a swift one, but if the owner is planning a home burial, then the other dog can be allowed to stay with its companion for longer. With a group of dogs, it is best to let them see the body one at a time, starting with the calmest and most sensible dogs and progressing to the more volatile. Supervise the reactions closely, and do not allow any dog to get hold of the body in its mouth. Most dogs sniff and are satisfied, but reactions can vary and it is important not to let ourselves be upset by them. Our own grief can make a difference too; we should try to keep matters as low-key as we reasonably can. Once they have all seen, we need to shut them away again while we remove the deceased, and do whatever we had planned by way of disposal. Now we can grieve properly as well. Some dogs will go to great lengths to give solace to their person, and others are so uncomfortable with the idea of their "safe place" being less strong and capable that they avoid us until we are more like our old selves. We should try not to take this personally – it's a pretty common reaction in humans, too.

If it is profoundly sad that we have our dogs for so short a time relative to our own lifespans, consider how much worse it would be if they outlived us. We give them the best lives we can, and need not feel guilty about the last gesture, in many ways the kindest of all, when their light begins to flicker and fade.

Photo: Jules Brittan.

Appendix

Further Reading

THIS LIST is by no means comprehensive but offers a good introduction to some of the best modern behaviour books, and introduces a feel for authors from whom the reader might like to read more. If an author or book is not mentioned, it is not intended as a criticism of their work, and readers are encouraged to explore more widely. Take note of which works have been updated because behaviour studies continually improve our knowledge and so newer editions of the same book might well reflect this progress. Older scientific studies are not mentioned here because in general these have been superseded by new ones; however the serious behaviour student will still have these on their must-read list and therefore is encouraged to compare 20th century conclusions with those of the present day. Read everything critically and take nothing as truth until you are satisfied with it. Where scientific observation and the reader's own experiences disagree, I would encourage readers to pass the disputed conclusions before the best judge of all – the dog.

General Behaviour

Brown, Ali
Scaredy Dog! Understanding & Rehabilitating Your Reactive Dog

Clothier, Susan
Bones Would Rain from the Sky

Donaldson, Jean
Oh Behave! Dogs from Pavlov to Premack to Pinker
The Culture Clash

Grandin, Temple
Animals in Translation
N.B. Not recommended for dog behaviour studies but explains space
issues and animals very well.

McConnell, Patricia
Other End of the Leash
Tales of Two Species
FEISTY FIDO! Help for the Leash Reactive Dog
I'll Be Home Soon

Parsons, Emma
Click to Calm

Prior, Karen
Clicker Training for Dogs
Don't Shoot the dog

Rugaas, Turid
On Talking Terms With Dogs: Calming Signals

Whitehead, Sarah
Clever Dog

Health and Nutrition

Billinghurst, Dr. Ian
Give Your Dog a Bone
Grow Your Pups with Bones

Dodds, Dr. Jean
The Canine Thyroid Epidemic

Drakeford and Elliott M.R.C.V.S.
Essential Care for Dogs
Essential Care in the Field

Engel, Cindy
Wild Health

Holt, Professor Peter
Understanding Canine Urinary Incontinence

Index